THE MURDER OF LAWRENCE OF ARABIA

Other books by Matthew Eden

Flight of Hawks

The Gilt-Edged Traitor

Conquest Before Autumn

THE MURDER
OF LAWRENCE
OF ARABIA

A NOVEL BY *Matthew Eden*

THOMAS Y. CROWELL, PUBLISHERS

ESTABLISHED 1834

NEW YORK

FIRST EDITION

Designed by Sidney Feinberg

Library of Congress Cataloging in Publication Data

Eden, Matthew.
   The murder of Lawrence of Arabia.
   1. Lawrence, Thomas Edward, 1888–1935—Fiction.
PZ4.E224Mu 1979   [PR9199.3.E33]   823'.9'14   78–69528
   ISBN 0–690–01790–1

79 80 81 82 83 10 9 8 7 6 5 4 3 2 1

Author's Note

This novel is a dramatic reconstruction of the last eleven weeks in the life of T. E. Lawrence, Lawrence of Arabia, who died on the 19th of May, 1935. It is based on his experiences during and after World War I, as written by him and in differing accounts by historians and biographers. The events and characters in this novel are historically accurate, except where the demands of fiction are stronger than those of history. Where one truth ends and another begins is, as always, for the individual to decide.

THE MURDER OF LAWRENCE OF ARABIA

1

From off the bare, desertlike emptiness of the North Sea a breeze cut across the Yorkshire coast and swept in gusts among the headquarters buildings and the long barracks of the Royal Air Force base outside the town of Bridlington. It tugged at the man in the baggy-kneed civilian suit who pedaled a bicycle down the smooth black road edged with whitewashed stones that led to the main gate.

He was a small man, stocky, with a dominant, well-shaped head that looked almost too big for his body, a wide, firm chin, and a strong, Arabic-looking nose. Red-brown from years in the sun and wind, his face was deeply crinkled at the corners of his eyes and mouth, and his sandy hair, flickered and turned by the wind as he pedaled, was graying at the sides. His lips were tight together, but the line of them was curved and soft-looking. The softness of a boy in the face of a middle-aged man.

Near the main gate an air force police corporal in a white-topped cap stood at the door of the guardhouse, checking the orders of an airman reporting for duty at the station, who stood waiting with his long blue-gray greatcoat buttoned to the neck, his kitbag and blue-gray webbing pack on the ground.

With the orders in his hand, the corporal looked up as the man in the civilian suit pedaled up to the guardhouse.

"Hello, Shaw," he said. "You off, then?"

The stocky man stopped and eased himself off the saddle, standing straddling the bicycle. "Yes, Corporal, I'm leaving at last, I'm afraid." His voice was high, too thin for the face with the strong-looking nose and chin, but it was cultured.

"Afraid?" The corporal smiled. "What d'you mean—you don't want to go?"

The airman waiting there looked at the man on the bicycle, who spoke like an officer and seemed sure of himself, like an officer. But the corporal had called him just Shaw. No mister. A gentleman ranker, the airman thought; he'd come across them once or twice. A funny-looking little bloke, this one was, hardly big enough to get both feet on the ground with the crossbar of the bike under him.

"No, I don't want to go at all," the stocky man said. "I most certainly do not."

"I could find a few who'd like to change places with you," the corporal said. "Who wouldn't be a civilian? Free to come and go as you please. Lovely!"

"You're young, Corporal. When your time comes, I suspect you'll think differently about it." The stocky man raised himself onto the saddle and tightened a checkered wool scarf around his neck.

"Well, you never know, do you?" The corporal nodded at the small black bag strapped to the back of the saddle. "Is that all the kit you're taking?"

"Yes."

"That's not much for a bike ride across England."

"It's adequate. One can survive with very little, you know, Corporal."

"Yes. You may be right. But I think I'd want a bit more than that."

"I'm an old man, remember." The stocky man smiled. "And I have to push this machine down to Dorset. The lighter, the better." He set one foot on a pedal and braced

2

the other to push himself away. "Goodbye, Corporal." He held out a hand.

"Bye, Shaw." The corporal shook hands. "All the best."

"Thanks."

The corporal and the airman stood watching him ride through the gateway onto the road that ran past the base.

"Know who that was, do you?" the corporal said.

"No. Who was it, Corp?"

"Lawrence of Arabia." The corporal handed the airman's orders back to him.

"That was!" The airman turned and stared at the gateway, but the man on the bicycle was gone. "That little bugger was Lawrence of Arabia?"

"Yes." The corporal was satisfied with the reaction. "Wouldn't think so, to look at him, would you?"

"No." Still staring at the open gateway, the airman remembered years ago, just after the war, about nineteen-nineteen, when he'd been a kid, seeing a photo of Lawrence dressed up like an Arab, all in white. That was a long time ago, sixteen years. Since then there'd been articles about him in the papers, but he'd never read any of them—he didn't read much except the sports pages—but now that he thought about it, he seemed to have heard, a few years ago, that Lawrence had joined the air force, in the ranks, using another name. But what he'd always remembered was that picture of him in white Arab clothes. Always remembered it. He'd thought Lawrence of Arabia was a bigger man, though. Taller. "Christ, I thought he was a lot bigger than that." The airman felt as though he'd lost something he had had for years. He was disappointed. He shrugged his arms in through the straps of his webbing pack. "Finished his time, has he, Corp?"

"Yes. Civilian now. Few nights ago they had a little do for him here, little retirement party. He was the only one who didn't have a good time. Sat there and didn't have a bloody drink."

"He sounded as though he didn't want to go."

"No, he didn't want to. Funny little bloke. Can't under-

3

stand him. Nobody here can. Nice, quiet little bloke, but nobody understands him."

"I'm surprised he wasn't bigger." The airman swung his kitbag onto his shoulder. "So long, Corp." He walked down the road toward the camp headquarters.

Lawrence pedaled on, moving south across the Yorkshire countryside, trying to concentrate on moving his legs and feet on the pedals of the bicycle, turning the wheels, not wanting to think of what was ahead for him. Nothing was ahead. He felt fit enough, but he was growing old. He hated to think about it, but it was there. He couldn't believe it was nineteen thirty-five. February the twenty-sixth, nineteen thirty-five, and in less than six months he'd be forty-seven years old. Forty-seven. It was terrible to think about it. He felt so useless now. Useless and unsure. Yes, he had to admit it: unsure. For so long, more than twelve years, his life had been secure and ordered, in the service, and there'd been no need to think about anything. No responsibility for anything but the duties that had always been comfortingly defined, for which he'd been paid his few shillings every week for so long. Now it was all behind him. And what was ahead? All that was ahead was Clouds Hill, his cottage in Dorset, and in a few days, when he was there— what? What was he going to do with the rest of his life, which might linger on for at least another twenty years? Twenty years, oh God, and none of them with any purpose or meaning. How would he endure it?

Best not to think about it. He looked down at his feet moving around on the pedals. Best not to think. But he felt so useless. And once it had been so different. Less than twenty years ago—and it seemed a century—it had all been so different. Through all these years he had tried to clean the memory of that time from his mind, but of course he never could, and nothing again would ever move him as he had been moved in those two years in the desert during the war. Sometimes the memories gave him such pride that he felt, even now, that there was nothing he could not dare. But sometimes there were memories that made him loathe the sight and feel of himself. Yet in those two years he had won such incredible fame that it would never completely fade. He felt that quite certainly. No matter how cheaply he valued that fame, because of his knowledge of himself and the motives that had driven him in those years, it seemed now that the rest of the world would never let him escape it. The thought of that warmed him and disgusted him. The disgust was with himself. He detested himself for the pleasure that the fame had always given him, and he hated the weakness that had driven him to gather it so consciously in Arabia in seventeen and eighteen.

In the early morning they halted their camels in a narrow valley, and while the two British sergeants and the eighty Bedouin of the Howeitat tribe sat waiting, the rising sun making their shadows long on the sand, Lawrence and Selim Shaalan climbed to the crest of a low hill and looked out from it. Half a mile away the sunlight glinted on the twin steel lines of the Hejaz Railway, curving north across the desert toward Maan.

Lawrence lay with his glasses focused on the line, traversing slowly back along it to the village, where there was a railway station and a garrison of Turkish infantry. Already he could feel the warmth of the sun on his back through his white sherif's robe. He could see no movement in the village, not even a Turkish sentry. He swept back with the glasses along the rail line. In front of where they lay, it ran out of sight behind a low ridge. During the night he and Selim had scouted there and had chosen that spot, close to the ridge, as the place to mine the track and lay their ambush for anyone who might survive the explosion and the derailment of the train.

"It still looks favorable," Lawrence murmured. "I see nowhere to better it."

"No." Selim stared out across the sand at where the low ridge hid the track, needing no binoculars. "That must be the place, Lawrence." He looked off along the rail line at the village. "And the Turks are still sleeping."

"Pray that they continue."

5

Lawrence eased himself back from the top of the hill, and they scrambled down to the men, motioning them to dismount and softly calling their orders.

They left the camels with some handlers, and the main body of men climbed the hill out of the valley and, keeping low, ran crouching down it and across the sand toward the single-track railway and the ridge that overlooked it. With one of the British sergeants, Johnson, was a crew of mortarmen he had trained, one carrying the tube, another the baseplate, and others moving forward with the shells. Around the other sergeant, Davis, Arabs hurried toward the ridge with two Lewis light machine guns and round pans of ammunition. Others carried the explosives and heavy rolls of thick, rubber-insulated wire that they would string out and bury in the sand between the detonators and the exploder box. All of them moved across the sand in a rushing, scurrying line, the mortarmen and machine-gun crews making for the ridge with the riflemen to set up their weapons there and command the track.

A demolition party with Lawrence ran out beyond the ridge, about two hundred yards, and dropped on their knees beside the rails, two men on either side digging into the sand with entrenching tools, chipping at the hard, wind-crusted surface and digging into the soft sand beneath, scooping out pits under the rails for the explosive charges, Lawrence and three Arabs kneeling beside the track, ripping the heavy paper from plugs of explosive gelatine and molding them into heavy charges in two sandbags.

The pits were dug, and gently Lawrence inserted detonators into the charges and attached the wires. He laid one sandbag charge in each pit and stepped back, motioning the men to cover them. As they shoveled the sand back in, he looked up and down the track and saw nothing. From here, the village they had seen from the high ground was out of sight along the track. He looked back to the ridge and no one was signaling from there to warn that a Turkish patrol was moving out of the village. Everything was well.

When the charges were hidden the men began backing away from the track, uncoiling the heavy blasting wire and

6

burying it in a narrow trench that they dug as they went, moving slowly back toward the cover of the guns on the ridge.

Lawrence waited at the track with one of the men. It had taken forty minutes to lay the charges. Moving slowly back to the ridge, burying the wire, would take at least as long. Then they would have to hide any sign that they had been here, and that would take longer. The men moving back with the wire were keeping to the footprints they had made in the rush out from the ridge, but still it would take time to cover the traces they left.

He watched the men laying the stiff wires in the shallow trench. Sometimes when they pushed the wires down, another section that they had buried broke up out of the sand, and one of them had to rush back and push it down again and lay a rock on it to hold it in place.

When the men were fifty yards from the track, still backing away, digging and burying, Lawrence, an empty sandbag in his hand, looked down at the loose sand under the rails on either side, where they had buried the charges.

Motioning to the Bedouin waiting with him, he bent to sweep at the loose sand with the burlap bag, but the Arab, a rifle slung from his shoulder, was watching the wiring party and had not seen him.

"Come, Shakir!" Lawrence snapped. "You have work too—and the Turks won't wait for you!"

"Yes, Lawrence!" Grinning, the Bedouin dropped to a crouch and swept at the loose sand with the hem of his riding cloak, smoothing.

Dragging softly the burlap bag over the fresh-dug sand, Lawrence brushed wavy lines in it, like the lines blown by the wind in the crusted sand out around them. With long-sweeping fannings of his cloak, Shakir blurred the sharp new edges of the lines until they looked weathered as the patterns of wind on the sand across the desert. Treading lightly, they moved after the others, walking backwards, smoothing and covering all the tracks behind them.

It took the wire-laying party more than an hour to cover the two hundred yards to the foot of the ridge, and Law-

7

rence and the Bedouin came slowly, bent-backed, behind them, brushing and sweeping at the sand. Then they took the wire up the fifty feet of the ridge, not burying it now, only covering it with handfuls of loose sand.

When they went over the crest the line of Bedouin riflemen were there, lying ready, with a Lewis gun at either end of the line, sited to cover the length of railway with cross fire. Just behind the riflemen, down the reverse slope, the mortar crew waited.

Selim hurried up, crouching, though he was out of sight behind the top of the ridge.

"Is it well down there, Lawrence?" He motioned out toward the railway.

"Yes. Now we must lie here and wait for the train." Lawrence could feel the weight of the sun now through his headcloth. They would not have to lie here long, he hoped.

"And pray the Turks do not find us first." Selim grinned.

"Pray well." Lawrence picked up the exploder box by the handle and, kneeling with it where the men had un-coiled the last of the wire, connected the two ends by the butterfly nuts to the top of it. He sat on the sand, the box between his knees, glancing back and forth at the far ends of the line of riflemen, where there were lookouts posted to watch for the smoke of a train or a dust cloud from moving Turkish troops.

When he had been sitting there twenty minutes, feeling the heat of the sun as it rose higher, he bent his head, his eyes in shadow under the edge of his headcloth. With the tips of thumb and forefinger he touched one of the butterfly nuts on the exploder box. Oh, God! He moved to jerk away from the heat of the metal but held for a moment more, then drew his hand back, feeling the blisters stinging, satis-fied that he had controlled himself. All his life he'd dreaded pain, but had felt the need to try to master it. Mastering it gave him great pleasure.

"Lawrence!" Selim hissed.

He jerked his head up, and Selim was pointing to the end of their line of men closest to the village. The lookout posted beyond the last rifleman was crouched below the crest of the ridge, pumping his rifle quickly up and down in one hand.

"He's seen something!" Lawrence bounded up from where he was sitting, motioning to the exploder box and snapping at Selim: "Stay and guard that!" and went running behind the line of riflemen, past the mortar crew, his glasses bobbing on his chest from the strap around his neck.

The lookout had turned away and, crouched low and peering over the ridge, was staring out along the rail line toward the village. Lawrence went down in a sliding dive on the sand beside him, bringing up his glasses with one hand.

"There, Lawrence!" The lookout pointed.

White smoke was rising from the village. One neat, thickening column of smoke.

Lawrence focused the glasses on it. It was a train, waiting at the station and gathering steam. From the smoke, it looked like a big one. He hoped it would be.

"Run and tell Selim—a train!" he snapped at the lookout.

As he lay watching the white woodsmoke through his glasses, waiting for it to begin moving, he heard an approaching soft metallic clatter behind him: rifle bolts being jerked as the word was passed from man to man along the line, and they checked the loads in their Lee-Enfields.

The column of smoke billowed and rose higher, drifting back over the village. Then it began to move. Lawrence watched until he was sure it was not just shunting in the village but was coming out to them, and when he saw the locomotive pulling out and the leading wagons behind it, he rolled on his side, looking back at Selim, and raised a hand.

Selim, crouched at the center of the line of men, waved back. Lawrence turned and brought up his glasses again, both elbows in the sand, holding the glasses firm with his right hand, steadying them with the fingertips of the left.

Now he counted twelve wagons strung out behind the locomotive, and still the end of the train was not in sight.

9

Thirteen. Fourteen. Fifteen. Sixteen wagons. And only one locomotive. It was perfect. Pulling a train as long as that, burning wood fuel, one locomotive could not make any speed. He would have time to choose precisely the right moment for blowing the track.

He watched the train as it drew out across the desert, the white smoke drifting back along the line of wagons. On the roofs of the first and last wagons were sandbagged machine-gun positions, and he could see the small figures of the crews crouched behind the guns, just their heads behind the sandbags. It was a train of closed freight wagons, and as it drew closer he could see firing slits cut in the wood sides. It was probably a troop train, and the Turks were all shut up in those box wagons like potatoes in an oven. They couldn't be traveling far like that. Even for Turkish infantry, that would be asking too much. Probably they were moving up to Maan. He would try to see to it that they never arrived.

The lookout scurried back and Lawrence told him to stay and watch the train and signal if it stopped.

"I believe it carries troops," he said. "If they are doubtful of this place"—and they should be, because it might have been created for an ambush—"they might stop before here and send troops to scout. If they do, warn me at once."

"Yes, Lawrence." The lookout went down on his knees, watching the slow movement of the train toward them.

Lawrence walked back to where Selim stood beside the exploder box. All along the line, the men lay waiting, and the mortar crew knelt around their weapon, one man holding a shell ready to slide down the tube, Sergeant Johnson, red-faced below the Arab headcloth he wore with his khaki shirt and shorts, kneeling at the elevating screw, ready to adjust the range if they should need it.

"Is it a large train?" Selim said.

"Sixteen wagons," Lawrence said. "A troop train, I believe."

"The best kind! No loot, but many Turks to kill. It is good, Lawrence."

Lawrence smiled quickly. He liked Selim, a sheikh of the Howeitat, a leader greatly respected by his men, and

not quite twenty-three years old. "Guard yourself, Selim."
He picked up the exploder box.

"You also, Lawrence."

They hurried together up the slope and lay just below
the crest of the ridge. Very clearly now, without the glasses,
Lawrence could see the white smoke and the locomotive
at the base of it. In a few minutes it would be passing in
front of them. Except that it would not pass. He hoped
nothing would go wrong, and that the explosion would give
them enough advantage—that and the surprise and the fire
from their mortar and machine guns. With all that, he
hoped, they would be more than enough for sixteen wagon-
loads of Turkish infantry. But if anything went wrong. If
anything went wrong, they were half a mile from their
camels. Half a mile across the desert, with Turks chasing
them, could be serious. But he must not allow himself to
begin thinking like that.

Now he could hear the train and see the dots of men
in the two machine-gun positions on top of the wagons.
Carefully he looked through the glasses, one hand cupped
over them so that the sun would not reflect on them, and
he could clearly see what type of machine guns they were.
Spandaus. Heavy belt-fed guns that the Germans had supplied their allies the Turks. With those, if they were handled
well, the Turks would have no trouble beating down the
fire of the two Lewis guns he had here on the ridge.

He turned to Selim. "Send word to the gunners. Tell
them to engage the machine guns on the tops of the wagons
the moment I explode the mines. With good fortune, the
explosion will finish the men on the first wagon, and in
that case both our Lewis guns must engage the gun on
the last wagon. It must not be allowed to dominate us."

"Yes, Lawrence." Selim gave fast orders to two men,
and they ran crouching to each end of the line to tell the
gun teams.

Pulling slowly, the locomotive rounded the curve that
the track made to pass the ridge, and, as the first wagon
came around, the men at the Spandau on top of it opened
fire, sweeping the ridge.

Lawrence and Selim and the men on either side of

11

them pressed closer to the ground as clouds of sand and chips of rock sprayed along the top of the ridge, just above their heads.

"Have they seen us?" Selim called in the noise of the firing. "How can they know we are here?"

"They don't! But this is a place for an ambush, and the Turks are having sport with their machine guns!" Lawrence looked along the line and saw some of the Bedouin with fingers on their triggers. Sweeping his hand down at them, he shouted through the sound of the clattering gun: "No one is to fire!"

The noise stopped. The men on the wagon were changing a belt, he guessed, and carefully looked over the ridge. The locomotive was very close to their mine. He hoped they would not open fire again until he had the train in position on it. Only three or four seconds.

Now the Spandau on the roof of the last wagon opened fire, but it was at the far end of the ridge, and no danger to him yet. The train was very close to the mine, and the men on the first wagon were still bent to their gun, working on the belt. It looked as though it had jammed. And the train was closer. Closer.

Both hands on the plunger of the exploder box, Selim watching him with a hand raised ready to signal the order to fire, he watched as the front wheels of the locomotive ran over the spot where they had buried the explosives. Another moment and the center of the locomotive was on it.

He slammed his weight down on the plunger and heard the hiss and click of the electrical contact in the box.

Selim dropped his hand, shouting: "Open fire! Open fire!"

The mine exploded with a red-black roar and the locomotive and first wagon disappeared in a cloud of black smoke that flashed wide on either side of the track and jetted eighty feet into the air.

All along the ridge was the snapping of rifles in the clear air, and the clatter of the Lewis guns. A quick, bouncing thump of the mortar firing, and the black shell arced over the ridge and burst redly in the sand just short of the wagons that were beginning to topple sideways off the track.

Metal and wood from the locomotive and the first wagon were falling far out in the desert, dropping heavily into the sand. A driving wheel whirred out of the black cloud and spun low over the ridge, landing close to the mortar position.

Fire from rifles and Lewis guns was chewing along the sides of the wagons, bullets chipping up white-clean wood splinters in the hot sun, ripping spurts of sand and cloth from the sandbags around the Spandau on the last wagon. One of the crew went down behind the gun at once. Another man began to traverse it onto one of the Lewis guns, and he was caught by a bullet that knocked him off the top of the wagon. Then the last two men seemed to burst apart in a storm of fire that shredded most of the remaining sandbags of their emplacement.

Half the wagons were still upright on the track, and at the firing slits were the red muzzle-flashes of rifles. Infantry were climbing out of some of the overturned wagons too, taking cover behind them and opening fire with rifles and machine guns.

A mortar shell burst on top of one of the last wagons and it blew apart with a red roar and there were rifles, splintered planks, and bodies flung out through the air onto the sand.

Close beside Lawrence a burst of machine-gun fire hissed along the crest of the ridge, and three Bedouin went down as the storm took them across their heads. Pressing himself suddenly lower, his chin deep into the sand, Lawrence saw the gun firing from behind one of the overturned wagons, in cover from the fire of the Lewis guns at either end of the ridge. He turned and made a hand signal to the mortar crew. Sergeant Johnson adjusted the elevation and one of the Bedouin dropped a shell down the tube. It arced out high over the ridge, black against the blue sky, and burst a few yards behind the overturned wagon. The Turkish machine gun kept firing.

13

Lawrence signaled again, and another mortar shell shot over the ridge. He watched it drop between the machine gunner and the loader. Gun and crew disappeared in the explosion.

Another shell dropped behind the overturned wagons, among the Turkish riflemen firing from there, and in the red flash and the cloud of sand and black smoke that humped into the air there were two broken rifles, a boot, and some limp-looking fragments in pieces of torn uniform. The sand and all of it showered down on the wagons. There were screams coming from where the shell had hit. Then men from behind the overturned wagons were running back from them, out into the desert, throwing down rifles, some of them unbuckling ammunition belts and throwing them down too as they ran. The Lewis gun at one end of the ridge began firing into them, swinging slowly back and forth along the mass of brown uniforms, and men were falling. Behind the running crowd were more and more dark bodies lying on the sun-bright sand. Arab riflemen were sniping at the running men too, and to escape the fire they broke into ones and twos, scattering in a wide arc from the broken train. And the machine gun and rifles still fired at them, until they were out of range, and then there were only about fifteen small figures still running. More than a hundred bodies were lying on the sand.

Now there was only weak firing from the wagons still upright on the track, but the rifle and machine guns along the ridge were still firing into them, and mortar shells dropped on them and around them. A door was dragged open in one wagon and slowly a hand came out fluttering a white handkerchief.

"Cease firing!" Lawrence jumped to his feet, waving his arms. "Cease firing!"

Selim shouted with him, kicking at some of the excited Bedouin who still lay firing into the wagons. Both of them ran along the ridge, shouting at them to cease fire, and at last it slackened and stopped.

In the quietness Lawrence stood looking down at the line of bullet-chipped, shell-blasted wagons. Into the open

14

doorway where the handkerchief had fluttered stepped a Turkish officer, with polished riding boots and no hat. He stood looking up at the ridge, gazing along it, then jumped lightly down. His boots made two small puffs in the sand when he landed.

Lawrence and Selim rose slowly, cautiously, at the center of the ridge and stepped down the slope, watching the firing slits in the wagons for a rifle muzzle that might swing toward them. Along the ridge the men were following them down.

The Turkish officer, a major, stood with his hands on his hips, waiting for them. Soldiers were climbing down from the wagons behind him, squat men with legs that looked short and thick in their puttees. They dropped their rifles in the sand as they climbed down and some of them, watching the Bedouin stalking down on them with their rifles ready, raised their hands, waiting. Some were bleeding from unbandaged wounds, and there was moaning from other wounded men inside the wagons.

The Turkish major, who had watched Lawrence in his white robe, Selim at his side, all the way down the slope and across the strip of flat sand, stepped out to him as he came close, and stood at attention, staring at Lawrence's face, surprised that he was not an Arab.

In French the major said: "I am Major Hassim."

"I am Major Lawrence, of the British army, adviser to the army of the Emir Feisal." It made him uncomfortable that the Turk was at least three inches taller than he was. Even without the riding boots he would have been taller.

"Major Lawrence, I surrender my command to you. Please accept my personal weapon." The Turk opened a big wooden holster on his belt and drew out a heavy Mauser pistol, holding it butt-first to Lawrence.

Lawrence tucked it into his sash, beside his long, curved dagger. "Have you a doctor, Major?"

"I regret, no." The Turk glanced back where his men stood in a loose line beside the wagons, at some of the wounded. Some who had climbed down, hit in the legs, were lying or sitting in the sand.

15

Along the line, where the Arabs were now very close in on the Turkish troops, there were shouts and jostling, some of the Arabs snatching wallets and cigarettes from the Turks and arguing among themselves over them.

Selim looked down the track, where two Bedouin, laughing, tussled with each other over something one had taken. He shouted at them and they came apart, one of them grinning and tucking something inside his robe.

"Let us kill them and go, Lawrence," Selim said. "Let the men take what they can find and leave here, before more troops come."

The Turkish officer, looking anxious, watched Selim, and Lawrence saw he could not understand Arabic but was nervous. There would be almost sixty Turks here, and more inside the wagons, too badly wounded to move. And they were all in his hands. Whether they lived or died was for him to decide with a word. He enjoyed the feeling. He didn't respect himself for it, but he did enjoy the feeling of power. The Arabs would wipe them out in a moment, without a thought, but they would not do it unless he ordered it. And he could give the order or not give it. Life or death for more than sixty men.

"No, Selim. Be sure that all are disarmed, then drive them off toward the village."

"To fight another day, Lawrence?" Selim hissed it, watching the Turkish major.

"They have surrendered to us and they are unarmed."

"More fools they are."

"No—only men who do not want to die."

"If we were unarmed and they held the rifles, they would kill us all—and not quickly, but for amusement, Lawrence. You know it!"

"Yes—but do we have to prove that we are no better?"

Selim said nothing, but slowly he took his right hand off his rifle.

"Remember that our main purpose is to destroy the railway and the trains," Lawrence said. "We have done good work today. We can afford to be merciful."

16

Selim spun away, calling to his men to search the prisoners and be sure they carried no weapons, then to drive them away toward the village. Laughing, the Bedouin moved in on the line of Turks, tugging at their uniforms and searching the jackets and trousers they stripped off.

"You are free to go with your men, Major," Lawrence said. "We give you your life today."

The Turk clicked his bootheels together in the sand, saluting. "I shall send a doctor from the village for my badly wounded."

"Yes. There is nothing we can do for them." It troubled Lawrence that the Turkish major had not thanked him for sparing all their lives. The man was proud. Foolishly proud. "Hurry, Major." He glanced at the Bedouin. Now several of them were wrestling among themselves for what they had taken from the Turks, but still laughing and playful. "It will be safest if you move your men away quickly." He wanted some response from this man—some sign that the Turk was grateful for what he had been given.

But the Turkish major said only: "I will take them at once." He clicked his heels again and turned away.

Lawrence watched him go. He felt cheated of the recognition that he should have had from the Turk. He had beaten the man, yet he felt he was the one who had lost something.

Arabs were up in the wagons now, gathering the rifles that the Turks had left. Others were picking up the ones that had been dropped in the sand.

"There is nothing more to do here, Lawrence," Selim said.

"No. Let us go back to the camels."

Carrying everything they had taken, some of them with two or three Turkish rifles slung from their shoulders, the Bedouin climbed back over the ridge, Lawrence and Selim among them, and all the way back across the half mile of desert to the camels Lawrence tried to forget the Turkish major and the feeling that somehow the man who had been at his mercy had mastered him.

17

Lawrence pedaled on. It was all far behind him now, Arabia and all the unbelievable, stupendous fame that had come to him because of what he'd done there—what he'd done and, yes, what he'd only claimed he'd done. So much of it had been fake. That towering fame of his had been built so much on constructions of his own, on his book and the fantasies he had spun for the American journalist Lowell Thomas in the few days Thomas had been with him in the desert in eighteen. And what that man had done with those stories! Thomas, with his vulgar genius for publicity, had created him. In those few years after the war Thomas had made him famous throughout the English-speaking world: Lawrence of Arabia, the Prince of Mecca, Uncrowned King of Arabia, and the Deliverer of Damascus. Oh, it had been unimaginable. It had seemed in those days that the public could never hear enough of him. They had wanted a hero from the war, and he had been the idealization of all that was heroic for them. And Thomas, with his film-and-talk shows, had entertained them for five years and crowned it all in nineteen twenty-four with his embarrassing book.

He himself was, of course, no better than Thomas. No, that wasn't good enough—he was worse, much worse. Thomas had been a journalist, nothing more, satisfying the commonest public taste—and he'd made a huge profit from his skill at it. He had never claimed to be anything but a showman. He himself, on the other hand, had always passed himself off as much more. He had spent so much time supplying Thomas with the carefully chosen stories that he wanted to be used in the creation of the legend, and then he had denied that the poor fool had ever had his cooperation. When Thomas, after months of captivating the Americans with his film of Lawrence of Arabia, had brought it to London, to Covent Garden, how many times had he himself crept into the place to hear the superlatives and listen to the applause. And, God, how he'd loved it, sitting there in the dark and knowing he had them. And every time the journalists pestered him for his reactions to the show, he'd told them he knew nothing of it, that Thomas had done it all without his knowledge. He'd even, after giving him so much to put in his book, insisted that Thomas print a caution that Colonel Lawrence had not been the source for anything in it. It had been a lie, of course. Why had he insisted on the lie?

Why? Because he was quite incapable of controlling his urge for self-dramatization. The way he had manipulated Thomas was nothing compared with the way he'd engineered the publicity for his own book, *The Seven Pillars of Wisdom*, when he'd at last published it. That had been masterful. First, after all the talk of it had been so discreetly circulated, there had been the limited edition, in twenty-six, two years after the Thomas book had established that the interest in him was as alive as ever. He'd published that limited edition in something like total secrecy, with not one copy sent out to a newspaper or magazine for review. And inevitably the publicity had come. It had all been so simply done. Delightful. Because of all that publicity, which he'd never failed to deplore to anyone who'd listen, there had, of course, been thousands of impatient readers waiting for the cheaper, abridged version, *Revolt in the Desert*, published a few weeks later. And so much of the stuff, complete or in abridgement, had been his own creation, fiction, designed to make himself exotic to everyone who read it. The little items of embroidery in the books— that the Arabs had called him Lurens, Aurans, and the rest, when the truth was that they'd never had any difficulty calling him Lawrence. They'd never had any trouble pronouncing that. But how exotic it had sounded that the Arabs had their own name for him! And no one who had read it in the books ever questioned it. Oh, God, but he had grown so tired of it, his compulsion to deceive.

Yet that nonsense with the books and the personal publicity had been relatively harmless. The memory of what he'd done to the Arabs was much more painful. That was the deception he found hardest of all to live with. He'd never be able to forget it. It had all been sham, all his time with them. Lawrence of Arabia, leading the Arabs

19

in their struggle for freedom from the Turks, had been just another of the fables he'd spooned out to Thomas—and, yes, that he'd written himself in *The Seven Pillars*. It was true that he'd wanted a kind of freedom for them. *A kind of freedom.* But there'd been nothing selfless about his motive. It was because of his liking for one of them that he'd wanted freedom for them—but freedom under British guidance, within the Empire. And with himself as counselor for whoever the Arab ruler would have been. Oh, yes, he'd wanted much for himself. He'd had that craving for power, to have millions of people expressing themselves through him, and because of that he'd used the Arabs. All of his reputation had been founded on fraud, and he had nothing but contempt for himself. All the dressing in sherifian robes had been simply because it was easier to handle the Arabs when you were dressed as one of them. It had helped win their trust. That was all. He wasn't proud of any of that. But most of all he despised himself for always having presented himself as other than he had been. Why had he never been able to say simply that he'd been a British officer sent to help the Arabs in their fight against the Turks, to help the British campaign in the Middle East? And why had he not said frankly that it had been the British intention to establish their influence in the area, never to give true freedom to the Arabs? Why had he felt compelled then—and even now—to glorify himself? God, it became harder and harder to go on.

Always, though, there had been that craving for good repute among men. Even in the desert, when he knew that he was being dishonest with the Arabs, that he was giving them much less than they thought, it had always been important to have their approval, to know that they respected him. That need for approval too had made him design the stories that Thomas had circulated so enthusiastically.

And he'd hated himself when he heard and saw the hero that Thomas had made of him, because he'd known it was mostly myth, far from reality. Yet he'd never been able to tell anyone what the truth was.

20

What a fantastic success he could have been in one of those advertising offices that made a profession of selling soap and chocolate to the public! What a flair he had for it!

Now where had it all taken him? A rather shabby middle-aged man riding a bicycle across England. Who would recognize him now, as he passed them? There was only anonymity for him now. Anonymity and nothing. Useless years ahead. He was so tired.

2

A policeman stood with his back to the black iron railing
outside 10 Downing Street, watching the tall man in the
black double-breasted topcoat and homburg hat crossing
the street from the side of the government offices in Whitehall. He saluted as the man stepped onto the curb, and
the Colonial Secretary, Sir Philip Cunliffe-Lister, nodded
and said: "Good morning," striding past to the front door.

He looked as though he had a lot on his mind, the
policeman thought, hearing the door close behind him.
They all looked like that these days, when they went in
the Prime Minister's residence and when they came out—
what with the Depression and all the men out of work.
He wouldn't change places with any of them in the government—especially the Prime Minister. Poor old MacDonald
looked worse every time he saw him, as though he didn't
have long for this world. And he wasn't a bad old fellow,
really, for a socialist.

A secretary showed Cunliffe-Lister into the Prime Minister's study. MacDonald, with his white wavy hair and
heavy white moustache, was sixty-eight, but he looked older.
His health had been bad for years and there was talk that
he would not stay much longer in office. More than three

years ago—soon after his Labour government had broken apart, unable to agree on action to improve the economy, and he had formed the National Government coalition, with the Conservatives the majority in it—he had wanted to resign, but the King had told him he must stay. He had stayed, but he had been more and more discontented and depressed, these three years. He felt degraded, staying in office only through the indulgence of the Conservatives, knowing they despised him for his socialism and his poor Scottish background, and knowing that most of his own party now detested his name because they thought him an opportunist and a traitor to his class for working with the party of privilege.

This man here now, Cunliffe-Lister—Sir Philip, if you please—was typical of them. Look at the smugness of the man as he sat there opening his beautiful black briefcase for this report that demanded such urgent attention that he'd telephoned first thing and said he'd like to come and discuss it before lunch.

Cunliffe-Lister took the report from his case and leaned forward in his armchair. "Here it is, Prime Minister. From the Palestine Police." He handed it across the desk.

"It's not long, is it?" Unwillingly MacDonald took it. He could see it was only two pages, but he felt he had to say something. A motion of protest. He wished he'd told Cunliffe-Lister he didn't have time for this today, but the man was very insistent always. All these Conservatives were, and he felt he couldn't struggle against them any longer. It couldn't go on like this. Before long he'd have to do something. He looked at the report.

It was very detailed, for what there was of it, but at the end there was very little that was concrete. From their undercover agents in three parts of the country—Nablus, Jaffa, and the Moslem Quarter of Jerusalem—the Palestine Police had had reports that the Arabs were preparing for a major uprising, with the aim of wiping out the Jews. The first report of the uprising had come five weeks ago, in Nablus, the center of Arab nationalism, and the police had worked to find confirmation from other sources. At last the two other reports had come and they had sent this warning to Whitehall, to the Colonial Office. But there was one vital element missing: None of the sources knew when the uprising would begin. The police agents had questioned their informants as closely as they could with safety, but they did not know when it would come.

MacDonald sat back and laid a hand on the report. "Is this something we must take seriously, d'you believe?" He would like to ignore it, just to forget it. There was so much else that needed his attention.

"The Palestine Police obviously think so. There's very little we can do, at this point—there's no precise information, as you can see—but I've sent them a message instructing them to inform me, as a matter of urgency, as soon as they have more specific information."

"Yes." MacDonald wished he were Cunliffe-Lister's age, about fifty, with all that energy. "Is there any more we can do—until we know more?" He could think of nothing. These days, he found it very difficult to concentrate on anything for long. He didn't feel well at all.

"Very little. But I suggest you ask the War Office to look at their available strength. If there were a flare-up suddenly, we might want to reinforce the Palestine garrison rather quickly. It'd be helpful, I should think, if the War Office had troops ready to move without too much delay."

"Yes. I'll have them look at that." MacDonald made a note on a pad. He'd never remember it if he didn't make a note. It was like that with him now. "I can't understand what the Arabs think they could gain from an uprising."

"They want the Jews out," Cunliffe-Lister said. "That's what they want, of course." There had been several Arab disturbances in Palestine since the British had taken control of it under the League of Nations mandate—a serious outbreak only two years ago, and two or three in the twenties—all because the Arabs feared that the Balfour Declaration meant the Jews would take their land. "I think we should expect trouble from them until we can convince them there's no danger that the Jews will be allowed to take Palestine from them."

"But haven't we given them enough assurance? We've

24

had the mandate more than a dozen years, and surely we've made it clear by now that we don't intend the Jews to establish themselves there." As far back as the summer of twenty-two that had been clear, when Winston Churchill, then Colonial Secretary, had published a White Paper that said Jewish immigration to Palestine should be limited to the capacity of the economy to absorb them. At the same time the part of the country east of the Jordan had been detached, creating Transjordan as a separate state. The Zionists had recognized that as the first British action to reduce the promise of the Balfour Declaration of nineteen-seventeen, which had favored the establishment of a national home for the Jewish people. And the Zionists had seen it accurately—for that had been the British intention, and it had been the direction of British policy ever since. "Only five years ago we had the Passfield White Paper, proposing a restriction on Jewish immigration and suspending their purchases of land from the Arabs."

"And you wrote Weizmann a letter that took most of the sting out of it," Cunliffe-Lister said. "I fancy the Arabs didn't fail to notice that."

MacDonald said nothing. It had been weak of him to write that letter to Chaim Weizmann. He should have held firm. Having published the White Paper, he should have seen to it that its intention was carried out and Jewish settlement was limited. But Weizmann, president of the World Zionist Organization and the Jewish Agency, with all their influence behind him, had been so firm, in his quiet English way, that he, the Prime Minister, had softened the official position—in writing. And what was the result of it? Now they not only had the Jews convinced, despite his letter, that Britain still favored the Arabs, they also had the Arabs quite certain that Britain's real sympathy was with the Jews. It was an impossible problem to solve. Had the government in power twenty years ago ever imagined what trouble there was going to be in Palestine? What could they have done differently to avoid it all? He couldn't think about it now. It was so complex, and he seemed unable to concentrate these days.

"Weizmann is a reasonable, understanding man," he

said. "He knows how difficult it is for us in Palestine. In common decency, I had to write him that letter—or his position with his own people would have been impossible. As it is, a lot of them call him an artificial Englishman and a traitor to his people." That was where MacDonald could sympathize with Weizmann; both of them had been called a traitor by their own people.

"And some of them are doing more than that, I must remind you," Cunliffe-Lister said. "More and more of them in Palestine are breaking away from Weizmann and becoming militant. They're talking increasingly of not just standing still and accepting it when the Arabs attack them, but of taking offensive action in retaliation. I tell you, if that becomes widespread, it'll be impossible for us. It'll be civil war out there."

MacDonald nodded. He didn't want to be forced to think about all this now. "I can't see what we can do. The Arabs are right to be nervous. There *has* been more Jewish immigration in the past year or two, hasn't there?"

"Of course there has. Much more." For about six years, from the late twenties to the early thirties, Jewish immigration to Palestine had averaged less than five thousand a year. Then, three years ago, Hitler had come to power in Germany, and the following year immigration had risen to something over thirty thousand. Last year it had been more than forty thousand. And this year there was every sign that it would be much higher. Yes, it was understandable that the Arabs were becoming nervous. If Jewish immigration went on at this rate, they were saying, in a few years, despite the fact that they'd still be numerically inferior to the Arabs, the Jews, with their wealth and ability, would be in a commanding position in Palestine. "But if the Arabs were foolish enough to resort to some sort of major uprising in protest, we'd be compelled to put them down. And then what?"

MacDonald said nothing. He was trying to think. Above the fireplace was a portrait of George V in admiral's uniform, looking like an authentic naval officer, with his full beard. MacDonald wished, as he did so often, that the King had allowed him to resign when he'd wanted to.

"We'd alienate them completely," Cunliffe-Lister said. "We'd have to crush them and it'd take us years to win them around. For years we'd have no stability at all in Palestine—far less than we have now."

MacDonald nodded. With Hitler in power in Germany, and Mussolini in Italy, war at some time in the next few years looked inevitable. And if it came, it was imperative for Britain to have stability in Palestine, to ensure the safety of the Suez Canal, their passage to that vast part of the Empire in the East. They had to be sure of Palestine. They would have to do something there.

3

"I feel so strange and aimless now," Lawrence said, sitting on the floor with his legs bent up, staring into the flames in the fireplace, his hands around his knees. "The past seven or eight days, since I left the air force, I've done nothing but ride my bike, visiting friends and looking at the country. I'd looked forward to going home to my cottage, but I can't even do that because of the journalists there, waiting for me. I can't face them, Williamson." He shook his head. "So I just ride about, wasting time. I don't know. It's all so pointless."

Williamson sat watching him from the couch, thinking how small he looked sitting there. Like a boy at a campfire. But what a towering man he was! "No. Nothing about your life is pointless. There are great things still for you to do. It's destiny for a man like you." It pleased him to be sitting here giving advice to Lawrence of Arabia. He felt honored to be able to call Lawrence his friend. For many years he'd admired him, ever since he'd read *Revolt in the Desert* and, a writer himself, had been taken by the style of it, but even more because he'd felt he and Lawrence had many attitudes in common. But he'd never written to Lawrence, hadn't wanted to presume. And then later, in twenty-eight, Lawrence had read a book of his and, unbelievably, had

28

written him a letter saying how much he liked it. So they'd become friends after all. It had delighted him yesterday morning when a friend who'd heard he was in London had sent a message to say Lawrence was here too, staying for a few days, not wanting to go to his cottage in Dorset because of all the journalists waiting for him there. "Give yourself time. For years you've buried yourself in the ranks, and it's only a few days that you've been out. Give yourself time to adjust."

"Oh, the jobs have been offered, Williamson. They've been offered." Staring into the fire, Lawrence laughed quickly. It was high and nervous-sounding, a giggle. "Before I left the air force they offered me Egypt, you know."

"They wanted you as High Commissioner?"

"Yes. I told them I couldn't consider it. Couldn't consider it."

"Perhaps you should. It would be challenging."

"They're constantly trying to present me with challenges. They've tried to have me take on Home Defence too—reorganizing Home Defence." Briskly Lawrence shook his head at the flames. "I told them I wasn't interested. In the mood that's on me now, I wouldn't consider anything at all."

Williamson sat watching him, wondering if he should say what he had to say. It had been in his mind for weeks, ever since he'd heard that Lawrence was leaving the air force and would be free. But it troubled him to see how dejected the man looked and sounded. He hoped he'd be the one to give some purpose to Lawrence's life. Nothing else lately seemed to have done it.

"What about politics?" Williamson said.

"Politics! D'you think I've the stomach for it? And d'you think any party would have me? There aren't many politicians who can tolerate me. The Labourites think I'm a spy from the middle class, trying to infiltrate the ranks of the workers; the Conservatives think I'm a Red. And I think most of them are impossible. A few, like Churchill, are able men and good friends, but most of them are fools. In any case, politics doesn't appeal."

"Not party politics, no, not all that haggling in the back

rooms to come to a compromise that's useless to man or beast—but what about some sort of direct action that could put a leader in immediate touch with the people?" Williamson hoped he could persuade him. Lawrence was the man the movement needed. He could perform a miracle for the movement.

"What sort of direct action d'you mean?"

"Do you know Sir Oswald Mosley?"

Lawrence looked up at him. "I've read about him, of course. Never met him." Mosley was the leader of the British Union of Fascists, the Blackshirts.

"And you've read about the Blackshirts?"

"Of course."

"How does the idea of joining them appeal to you?"

"I've never given it any thought. Why do you ask?"

"I'm a Blackshirt. I was one of the first to join Mosley in thirty-two."

"Oh?" Lawrence rested his hands on the floor and leaned back on them. "Why?"

"Because the Fascist movement is strong and clean. Muscular."

"Anti-Semitic too." That repelled Lawrence. He knew he was many undesirable things, but not anti-Semitic.

"No, no. Not seriously. Mosley uses some anti-Semitic talk to attract the masses, but it's nothing more than that. He wants great things for Britain. He believes all of us should contribute unselfishly to the common good. He wants a classless society—classless but authoritarian, with strong leadership." Williamson leaned over from the couch, looking down at Lawrence. "But I see in it a hope for much more than that."

"What, exactly?"

"World peace. If there were a Fascist Britain, what would be more inevitable than an alliance with Hitler? Britain and Germany allied together! Can you see it, Lawrence? It would bring in a new age. No more war in Europe. The two greatest European powers working together in friendship. Doesn't the thought of it excite you?"

"If it could be made to happen, it would be worth working for, God knows." Lawrence leaned forward again, fingers locked around his knees.

"Then will you join us? Will you?"

"What possible use could I be?"

"What use! Lawrence, you could be an inspiration to the movement."

"Surely you're not asking me to lead the Blackshirts?" Lawrence giggled quickly. "Does Mosley know about this?"

"No, no, that's not what I'm suggesting. But your name could make the movement shine. With you as a member, as an avowed supporter of Mosley, the imagination of the entire country would be caught."

Staring into the fire, Lawrence shook his head. "All I want is to go home to my cottage. When I'm there wild mares won't drag me away. Not for the foreseeable future."

"But will you think about this?" Williamson had thought for a moment that he might be able to persuade Lawrence. He still hoped it might be done, but perhaps not now, not today.

"I'll think about it, of course. I've time for nothing else but thinking."

"It's worth struggling for, isn't it—the possibility of peace, no more war? No more of those terrible bloody nightmares that we both went through?"

"If it could be made to happen, there'd be nothing in this world more worth the effort." Lawrence looked up at him. "I'll certainly think about it."

"Mosley's speaking at the Albert Hall this month, on the twenty-fourth. Why don't you come and hear him? I'll introduce you. If he doesn't convince you, I can't imagine who could."

"I'll think about it, but I'm not saying I'll come. I hope I'll be home at Clouds Hill by then, and London's a very long ride from there on a push-bike, which is what I'm reduced to these days."

"But you will consider it? My proposal, I mean."

"Of course." Yes, he'd consider it. It was tempting, certainly, the thought that he might be the mainspring for the kind of movement that Williamson spoke of—but he

31

couldn't believe that he was the one for it. It would be too much for him. All he wanted was to get to Clouds Hill and stay there, to do nothing.

They walked outside to Williamson's six-cylinder Alvis. Lawrence stood watching him drive down the road until the car turned a corner. It was a cool day, even for March, and he didn't like cold. He walked back inside and sat by the fire again, now on the couch.

For a moment he felt terribly lonely, with the quiet in the room after the sound of voices. But he wanted to be alone, didn't he? Yes, he wanted that—and yet he didn't. It seemed that all his life so far had been a contradiction. His life so far. And how much was left of it? Could there be much more? The days it had taken him to ride down here from Bridlington had probably depressed him, having to move so slowly on the bike. But he might have no alternative to traveling like that. With the few shillings a week that his investments were going to give him, it wasn't practical to consider riding the motorbike very often. And, God, he did love riding that Brough Superior wide open on a good road, with the wind ripping through his hair. He'd have to ration his time on it, though. Just couldn't afford the petrol.

But he'd have to do something. If he stayed at Clouds Hill day after day, inventing odd jobs to keep himself from thinking, he'd certainly go mad. And no one had rushed to him with offers of employment. The jobs in Egypt and Home Defence were complete fabrications, of course. Poor old Williamson had accepted them without raising an eyebrow. So had everyone else he'd told about them in these past few weeks. But there wasn't a word of truth in any of it. Who in the government would ever consider him for those jobs or any other? But why did he still have this compulsion to tell such lies? Oh, it was much too late to think about motives. He really didn't want to look too closely at himself. Not today.

Perhaps he should think about Williamson's suggestion. Could he really do something useful with the Blackshirts? Would men rally around him again, even now, after all these years? Did his name still have the power? Oh, yes, there wasn't much doubt of that. But did he any longer want power? He'd been hiding from it for too many years, burying himself in the ranks. And could he really associate himself with any movement that might ally itself with a man like Hitler? There was a man, with his vulgar pursuit of power, who personified everything that he himself turned away from: the blatant display of ambition. He himself had always hidden his.

And what Hitler was doing in Germany made him very uneasy. What he was doing with the Jews. That was disturbing. And it was even more disturbing that so many of them were leaving Germany now and going to Palestine. The news from there was depressing too. Arab and Jew were going to be at each other's throats there, it seemed. And once he'd thought it might be so different—when Feisal and Weizmann had met, late in the war, and he'd been there as a bridge between them.

Emir Feisal, leader of the Arab army, and Dr. Weizmann first met in early June, nineteen-eighteen, at Feisal's camp at Wahida on the plateau northwest of Akaba.

Weizmann was touring the Middle East with the Zionist Commision from London, explaining to influential Arabs and Jews the Zionist hopes for a national home for the Jews in Palestine. Feisal had heard reports of the tour, and he sat talking about it to Lawrence the day before Weizmann's party arrived.

"Dr. Weizmann has been saying that the Arabs should not believe those who tell them that it is the Jews' intention to take supreme political control in Palestine when the war is ended," Feisal said. "Can he be believed, Colonel Lawrence?"

"Most certainly, Your Highness—and for the very good reason that my government would never let the Jews take control of Palestine. For that reason, even if there were no other, you can believe Dr. Weizmann."

Feisal's slim hands were on his lap, one over the other, his long fingers laced together, and his back was straight

33

in his chair. He was thirty-two, only two years older than Lawrence, but it always seemed to Lawrence that he was dignified far beyond his years, with his high cheekbones and neatly pointed black beard.

"Is that really so?" Feisal's long fingers moved when he talked, tensely. "In spite of Mr. Balfour's declaration only six months ago?"

"Not in spite of it—because of it, Your Highness. Balfour was very specific that nothing should be done to prejudice the rights of the Arab community in Palestine."

Feisal sat watching him. He trusted Lawrence, but he was not so confident about the British government. Early in the war, to persuade him to help them against the Turks, Britain had promised Feisal's father, Sherif Hussein, that they would support Arab independence once the Turks had been driven from all Arab land. But last year there had been the Balfour Declaration. And earlier, in nineteen-sixteen, the British and French had secretly signed the Sykes-Picot Agreement, for dividing most of the Arab lands between them when the war was won. Six months ago the Turks had heard of it and, hoping they would undermine Arab support for the British, wrote of it to Feisal, as proof that the British were not to be trusted. Feisal had sent the letter to Hussein, but the old man had not doubted the British. A British promise is like gold, he had said; no matter how hard you rub it, it still shines. Even so, Hussein sent the Turkish letter to the British, for reassurance from them. The British had given it. They wrote Hussein: "His Majesty's Government reaffirm their former pledges to His Highness in regard to the freeing of Arab peoples. Liberation is the policy HMG have pursued and intend to pursue with unswerving determination." So the Arabs had fought on against the Turks. But Feisal was still uneasy.

Lawrence sensed his skepticism. "The Jews do not desire to control Palestine, Your Highness. What they desire is to feel that in Palestine a Jew may live his life and speak his tongue as he did in ancient times. Nothing more." He hoped it would be nothing more. No, it could never be

34

more. London knew that if they allowed the Zionists more than that, they would make enemies of the Arabs, and that would be disastrous.

"I shall see," Feisal said. "I shall be most interested to meet Dr. Weizmann and hear him."

"I think it will be reassuring for you, Your Highness." It relieved Lawrence that Feisal had not refused altogether to see Weizmann. He could not blame Feisal for being suspicious. Somehow, though, Feisal, most influential of the Arab leaders, had to be persuaded to accept some Jewish colonization of Palestine. Lawrence had been ordered to do all he could to reassure him. The order had come from London and the reason for it was compelling: In the two years of war that had passed since the Sykes-Picot Agreement, which also proposed an international administration for Palestine, the British had decided that Palestine must be controlled by them. The Turks had come close to overrunning the Suez Canal, and Britain was determined that that would never happen again. To protect the canal from the north, they wanted Palestine, and against the French insistence on internationalization, which they were sure would come at the peace conference, they wanted the support of Arabs and Zionists for a British mandate. That had been one of the reasons for the Balfour Declaration, to ensure that the vast influence of the Zionists, especially the Americans, would come down on Britain's side. And now Lawrence had to see that Britain did not lose the support of the Arabs; he had to persuade Feisal that Zionism was no danger.

"The Jews have exerted a major influence on the course of the war, Your Highness," he said. "Particularly in matters of finance. All nations need them. Even the Arabs."

"Do you suggest we could obtain such help from the Zionists, Colonel Lawrence?"

"Yes, Your Highness. A great sum of money will be needed after the war, to establish an independent Arab government and to maintain it. I would say that in exchange for your approval of some form of Zionist presence in part of the Arab lands, in Palestine, the Jews might provide be-

35

tween fifteen and twenty million pounds."

"Money, yes, they might provide that in exchange for land."

"And they could provide advice and assistance, Your Highness. It would be essential until the Arabs develop their own skills—and better to take counsel from the Jews, who would be neighbors, than from a foreign power."

Watching him, Feisal said softly: "Yes, we shall be reluctant to accept assistance from a foreign power."

Lawrence could see that all of it had made an impression. But Feisal did not say how he regarded the thought of working with the Zionists; he merely sat considering it all.

The next day Feisal met Weizmann, and Lawrence was there to interpret for them, because although Feisal spoke some English, he did not trust his command of it for delicate conversations such as this.

It was not a long meeting, something less than an hour, and Feisal was cautious. Weizmann, stocky, with a bald head and a black goatee, tried hard to charm him.

"I congratulate you, Your Highness, on the brave and skillful campaign that your army has fought against the Turks," Weizmann said.

Lawrence translated.

"Thank you." Feisal nodded, stately in his dark robe and headdress. "I look forward to the final victory."

"May it be soon," Weizmann said.

"If God wills it."

"It will come. And then, Your Highness, will come the task of building a strong and prosperous Arab kingdom."

As he translated, Lawrence watched Feisal and saw that he sensed where it was all moving.

"It is a great challenge," Feisal said. "There will be many difficulties, but I am hopeful that we shall overcome them."

"I understand, Your Highness, that your main interest is with Damascus and northern Syria."

"I have an interest in all the Arab lands that shall be freed from the Turks."

"Including Palestine?"

"Yes, of course."

"My people also have an interest there," Weizmann said.

"I know of it."

"Is it possible that we could both satisfy our interests in Palestine, Your Highness?"

Feisal's hands moved loosely as he said quickly: "Everything is possible, but there would be much to discuss."

"And there is much room in Palestine."

Feisal bent his head. "Much," he said softly.

"My people believe there is room there for four or five million Jews, if the land were fully developed. And the lives of the Arabs there would be greatly improved through the work of Jewish settlers."

"Your people are diligent workers, Dr. Weizmann."

"And we could help in other ways, Your Highness. The creation of a strong, independent Arab kingdom will require much money and technical advice. We Jews would be able to help. We could give the necessary money and organizing ability. And such assistance would be without debt or obligation. We shall be your neighbors and will not represent any danger to you, as we are not and never shall be a great power."

"What you say is persuasive, Dr. Weizmann. It merits much thought," Feisal said, and Lawrence could see he was not yet convinced. It would take time.

When their talk ended, Feisal suggested that he and Weizmann should go outside and be photographed. They posed together, Weizmann wearing an Arab headcloth with his white linen suit and dark tie. And then the Zionist party left.

"He is a persuasive man," Feisal said, when he and Lawrence were inside again. "He said much that commends itself to me."

"I think his proposals should be seriously considered, Your Highness. There could be great advantage for the Arab people in accepting such help from the Zionists. I believe it."

37

Feisal nodded, thinking. "There is much more to discuss. I shall meet Dr. Weizmann again."

They met again six months later, on the eleventh of December, nineteen-eighteen, at the Carlton Hotel in London, when Feisal was in Europe for the Paris Peace Conference. Again Lawrence was their interpreter.

"Your Highness," Weizmann said, "I should like to explain in summary the wishes of my people. These are that you and the other delegates to the peace conference should recognize the Jews' national and historic rights in Palestine, and that we be given a share in the government of the country commensurate with our contribution to the economy and our ability. Our desire is that four or five million Jews should be settled in Palestine, and we are certain that when the land is developed this can be done without any prejudice to the rights of the Arab population. In return, we would be willing to render the Arab people every assistance, in money and such guidance as might be required in the establishment of an independent Arab state in Syria."

Feisal replied in Arabic.

Lawrence translated: "I tell you on my word of honor, Dr. Weizmann, that I will do everything to support Jewish demands, and I will declare at the peace conference that Zionism and Arab nationalism are fellow movements, and that complete harmony prevails between them."

Feisal and Weizmann agreed that they would write this agreement into a document and sign it before the peace conference opened.

By the third of January the document was ready—and Feisal read words that he had not heard in his discussion with Weizmann. "Jewish State" and "Jewish Government" in Palestine were written into the document.

"This I cannot accept," Feisal said. "These must be changed to 'Palestine' and 'Palestine Government.' I will not sign otherwise."

The changes were made and Feisal seemed satisfied. But at the bottom of the last page he wrote that the conditions of the agreement would be met only if the Arabs were given their independence as promised by the British government.

"If the slightest modification or departure were to be made, I shall not then be bound by a single word of the present agreement, which shall be deemed void and of no account or validity," Feisal wrote.

The agreement was signed, but in it was no mention of Zionist financial support for any independent Arab government.

And that was a time when I deceived not only Arabs but Jews too. Lawrence sat staring into his fire. How different it might be in Palestine now if I had worked for it differently sixteen years ago. But I cheated them both, Feisal and Weizmann, interpreting for each of them not precisely what he had said but what it would please the other to hear. Feisal had never accepted Zionist demands or said he would ever support them, and he hadn't known that the Jews' intention was to establish a government in Palestine.

But was I to blame for it? The politicians in Whitehall had wanted an agreement between the Arabs and Zionists before the opening of the peace conference, so that both sides would go to Paris ready to support the British mandate in Palestine. And how could any agreement have been reached between Arabs and Zionists except by distortion? But did I have to agree to be a party to it? Couldn't I have refused? Yes—but there was my own ambition still. There was always that. I had hopes that something could, against all logic, be agreed between Feisal and the Zionists, and my own plans might in time become real—that I would become the adviser to Feisal as the ruler of an independent Syria.

That had never happened. Feisal, at least, had never compromised his beliefs, and in the weeks after the signing of the agreement, when he realized all that had been attempted against him, he said in a statement that the Arabs would fight to the last ditch against Palestine being other than part of the Arab kingdom, that they would fight for the supremacy of Arabs in the land. Feisal was dead now, but they were fighting in Palestine, and he, Lawrence, might once have had the influence to arrange it all differently. If only he had been a different man.

4

It was morning, and the *souk* in Nablus, in central Palestine, was busy, with Arab women buying meat and vegetables at the stalls. At the tables outside a café, the men sitting with their small cups of strong black coffee watched a British army patrol walking by, four soldiers with rifles slung on their shoulders.

Two Arabs at one of the tables just glanced at them, sipped their coffee, and went on talking.

"Soon they will not be passing us so carelessly," the older man said. "When the revolt begins, they will look at all Arabs with respect."

"Soon!" The younger man snorted. "Three weeks ago you said it would be soon. When will it begin?"

The older man sipped his coffee. "In time. Not next month, but in time."

"I begin to doubt this. I doubt all this talk of an uprising."

"It will come. It *must* come, Nasir. Every month now, more and more Jews come into our country. They buy our land from Arab landlords who live far away, and then they come and take it from Arab peasants and poor farmers who have worked on it all their lives. The Jews are taking more and more. It must end. If we do not act, the Jews will take all Palestine from us." The older man sat back from his empty cup. "The revolt will come." He looked confident. "And we will have a great leader."

Nasir forced himself to show curiosity. "Great enough to ensure victory against the Jews?"

"Of course."

"I hope so—but what Arab is there in Palestine who has the experience to lead an uprising?"

"Not an Arab. An Englishman." Now the older man was very confident.

Nasir leaned across the table. "An Englishman?" he hissed. "Rasim, are you serious?"

"Of course."

"What Englishman would lead Arabs in such a revolt? It would not be only Jews who would die; the British troops would also be against us, trying to protect the Jews—and they would die too."

"Yes." Rasim nodded. "But there will be an Englishman. I have been told this."

"And he would be a man competent to lead us?"

"Yes. He is one who has led Arabs in the past—with great honor."

"Who is this man?"

Rasim looked into his empty coffee cup.

Nasir thought he had gone too far; he had startled the man. "I thought so. There is no leader—certainly not an Englishman. That is foolishness."

Rasim looked up. "No," he whispered. "There is such a man."

"Then who?"

"Lawrence."

"Who?"

"Colonel Lawrence."

"Lawrence? The Englishman who fought with the Arab army in the war?"

"Yes," Rasim said. "Colonel Lawrence."

"This cannot be. I thought this man was long dead."

"No, he is not dead. He is coming."

"Perhaps." Nasir smiled indulgently. "If you tell me it is so, I believe it, of course." But he still smiled.

"No, you do not believe. You think I am a fool. But you will see."

Nasir finished his coffee. "Yes." He looked at his watch. "I will be patient, and I hope I will see all you have told me." He pushed his chair away from the table. "I must go back to work, Rasim."

"We will meet another time."

"Yes. Soon."

Nasir walked away from the café and out of the Arab market, toward the center of the town, where he had a barbershop.

Later in the morning an Arab came into the shop, and while Nasir cut his hair he told him what he had heard in the café. The Arab was a sergeant of the Palestine Police, working undercover in intelligence, and Nasir was one of his agents.

"You are sure of the man who told you this?" the sergeant said.

"He is the one who has been telling me of this uprising for some time now. Have you believed him so far?"

"We have no reason to doubt the reports."

"Then believe this one too."

"But—Colonel Lawrence!" the sergeant whispered.

"That is what he said."

The sergeant looked into the big mirror at Nasir cutting his hair. "I will report it—but I hope it is no joke."

"It is not a joke. The man who told me is certain of it. Take it with seriousness."

Three men sat around a table in a room in Jerusalem, the glare of the afternoon sun softened by heavy drapes drawn close across the window. They were the senior commanders of the Haganah, the defense organization of the Jewish Agency. To guard against the risk of civil war, the British order was that only the army would defend Jewish settlements against Arab attacks and that any Jewish self-defense would not be tolerated. So the Haganah was illegal, and the commanders always met secretly, often changing their meeting place. This day it was above a bookshop off Ben Yehuda Street, in Ohel Moshe, one of the Jewish sections of Jerusalem.

Weeks ago they had heard the rumors that the Arabs were planning a major uprising. Now, two hours ago, one of their members, a Jewish police inspector, had told the senior commander, Josephson, of the report that Lawrence was coming. It had shocked Josephson, and at once he had called the others to this meeting.

Sitting there, Ben-Shemin, a thin-faced man, about thirty-five, said: "Is this to be taken seriously? I can't believe it."

"I know it sounds incredible," Josephson said, "but we must take it seriously. The police are. They're sending an urgent message to London."

The third man grunted a laugh. "Do they think London doesn't already know about it?" He pulled deeply on a cigarette and, jerking his head back, blew the smoke impatiently at the ceiling. He chain-smoked Turkish cigarettes, and already the room was heavy with the smell of them.

"What do you mean?" Josephson said.

The man flicked the end off his cigarette into an ashtray and drew on it again, staring through the smoke at Josephson. His name was Lehrs, and he was thirty, the youngest of the three. "I mean the British government is sending Lawrence. It must be obvious to you."

The other two sat looking at him from their sides of the table. This had not occurred to them.

"No," Ben-Shemin said, shaking his head. "That can't be. You don't like the British, Avi—I know that—but to suspect them of something like this . . ." He shook his head again. "I think that goes too far."

"Do you? Perhaps you haven't thought enough about it." Lehrs leaned across the table, brushing aside blue smoke. "Do you imagine that Lawrence would be coming here as a private citizen, independently, to help the Arabs in one more of their pathetic little uprisings?" He puffed quickly, flicking the smoke irritably with his hand. "No, my friend—the British are sending him."

Ben-Shemin was concerned. He looked at Josephson. "What do you think, Meyer? Is this possible?"

Josephson was staring at Lehrs, thinking about what he had said. "I don't know. I don't know what to think. When I first heard this about Lawrence, I thought it was nonsense. I thought it ridiculous that a man like him, who has done nothing for so many years, would come here for something like this. I thought it was another of the wild stories that the Arabs tell one another to keep themselves excited. But now, I'm not so sure. I think that if Lawrence were being sent by the British government, it might be true."

"Of course it's true!" Roughly Lehrs butted out the end he had just used to light another cigarette. "Do you think he'd get here unless he were being sent by those bastards in Whitehall?" He looked from one to the other. "Of course not! They'd never let him come here and stir up the Arabs if it wasn't what they wanted."

"You both think this?" Ben-Shemin said.

Quietly, as though he was thinking aloud, Josephson said: "I think it's possible. If this story is true, and he's coming—yes, then I think he's being sent by the British, as an agent."

"Doesn't it make sense?" Lehrs said. "For years the British have been trying to keep us from gaining strength here, but they've never had the guts to make any move against us that would be too obvious—just their sneaking politicians' games. But what if they secretly incited the Arabs to attack us—really attack us, up and down the country, and drive us into the sea?"

The others said nothing.

Then Josephson said: "I think it's possible, Avi. You might be right about it." The more he thought about it, the more he agreed with Lehrs.

"What will you do, Meyer?" Ben-Shemin said. He did not want to believe any of this, but he knew it was possible. The British were capable of it, he had to admit.

"I'll send a report to the Jewish Agency." Josephson

45

shrugged. "What more can we do, at the moment? I'll give them the report about Lawrence, and what we suspect, and they can send it on to London, for Weizmann."

"And Weizmann will have lunch with one of his friends from Whitehall and politely ask about it, and his friend will deny it." Impatient, shaking his head, Lehrs flicked ash from his cigarette.

"At the moment, there's nothing else we can do," Josephson said.

"Of course not!" Lehrs puffed quickly. "Weizmann talks to them in London, one Englishman to another, and we sit here and take it from the Arabs. No, there's nothing else we can do."

Josephson sat looking at him. "Be patient, Avi."

Lehrs nodded quickly, shifting his chair, looking around the room, restless. "Yes, yes. Be patient."

Still watching him, Josephson wondered how much longer Lehrs would be content with the Haganah's passivity, its policy of self-defense and no more. In the last few months there had been times, like now, when he looked as though he could not tolerate it. Sometimes he seemed to want to go out and fight for what they might not be able to win peacefully. Josephson looked at his watch. "Is there anything more to say?"

Impatiently Lehrs shook his head.

"No," Ben-Shemin said.

"I'll send the report," Josephson said. "You two go."

Lehrs rose. They always left a meeting one at a time, at five-minute intervals. "We'll have to find out how soon the Arabs plan to do all this to us."

"We'll find out," Josephson said.

Lehrs looked unconvinced. "Shalom." He nodded at them.

"Shalom," they said.

He walked out and carefully shut the door. The other two sat looking at it.

"He's becoming impatient," Ben-Shemin said.

"I know it," Josephson said. "But he's all right." Many of their people had become impatient over the last few years, losing confidence in Dr. Weizmann's quiet, diplomatic way with the British government and his insistence on nonretaliation for Arab attacks. Many of them had become convinced that those methods would never win them a homeland in Palestine. Three or four years ago some of the most militant Haganah members had broken away and formed Haganah B. In the last few months they had begun calling themselves the Irgun Zvai Leumi—the National Military Organization—and the Irgun was ready to fight the Arabs for their place in Palestine.

"I hope he's wrong about the British sending Lawrence," Ben-Shemin said.

"So do I—but time will tell." Josephson was uneasy. He felt it was likely that Lehrs was right.

Lehrs walked in the bright sun down the wide strip of King George V Avenue. He was glad to be out of the meeting place, away from Josephson and Ben-Shemin. For months he had found it more and more difficult to sit in the same room with them and their passive acceptance of everything the British and the Arabs were doing to their people. But he had to go on with them—and he had to try to control himself much better than he had today. It was hard to believe that there'd been a time when he was like them, willing to wait forever—which meant till Weizmann performed a miracle in London and persuaded the British government to fulfill the promise they had made to the Jews in nineteen-seventeen. But he was no longer willing to wait. Three months ago he had joined the Irgun. He had not wanted to stay with the Haganah, but the Irgun had told him he would be useful there, because the Haganah, with members all through the Jewish population, had a much larger intelligence-gathering organization than the Irgun, and Lehrs, with access to all that, would be invaluable. He wondered what the Irgun would do with this news about Lawrence.

5

When the Palestine Police report mentioning Lawrence arrived at the Colonial Office, Cunliffe-Lister at once telephoned the Prime Minister, and within an hour he was at 10 Downing Street, in MacDonald's study. Sir John Gilmour, the Home Secretary, was there too when he walked in.

"This all sounds very strange," MacDonald said as Cunliffe-Lister opened his briefcase. "Gilmour and I were just talking about it."

"It hardly sounds feasible," Gilmour said.

"Here's the police report." Cunliffe-Lister took it from his case in a brown envelope with the flap held down by pink string wound around a metal tag. He pulled out the report and handed it across MacDonald's desk to him. "There's very little." It was one and a half typed pages.

MacDonald sat reading it. He wore round horn-rimmed glasses.

He looked up at Cunliffe-Lister. "I don't know what to think about this." Years ago—at the end of the war, it must have been, and it seemed a very long time ago now, when his dear wife had been dead only seven or eight years—he'd read some of the newspaper articles about Lawrence of Arabia, and he remembered thinking that he

48

seemed an extraordinary man. He couldn't believe the man would do something like this—against his own country.

"May I see it?" Gilmour held out a hand for the report. MacDonald passed it to him.

Gilmour read it quickly. "What d'you think, Philip?" He ignored MacDonald. Like Cunliffe-Lister, he was a Conservative member of the government, and they both thought MacDonald—at his age, with his poor health—was incompetent and should resign.

"It certainly sounds strange—but, as you see, the police say the agent who made the report is a very reliable one."

"Hasn't this man Lawrence retired from the RAF very recently?" MacDonald said. It seemed to him that he'd read something about it, but he couldn't be sure. These days he forgot so many things.

"Three or four weeks ago," Gilmour said. As though the Prime Minister were not in the room, he said to Cunliffe-Lister: "Can Lawrence be up to something?"

"I haven't the faintest. I've never met the man. Don't know a thing about him—except the odd article I've read. Seems an eccentric."

"He is. I knew a chap who was with him in Cairo during the war—before he went out to Arabia—and he told me he was damn strange. And he's quite definitely a self-serving exhibitionist."

"I shouldn't be surprised if you're right," Cunliffe-Lister said.

MacDonald sat listening to them. They were talking to each other as though he were not here—and he was, after all, the Prime Minister. A few years ago he would never have accepted such behavior. It was unacceptable now, but he cared too little to object. He was too tired.

"I'm certain I'm right." Gilmour was saying. "Have you, by any chance, read that book of his, *The Seven Pillars of Wisdom?*"

"No, actually, I don't think I have."

"It'd tell you everything about Lawrence. It was a self-indulgent piece of romancing. Reading it, you'd think he was the only British officer serving out there with the Arabs. The only purpose of the book, so far as I could see, was to make that little upstart look heroic. Evidently it succeeded."

"He's certainly something of a hero." Cunliffe-Lister picked up the Palestine Police report from the corner of MacDonald's desk. "But d'you think he could be capable of doing something like this?"

MacDonald sat watching Gilmour, waiting for what he would say. Of the two, he liked Gilmour less. He was older than Cunliffe-Lister, almost sixty, and a harder man.

"Yes," MacDonald said. "That's what I want decided." He felt he had to say something, to assert himself. "That's why I asked you both to come here." It gave him some satisfaction, at least, to remind them that they were here because he had called them.

"I think this is precisely the sort of thing that Lawrence might do," Gilmour said. "I'd say it could very easily appeal to him. The man's egocentric, no question about that, and if the Arabs have asked him to go and help them, it would certainly flatter him and he wouldn't be able to resist." He nodded decisively. "I'm strongly inclined to believe this report."

"But he'd be working against his own country," MacDonald said. "Against the national interest."

Gilmour looked at him and said nothing.

"Well? Do you think he'd do this?" MacDonald felt quick anger at the way Gilmour was looking at him, as though he were of no importance. He was still the Prime Minister, no matter what Gilmour and his party might wish, and he would be respected. "I'm asking if you believe Lawrence would lead Arabs against British troops?"

"I was under the impression that I'd made it quite clear." Gilmour stared across the desk at him. "Yes. I believe he would."

MacDonald stared back at him through his horn-rimmed glasses. A few years ago he'd never have allowed a man to speak to him as Gilmour just had. But he wouldn't give Gilmour the satisfaction of reacting. He wouldn't give him the satisfaction.

"It's going a bit far, John—even if Lawrence is as you say he is," Cunliffe-Lister said. "To fight against his own country . . ." He shook his head.

"Yes, I'm aware it is. But I'm thinking now of something I read in that book of his. It struck me forcibly at the time, and I thought the man should've been charged with treason, not applauded as a hero. I've never forgotten it and it's always irked me."

"Would you be kind enough to tell me what it was?" MacDonald said.

"Yes. He was apparently suffering some kind of guilt, toward the end of the war, because he knew that, what with the Sykes-Picot Agreement and one thing and another, the Arabs wouldn't get the independence they'd been fighting for—so he decided he'd take them in a dash up to Damascus, to take control before our army arrived, and have them so firmly established as the government of Syria that we wouldn't dare to move against them and risk provoking another revolt—against us, this time, rather than against the Turks. And that way, Lawrence said, he'd—and these are his words, which infuriated me when I read them, and still do—'be able to defeat not merely the Turks on the battlefield, but my own country and its allies in the council chamber.' That was his instinct, you see: to work for the Arabs, for whatever self-serving reason—because certainly it wasn't out of feeling for them, or he couldn't have written about them as he did—against his own country. As it happened, he was unsuccessful in nineteen-eighteen, but he was ready to work for the Arabs then, and I don't for one moment doubt that he'd be ready to do it now."

Much as he disliked Gilmour, MacDonald had to admit that he sounded convincing. Clearly he didn't like Lawrence but, even making an allowance for that, he was convincing.

"D'you think Lawrence thought of himself as some kind of messiah to the Arabs?" Cunliffe-Lister said.

51

"Yes, I'd say that's about it. And I think he'd find it very appealing to go out there and help them now." Gilmour nodded at the report. "I believe we should treat that seriously."

There was silence in the room.

"Then it's dangerous," Cunliffe-Lister said.

MacDonald looked at him, and at Gilmour. Yes, it would be dangerous if a man like Lawrence went out to Palestine and did this. There could be terrible complications. It was a very delicate problem, Palestine. For years it had caused him trouble, and he felt less and less fit to deal with it.

"Yes, it is dangerous," he said. "We can't have the Arabs incited to revolt."

Gilmour looked coldly at him. He could see MacDonald was losing his grip on the conversation. It happened more and more often these days. The man could concentrate for only brief periods, and they were becoming briefer. His mind wandered. He came and went. This couldn't go on much longer; he wasn't fit to run the government.

"It isn't a question of the Arabs' being incited to revolt," Gilmour said. "It isn't necessary to incite them. They're constantly ready to revolt, it seems to me. Obviously they're ready for it now—without any help from Lawrence. But they've apparently asked for his help. The danger is"—he glanced at Cunliffe-Lister—"and I'm sure this is what you had in mind, Philip—that if he goes out there, it'll be assumed by everyone that he's been sent by us."

"Exactly," Cunliffe-Lister said. "If it became known that he was out there."

"Oh, it'd become known soon enough. Given Lawrence's addiction to personal publicity, it'd become known the day he arrived, I imagine." Very carefully, so MacDonald would understand it, Gilmour said: "That's the danger, Prime Minister—that Lawrence would be taken as an agent of the British government, sent surreptitiously to help the Arabs. Then our policy, which has been subtle encouragement of the Arabs, support for their position, would appear blatant." He glanced at Cunliffe-Lister and back at MacDonald to make sure that the old man was still following him.

"And at once we'd have opposition from the Zionists around the world—most particularly in America. I hardly think I need to elaborate. We most certainly don't want to antagonize the American Zionists. No more than we already have, that is."

"Absolutely not," Cunliffe-Lister said.

No, MacDonald thought. No, they must not antagonize the American Zionists. And it would antagonize them if they thought his government had sent Lawrence to help the Arabs against the Jews. Yes, that was very plain. It had been policy for years—as this man Gilmour had just said—to appease the Arabs at the expense of the Jews. That had to be done. The only way to ensure the safety of the base in Palestine was to satisfy the overwhelming majority of the population: the Arabs. He understood it all very well—as he should, because he'd certainly spent a great deal of time with this terrible problem, over the years. Especially in the past year or two, with the probability of a war with Germany or Italy, or perhaps both—not in his time in office, he hoped, but some time in the future. There might be no way to avoid that. Then Palestine would be vital, for the protection of the Suez. Yes, they'd discussed that several times in this room. Did this man Gilmour think he didn't understand the problem?

Gilmour and Cunliffe-Lister were sitting watching him.

"We're agreed, are we not, Prime Minister?" Gilmour was being elaborately patient. "In the event of war, Palestine would be of supreme importance to us—but so would the friendship of America. And if the American Zionists were convinced that we'd come out unreservedly in support of the Arabs—to the extent of sending a man like Lawrence out there, unofficially, to lead them—then they'd use all their very considerable influence against us in Washington. That would be disastrous. I'm sure you agree."

"Of course I agree!" MacDonald snapped. He wouldn't tolerate this man Gilmour's condescension!

"What d'you suggest we do, Prime Minister?" Cunliffe-Lister said.

"We shall have to do something. That's evident." Mac-

Donald thought he sounded very decisive.

The other two sat waiting to hear what they should do.

"I suppose we could prevent Lawrence from leaving the country," MacDonald said. On the other hand, he wasn't certain that they could do that.

"No, no." Quickly Gilmour shook his head. "We have no legal means of stopping him. What possible reason could we give? None. And if we tried to bring pressure against him, to prevent him, this affair would become known to the press at once. Lawrence himself would almost certainly publicize it. There's no telling how it would become distorted." He shook his head again. "We daren't risk that."

"No, I suppose not."

"I think we're rather ahead of ourselves," Cunliffe-Lister said. "We don't know with absolute certainty that Lawrence is going. This is still only a report that's come from an agent in Nablus. It might merely be that an Arab who knew Lawrence during the war, or perhaps only heard of him, was talking about him and wished he were there to lead them now. And the rumor spread."

"Perhaps," Gilmour said. "But we can't assume that."

"No. But we don't know what contact, if any, Lawrence has had with the Arabs. He's hardly had much time, barely out of the RAF. If he were to be going there, there'd be some discussion beforehand. I don't imagine they'd simply write him a letter, inviting him."

"No. They'd discuss it, of course. And I doubt if they'd ask him out there to do that—not if they wanted to keep it quiet. Lawrence couldn't go there without the press hearing of it. No, they'd send someone to have talks with him here."

"I should think so," Cunliffe-Lister said.

"And what should we do about it?" MacDonald said. He couldn't decide what they should do—but they had to do something. He could see that clearly enough.

"For the moment, I think we should place Lawrence under surveillance," Gilmour said. "If he's meeting Arabs, we must know about it."

Cunliffe-Lister looked nervous.

"Surveillance?" MacDonald said.

"We should know where he goes, whom he speaks to, whom he meets," Gilmour said. "If we see nothing suspicious after a few weeks, then we'll know this was just a rumor, and we'll have no cause for concern."

Cunliffe-Lister looked easier. "If it was discreetly done, I imagine it'd be a useful thing."

"I'll have MI-5 do it," Gilmour said. "It'll be discreet, I assure you. Do you approve, Prime Minister?"

"I think so." Tiredly, MacDonald nodded. If these two agreed on it, he would too. He wanted to rest. "Yes, I approve. Have it done, Gilmour. Give me frequent reports on this." That was the thing; he should have frequent reports, to know what was happening.

"Very well." Gilmour leaned forward in his chair, to rise. "I'll have the surveillance begun immediately." If Lawrence was involved in anything, MI-5, the security service, would find it.

6

The scar-faced man stepped out of a taxi at the corner of Shmuel Hanavi Anenue, in the north of Jerusalem. He stood watching the traffic that had come up behind the taxi, to see that no one in any of the cars was paying too much attention to him. Then he turned up a side street and walked north, into Nahlat Shimeon, one of the Jewish districts.

When he had been walking slowly for almost ten minutes, moving almost in a circle through the streets, stopping from time to time and watching behind him, he knocked at the door of a house very close to the edge of the city, turning to look behind him for the last time while he waited for the door to open.

The scar on his face, a jagged white line in his tan, was across his right cheek from the jawline to the corner of his eyebrow. He also wore an artificial right hand, wooden, covered with a black glove. His name was Yehuda Matot and he was one of the commanders of the Irgun. Two years ago, when he was twenty-six, he had been almost killed by a bomb set by Arab terrorists, but at the hospital he had struggled very hard to stay alive, and after some weeks he was safe, with his injuries. Then they told him that his wife had been killed outright by the bomb, and

he had shouted at the doctors, cursing them because they
had not let him die too. Now for two years he had lived
without caring about anything except to see a Jewish homeland in Palestine. He felt with certainty that he would not
live to see it, but he was ready at any moment to die fighting
for it.

He heard the faint click of the lock and turned at once,
as the door opened.

A woman held it open for him. "Shalom," she said.

"Shalom, Ruth."

"They're waiting for you."

She shut the door behind him and went back to a seat
at the window, to watch the street from behind a curtain,
while he walked through the house to a room at the back.

Two other men were sitting in armchairs, and they
stopped talking when he walked into the room. One of
them was Yassky, the other was Ben-Joseph, and when Matot sat with them, in another armchair, they looked like
three friends together for an afternoon. But the three of
them were the high command of the Irgun, and this house
was one of the meeting places they used. It always gave
them satisfaction to come here, and some amusement, because it was only a few yards from the compound of the
Palestine Police training school.

"It sounded urgent," Matot said to Yassky, who had
called the meeting. "What is it?"

Yassky, the senior commander, with a heavy black
moustache, said: "I was telling Ben-Joseph about it before
you came." He did not like it that Matot was five minutes
late.

Matot said nothing but looked irritated, waiting for him
to begin it again.

Yassky told of the report that had come from the Haganah meeting the day before, that Lawrence was coming.
It had not come to him until late last night, when Lehrs
had decided it was safe to make contact, and now he did
not tell the others who had told him. There was deep bitterness between the Haganah and the Irgun, and just as they
had Lehrs working in the Haganah, the Haganah might

have a sympathizer among them. One could never be too cautious.

When he heard about Lawrence, Matot thought he would explode. "Damn the British!" He hit with the side of his wooden hand on the arm of the chair. "How can any of our people still be uncertain about what those bastards intend to do to us?"

It did not occur to Matot or the others to doubt that if Lawrence was coming he was being sent by the British government, as an instrument of British policy, which they knew was against the Jews.

Ben-Joseph said to Yassky: "Is this from a reliable source?"

"Very reliable, Jacob. This talk of Lawrence is circulating among the Arabs. Perhaps it's just Arab talk, I don't know—but they're talking about it."

"Do you doubt it?" Matot snapped. "My God, man, do you doubt this?"

Ben-Joseph said nothing to him. Sometimes he thought Matot was perhaps a little insane. He himself had a reputation as a wild young man with a violent temper, but Matot had a way of making him feel old and cautious.

"Yehuda," Yassky said firmly. "We came here to discuss this, not to waste time screaming. I want us to agree what action to take, and I want it agreed quickly."

Matot smiled thinly at him.

"What do you think we should do, Mordechai?" Ben-Joseph said to Yassky.

Quickly Matot said: "Do? Why must we do anything? Does it mean anything to us if Lawrence comes?"

"What do you mean?" Yassky snapped. He had been disturbed by this story of Lawrence and he was in no mood for any of Matot's outbursts. He wanted reasonable discussion.

"I mean it's not important." Matot's wooden hand pounded his chair arm. "Who is this man? Perhaps he was something during the war, but that was twenty years ago—and perhaps he was nothing even then. Among the Arabs, anyone of average intelligence can appear to be a god. And he would certainly be very little help to them now. He must be an old man."

"Not too old," Yassky said. "Less than fifty." That was older than any of them, but not too old to be effective.

"I don't think it's important," Matot said. "If the British believe sending him here will help the Arabs against us, let them send him. I tell you he will be no danger to us."

"I don't agree with you, Yehuda. I've read of Lawrence. He was a leader among the Arabs—and they've produced very few leaders. If he comes—even if he does nothing but give them his name to rally around—he'll be of great value to them. And he'll be a danger to us. I want this to be considered as a threat. A dangerous threat." Yassky wanted none of Matot's heroics.

"What do you suggest we do?" Ben-Joseph said.

"First, we must know more about this," Yassky said. "We must know if Lawrence is coming or if this is just another Arab story."

"And how do you suggest we find out?" Matot said.

"We must send someone to England."

Ben-Joseph looked startled, but Matot smiled. He liked this. He had been ready to argue with Yassky, but he liked the thought of sending their fight to England. He liked it very much.

7

Harding, the director general of MI-5, had always been skeptical of most that he had heard of Lawrence. But he admitted that he was skeptical of just about everything and everyone. Either he was that way because of the conditioning of so many years in his work, doubting everyone, or he'd found his way to this work because he was by nature skeptical. From time to time he'd wondered about that. But now, at fifty-eight, he told himself it was academic, why he was the way he was. He was skeptical, that was all.

About Lawrence, though, his feelings were definitely mixed. He'd never met the man, but he'd always had great respect for him, not because of all that had been written about him but for the way he'd used publicity so cleverly to present such a careful picture of himself to the public. Yes, he respected Lawrence greatly for that. And for his talent in concealment, suppressing everything of himself that might be seen unfavorably—and there must be some of that in him, as in everyone. Even discounting a great deal of the popular myth, which Harding was convinced was nothing more than that—and he'd thought so years ago, soon after the war, when he'd gone along to Covent

Garden for a lecture on Lawrence by the American journalist chap Thomas—with all that, he imagined there had to
be enough essential truth among all the publicity to make
Lawrence an unusual man. He admitted he was fascinated
by the mystery of the man.

So the assignment appealed to him, when he sat in
Gilmour's office and listened to him explaining why they
suspected Lawrence might be involved in something shady
with the Arabs in Palestine, and why they wanted a watch
maintained on him.

But there was a risk here, too, and Harding saw it at
once.

"It might be difficult, if he were to become aware that
we were keeping an eye on him, Minister," he said. "He's
been a national hero—an *inter*national hero, for that matter—since the war, and if he were to become aware of
our interest, and made it known to the press, it'd be a scandal throughout the country. The public would sympathize
with him, of course. They'd be behind him. It'd be very
uncomfortable."

"I'm aware of that, Harding—and you'll have to impress
on your people that they be extremely careful. Lawrence
mustn't have the slightest suspicion that he's being watched.
Now that's imperative."

Harding nodded, brushing a fingertip over his gray
moustache. He didn't much care for the risk. Keeping an
eye on Lawrence, reading reports that perhaps would reveal something of the truth of the man, yes, that was something he looked forward to—but Lawrence had, as well
as his talent for publicity, many powerful friends, several
politicians among them, and he could make a great deal
of trouble if he wished. And he would certainly do it if
he became aware that MI-5 had him under surveillance.

"Of course, we usually try to ensure that the people
we watch don't become aware that we're watching them,
Minister," he said coolly. He didn't much care for Gilmour's
implication that his officers needed to be advised of the
need for delicacy—they were rarely clumsy—but that was
beside the point. What was very much to the point was

61

that Gilmour understand the risk here—the political risk for him and for any other member of the government who was involved in this, if it became known. "I simply thought it was my duty to point out that Lawrence is very far from being an ordinary subject for surveillance. Very far from it."

"I'm aware of it, Harding. I know how much noise the little man's capable of making—but if your men find that our suspicions are justified, and he *is* up to something with the Arabs, then we shall have him where we want him. I doubt very much that Lawrence will be in any position to complain to the press."

From the way Gilmour spoke, it was clear to Harding that he had very little regard for Lawrence. He hoped Gilmour hadn't let his personal feelings influence his judgment when he and MacDonald and whoever else had been a party to it had decided on taking this action against Lawrence. As for himself, he'd carry out the order, of course, and hope nothing went wrong. He was, after all, as he so often reminded himself these days, close to retirement.

But when, later in the day, he briefed the two officers who would be in overall charge of the surveillance, Harding was careful that they understood the importance of taking great care.

One of them, Quint, he knew it was unnecessary to caution. He'd known Quint for more than twenty years; the man was fifty and had joined MI-5 when it was created, a few years before the war, and, except for four years out for service with the Grenadiers during the war, had been in ever since. They'd worked together several times in their early days. He could be sure of Quint.

It was the other man Harding was less certain of—Richmond. He'd come into security five years ago, straight from Cambridge, and he was a very personable fellow but perhaps in need of a bit of experience. That was why he'd had Quint take him under his wing. If a tough old bird like Quint couldn't take some of the schoolboy shine off Richmond, no one could.

And when Harding sat telling them how vital it was that Lawrence did not become aware of their surveillance, he was certain he saw something in Richmond. A slight reaction, disapproval.

"Is there something about this that troubles you, Richmond?" he said.

"No, sir." Richmond, tall and slim, with blond wavy hair, was twenty-eight, but he looked much younger.

"Are you quite certain? You looked a bit uneasy."

"No, sir—but I find it hard to imagine that a man like Lawrence would do something like this. I mean, if he did this, he'd be fighting against his own country."

Quint glanced at Richmond with no expression, but Harding knew what he was thinking. Quint, with his black hair parted in the center, brushed back and stiffly brilliantined, his twice-broken nose and his big shoulders, very rarely showed what he was thinking. He simply looked very tough—but not nearly as tough as he actually was. Quint would stop at nothing. He was, Harding well knew, completely cold and ruthless. Quint had seen it all, and nothing would make him hesitate to do what he considered was his duty. Yes, young Richmond could learn a great deal from Quint.

"Yes, he would," he said to Richmond, still thinking of Quint. "D'you suppose that would be unthinkable for someone like Lawrence—to fight against his own country?"

"I really don't know, sir."

"Do you know Lawrence, Richmond?"

"Only from what I've read, sir. I've never met him, of course."

"Quite." Harding knew the signs. He was sure that Richmond was one of the thousands—hundreds of thousands, probably—whose imaginations had been caught by Lawrence. Richmond probably assumed quite naturally that the man was incapable of wrong. It might be a complication. He'd have to have a private word with Quint and tell him to be very careful with Richmond. "Nevertheless, we think it's quite possible that Lawrence is, in fact, prepared to, as you put it, fight against his own country."

"I see, sir." But Richmond sounded as though he still found it hard to believe.

"What about you, Quint—any questions?"

"No, sir."

"No reservations?" One corner of Harding's mouth moved: a secret smile for Quint.

Quint did not smile. "If Lawrence is up to something, I'm sure we'll find it. No, I've no reservations. I imagine Lawrence is capable of anything." He glanced at Richmond. "We'll have no difficulty."

"But carefully," Harding said. "It's delicate, I don't need to tell you."

"No." Again Quint looked at Richmond. "I think that's understood."

Richmond nodded. "Absolutely."

Quint sat watching him, disapproving. It was not that he disliked Richmond, just that he did not think he was serious. He would much rather work alone than have Richmond with him, but he understood why Harding had put them together like this. Someone had to do something with Richmond.

"How soon do we begin, sir?" he said.

"Immediately," Harding said. "I've selected the men who'll work on this, and told them they'll report to you. I'll leave it to you to brief them."

"Yes, sir," Quint said. "If there's nothing else, I should like to begin."

"That's all. Do begin at once, by all means."

Watching them walk to the door, Harding hoped again that nothing would go wrong and the press would not hear of this surveillance of Lawrence. God, that would be a scandal that would go with him as long as he lived. And he knew that the politicians who had ordered it would leave him to carry it all alone, if they could find a way. He had no doubt of that. It was possible that he wouldn't, after all, be allowed to retire gracefully.

8

Except for a few days in the middle of the month, Lawrence had stayed away from his cottage for most of March. To avoid the newspapermen who waited there, he had pedaled his bicycle through the south of England, looking at the country and trying not to think.

Now, in early April, he had thought it safe to come back, but pedaling down the road toward the cottage, he saw two cars parked ahead, against the grass verge. A man climbed out of one and stood watching him. More men came out of the cottage garden. They all stood waiting at the side of the road. More than a dozen of them, he saw. He pedaled on toward them. He couldn't understand why they had all come back. But, yes, he could: The more you showed yourself shy to them, the more vigorously they persisted. It was an infallible technique that he'd used often enough when he wanted to draw attention. But now he honestly didn't want these men here. For the moment he wanted nothing but to be alone.

When he was close to his garden gate they moved out around him, suddenly, as though each one had been waiting for someone else to make the first move.

"Colonel Lawrence!"

He turned to one who called, and when he saw the man focusing a camera he looked away again. The last thing he wanted in the press was a photograph of himself as he was now: tired-looking, old, and shabby. Let the public keep him as he'd been in the photographs they all remembered, in his white sherif's robe.

Wheeling his bicycle, he pushed his way through the crush of them all pressing in on him, the ones at the back trying to push through to get to him.

"Colonel Lawrence! May I ask . . . ?"

He pushed through them, not looking at any of the faces around him.

"One moment, sir! Just a moment!"

When he was in the garden he turned to them and stopped. If he didn't answer some of their questions now, they'd stay here, outside the cottage, trying to interview him and photograph him every time he went outdoors. Better to talk to them now and hope it would satisfy them.

"Sir, is it true that you want to take over the leadership of the Blackshirts?"

Lawrence smiled, and he knew these journalists would describe it as a "mysterious" smile. So they'd heard the story that he'd been asked to take over the Blackshirts. He'd mentioned that to only a few people, expanding slightly on the conversation he'd had with Williamson a month ago. Now it would be reported in the press.

"I was under the impression that Sir Oswald Mosley was the leader of the Blackshirts," he said.

"Yes, sir, but there's a rumor that you've been approached to replace him."

Lawrence shook his head. "I don't know anything about that." But again he smiled the mysterious smile, to make them imagine all he might be hiding from them.

"Do you have any ambition to become dictator of England, Colonel Lawrence?" another one said.

Lawrence looked at him. God, was there no limit to the tales they would dream and write about him? Dictator of England! But was it so far removed from the stories he'd spread about himself, over the years? He really didn't have the right to complain of fellows like these who came and disturbed him with their inventions about him, when it had pleased him so much in the past to circulate his own— and pleased him to have men like these magnify his stories and perpetuate them. He'd started it all—and he was still doing it. He'd told this story about the Blackshirts, knowing how it would travel. And he had to admit it was flattering that they were all here, eager to hear his answers to their questions.

"Dictator of England?" What could he say to this? If he denied it too emphatically, the story might die here— and it was a fascinating notion, too appealing to kill off here and now. "It's not something I'm giving a great deal of thought to." Again the smile, which they could take to mean either that he thought the whole subject frivolous or that he knew much more than he was telling.

He turned, pushing his bicycle to clear a way through them and cross the last few yards to the door of the cottage, so he could go in and shut them out.

A small red-faced reporter grabbed the handlebars of his bicycle to stop him.

"One moment, Colonel Lawrence—please!"

Lawrence wrenched at the handlebars and the reporter held on.

"There must be more to this than you say, sir," the reporter said. "For several days there's been a rumor that you're going to lead the Blackshirts and . . ."

"Please let go!" Lawrence jerked the handlebars.

The reporter held on. "I must insist, sir, that there . . ."

Lawrence's right hand moved very fast, and he punched into the reporter's face, feeling the jolt when his fist hit the bone of the eye socket.

The reporter staggered back, and jerking the handle-bars loose, Lawrence pushed his bicycle clear of the crowd and wheeled it to the cottage. Feeling them all watching him, in the sudden quiet, he wheeled the bicycle inside and shut the door.

"What the hell made him do that?" one of the reporters said.

The one Lawrence had hit was standing with his head down, both hands over his left eye. Another one was offering him a handkerchief.

"He must be bloody mad," one of them said.

"Christ! Did you see it?" a photographer said to a neatly dressed reporter. "I'd just looked away."

"Yes, I did. Served him bloody right, I'd say, for holding Lawrence's bike like that."

"Yes—but it was a bit strong, wasn't it? He could've asked the bloke to let go."

"I thought he had," the reporter said.

"Well, even if he had . . ." The photographer was looking at the man who'd been hit, now with a handkerchief pressed to his eye.

The neatly dressed reporter said nothing. He thought he might have made a mistake sounding unsympathetic about the silly bastard that Lawrence had punched. But if he'd been Lawrence he'd have punched one or two more of them. He'd been standing here for six hours with them, waiting for Lawrence, but he felt no closeness to them. He'd have to try, though, because he and the other MI-5 officers who'd been assigned to watch Lawrence would be here among them as long as there were journalists here— and in a few days, when they'd all gone again, he and the other MI-5 men would still be here, but hidden somewhere. For the moment, though, these journalists were excellent camouflage.

Standing back from the window of his downstairs room, Lawrence watched them in a group on the far side of his garden. The one he'd punched was still holding his eye. God, it was years and years since he'd hit anyone like that. He hadn't thought he still could. His hand hurt from it. For a moment, when he felt his fist hit, he thought he'd broken his fingers. He wished he hadn't done it. He didn't want a reputation for violence among the journalists. To be coy with them was one thing, to keep them interested. Hitting them was quite another; it could sour them on him, perhaps keep them away altogether—and he really didn't want that.

He turned from the window, tugging off his jacket and shirt as he walked to the bathroom to wash. Around his ribs were old scars, thin welts that curled around his sides from the back. At the washbasin he slipped off his shoes and socks, then his trousers, and there were more scars across his buttocks and the backs of his thighs, the flesh of his buttocks ridged and pitted where many of the newer scars overlaid the old ones.

Touching them lightly, he turned and looked down at them, brushing them gently with his fingertips. What would those journalists outside think if they could see them? What questions would they ask—and what stories would they write? Oh, God, what stories would they write about him if they knew the secret of these scars? Nothing heroic. He'd be no hero any longer if they knew what he'd been subjecting himself to, for so many years, to get these. But it went back to the war, after all. It had begun honorably enough, that November day in nineteen-seventeen when he'd gone to scout inside Deraa. If he'd known how his life was going to be changed by what happened there, he would never have gone. Never.

That November the British army under General Allenby was pushing slowly, very slowly, north against the Turks, through Palestine; and the Arabs were raiding out of the desert, blowing up sections of the railway, the Turks' supply line.

Deraa was a small town but an important rail junction, south of Damascus, with lines running out of it to the north, south, and west. It had to be isolated, taken out of theTurks' rail system, so they could no longer send trains out from there to supply their troops all through Palestine.

There were two ways to put it out of action, Lawrence decided: by cutting the rail lines into it or by capturing it. Cutting the lines in three directions would take time and would not be permanent—the Turks would repair one line almost as soon as he could blow another—so taking the town seemed to him more effective. But he had to know the state of the Turkish defenses, and there was only one way: He would have to go into Deraa and make a reconnaissance.

On horseback, he and a group of Bedouin rode south along the line and stopped a few miles outside the town. Lawrence dismounted, and with one of the older men, Faris, he walked on.

It had rained the night before, and the track was muddy. It was hard walking. Lawrence limped from a right foot that had been injured at a train-mining a few days before, but to walk straight on the trail they had to spread their bare toes and grip the soft ground, pushing themselves off on the next step. Every time he dug the toes of his injured foot in, Lawrence felt the pain jarring up through his body. Still he tried to spread his toes wider, wincing from the pain but insisting on it. He had to feel it and be able to master it.

Slowly they climbed the curving railway embankment, and then looked out across the flat ground to Deraa station.

"There can be no surprise attack across there," Lawrence said.

"The Turks' machine guns would finish us long before we were close enough to threaten them," Faris said.

"We will look closer. There must be an approach."

They walked out across one side of the Turkish defenses, seeing the barbed wire and trenches. At the end of the line of wire was an airfield, with German fighters, Albatros, in open hangars. They crossed the corner of the field, making for the town.

A man called out in Turkish.

They walked on, not looking around.

Someone grabbed Lawrence's arm, and he turned. It was a Turkish infantry sergeant.

"You are needed by the Bey," the sergeant said, still gripping him.

Lawrence could sense Faris shrinking aside, not to become involved. There was nothing they could do. If Lawrence tried to break away, the sergeant had only to shout. Turkish troops were all around. And there would be no gain in struggling here and having Faris captured too. Faris, at least, could slip away now and tell the men what had happened.

Lawrence let himself be led away.

The sergeant marched him through a gate into a Turkish army compound. The Turkish flag, white crescent and star on a red field, drifted softly on a staff at the edge of the parade square, and around the sides were some mud buildings and long barracks.

On the earth floor of a verandah outside the guardhouse sat a Turkish officer, one booted leg folded under him. The sergeant, tugging at Lawrence's arm to stop him, came to attention and reported where he had found this man, his prisoner.

Sitting studying Lawrence, the officer said: "Who are you?"

"Ahmed ibn Bagr is my name, sir," Lawrence said.

"You are fair-skinned. Are you Circassian?"

"Yes, sir—from Kuneitra."

"Are you a deserter from our army?"

"No, sir,"

"I think you are a liar—but for the moment it is not important." The officer nodded to the sergeant. "Take him into your section. See that he is cleaned and fed, and hold him until the Bey sends for him."

The sergeant led him into the guardhouse. Ten or twelve men in lumpy-looking Turkish uniforms lay on wooden cots, and the sergeant shouted orders at two of them. They jumped up and grabbed Lawrence. One of them took his belt and knife, then they led him out to a trough and made him wash. They led him inside again, to a rough table at one end of the room, and gave him a tin plateful of cold mutton. Then they told him to sit on one of the cots, and they sat watching him.

He wondered what they were going to do to him. It was impossible that they knew who he was. If they did, he wouldn't have been treated as softly as this.

One of the Turks said: "Do not worry. It is not bad,

given leave"—he grinned at the other soldier—"if you please the Bey this evening."

That was it! Lawrence looked from one to the other of them, and could see it. He had been picked off the streets because he looked like material for the Turkish army. But was there something else? What had this man meant— please the Bey? He felt uneasy.

"Who is the Bey?" he said.

"The governor. Nahi. And if he does not like you, you will be sent to Baalbek, for infantry training."

Lawrence sat wondering what he might have to do to please the Bey.

In the evening three soldiers marched into the guard-house and took him out, one on each side, one leading. They marched him through the town to a two-story house in a garden. A guard with fixed bayonet stood outside the front door.

The three soldiers took Lawrence inside and upstairs to a bedroom. A big man in a nightgown sat on the edge of the bed, watching him. He waved a hand at the soldiers, shouting at them to get out. This was the Bey, Lawrence thought.

One of them shut the door as he backed out. Lawrence, standing watching the Bey, heard it shut, sounding very heavy. He felt helpless.

"Sit down," the Bey said.

Slowly Lawrence lowered himself, crosslegged, looking up at the Bey on the edge of the bed.

The Bey sat staring. He had the stubble of a beard, and his hair was cropped very short.

"Stand up," he murmured.

Lawrence stood.

"Turn." The Bey made a turning motion with his hand.

Slowly Lawrence turned in a circle, and as he came around to face the Bey again the big arms came out and gripped him and, throwing himself backward on the bed, the Bey dragged him over with him.

Lawrence grappled with him, heaving over and breaking loose, and jumped to his feet.

The Bey sat up. "Come," he whispered. "Do as I desire." He smiled. "I will make you my orderly, my personal servant. You will live well, and I will see to it that no other man touches you." He held out his arms. "But come to me."

"No." Lawrence stood with his fists tight at his sides. His stomach felt as though it had melted.

"Take off your trousers!" the Bey shouted.

Lawrence did not move.

The Bey snatched at him, and Lawrence grabbed his hands and pushed them away.

"Guards!" Shouting, the Bey clapped his hands. "Guards!"

The door slammed open and five soldiers rushed in.

"Hold him!" The Bey waved a hand at Lawrence. "Strip off his clothes!"

Two of them gripped him by the arms and the other two ripped off his clothes. The Bey watched, sitting on the edge of the bed. Then he got up and walked across the room.

Lawrence knew what was going to happen. He could see it in the Bey's face.

He felt the man's hands on him, stroking him.

He felt himself becoming excited, stiffening into erection. Oh, God! He jerked his knee up into the Bey's crotch.

"Ah!" The Bey doubled over, both hands pressed into his testicles, pressing hard to ease the pain, doubling over further and backing to the bed, his eyes and lips squeezed shut.

The two men holding Lawrence gripped him tighter. One of the others, a corporal, stood at attention, frightened-looking, watching the Bey lower himself gently to the side of the bed, holding himself and groaning softly, rocking back and forth with the pain.

There was no sound in the room except the moans.

The soldiers stood holding Lawrence tightly by the arms.

Lawrence watched the top of the Bey's bent head, the

73

close-cropped hair. He could think of nothing but what he had begun to feel when the man had fondled him. He could not believe it. He was fascinated by what might happen next, what they might do to him.

The Bey looked up and, staring at him, took off one of his soft slippers. Carefully he got up and walked over. He hit at Lawrence's face with the slipper. Lawrence jerked his head back, and the corporal jumped in behind him, grabbed him by the hair, and held his head still. Again and again the Bey hit him with the slipper. Then he grabbed him by the head and one shoulder and, dropping his face suddenly, bit him on the neck. Lawrence felt the ripping pain. The Bey's head came up from his shoulder and Lawrence saw the blood, his own blood, on the man's lips, and the heavy look in his eyes.

Then the Bey's big hands were clamping his face, gripping his cheeks, and the thick lips were forcing, pressing on his. Oh, God!

The Bey took his face from Lawrence's and, watching him, reached with his right hand to the scabbard of one of the men holding Lawrence, and drew the bayonet.

This was going to be the end of it all. Lawrence was sure now it was going to come.

With his left hand the Bey reached out and stroked below Lawrence's chest, over the ribs. He squeezed the flesh between thumb and forefinger, raising a fold of it, and slowly pushed the bayonet point through. Gently he twisted the blade, watching the blood run down over Lawrence's belly, down his leg.

Smiling, the Bey rubbed his fingertips in the blood and wiped it over Lawrence's belly, gently rubbing.

Again Lawrence felt himself tensing. The man was exciting him again.

"No, please," he whispered.

Staring at him, a hand still on him, the Bey said softly: "I know what you wish. Understand that. Why refuse to do what we both desire?"

They stood with their faces very close together. Lawrence felt one of the soldiers beside him move, shifting

74

his feet, and he could sense the man was uncomfortable. Still staring into the Bey's big eyes, he felt he might not be able to control himself. He might not be able to refuse. There was so much that he wanted to know, that he wanted to experience.

"No!" He shook his head, lips tight.

Slowly the Bey backed away to the bed, and sat down. "Take him out," he said quietly, waving tiredly at the door. "Deal with him."

The guards dragged him out, tugging and kicking him along the landing, and pushed him face down across a bench. The corporal shouted an order, running downstairs, and they stretched Lawrence along the bench and held him there, two men tugging on his ankles, two on his wrists.

Heavy boots came pounding up the stairs. Lawrence strained his head back to look, and the corporal bounded up heavily to the landing, gripping a silver-handled riding whip. It looked Circassian, with a black hide thong that tapered to a point at the end.

Grinning, the corporal swung up the whip and the lash flicked out. Lawrence had been waiting for it and did not jerk his head. It cracked on the wooden floor close to his face.

"Ha! You do not move!" The corporal snapped the whip back. "Soon you will. Soon you will be begging to go back to the Bey." He braced his feet, flexing the whip. "Hold him!"

The four soldiers stretched Lawrence tighter, and he felt the rough wood of the bench hard against his flesh.

The sharp hide thong lashed across his back.

Lawrence felt his body jerk, but he kept his teeth ground together. He'd felt pain like this before.

Again the lash cut across his back. He tried to press himself tighter into the wood of the bench, concentrating on the roughness of it, not to think of the pain of the whip.

Keeping his lips tight, not to make a sound and give them the satisfaction, he heard the dry hiss of the lash coming again. It cut across his spine and he felt himself quiver. But he'd felt pain like this before. He had to keep telling

75

himself that. He'd felt pain like this before, and he could accept it now without breaking.

Again the lash cut across his back. It was the ninth. He concentrated on counting the cuts as they came. He was sure he could feel blood on his back, something sticky in the hot pain. And the lash was sounding wet now, when it landed.

Ten now. But the corporal wouldn't be able to go on forever. He would stand the pain longer than the corporal would be able to go on lashing him. He would lie here without a sound, until the corporal was too tired to lift his arm. He'd felt pain like this before.

Now twelve, and the lashes seemed to be cutting deeper, the hide strip sounding soggy when it curled across his back.

Thirteen, and it was like nothing he'd ever felt before. Like none of the whippings he'd taken from his mother when he was a child. Whippings across his bare buttocks. But he'd deserved to be beaten by her. He was worthless. Illegitimate. It had always been nothing more than he deserved, to be beaten by his mother. It was right that he should suffer for the sin of his unmarried parents. He knew how to accept pain and hold himself without breaking under it. His mother had never been able to break him.

Eighteen lashes now, and it was much worse than anything he'd felt before. He'd been ready for pain that ripped at his bare flesh like steel claws, as it always had when he was a child. But this was much more. This soggy-sounding, bloody-feeling lash was tearing apart his whole being with waves of pain that ripped and quivered up his spine and crashed together inside his brain.

Now he'd counted twenty, and there were more, still cutting at him, the lash tearing and tugging at his flesh.

A clock was ticking loudly, hollowly, and he tried to concentrate on it. There was no sound but the lash and the loud ticking, and the corporal's deep intakes of breath every time he braced himself to bring the lash down again.

The rhythm of the falling lash was not in time with the ticking of the clock. Why couldn't the corporal keep time with the ticking of the clock, so he could brace himself for the cut of the leather when it came?

But he couldn't brace himself now. No longer.

And he heard himself screaming now. In Arabic. He must be sure to do that. He must force himself to scream only in Arabic. If he let himself go so far that he called out in English, he'd be finished. What they'd done to him so far would be nothing against what they'd do to him if they discovered who he was.

The lashes stopped.

It was finished, he thought. But one of the soldiers had let go of an ankle, and he knew that the corporal had handed the whip to him, to go on.

It began again, and went on and on, the soldiers taking turns to lash him, the lash cutting and cutting.

He thought he must have lost consciousness. He was off the bench, on his back on the floor, feeling it rough and hard against the ribboned, bleeding flesh.

Something smashed into his right side, as though it would break through his ribs. He opened his eyes and the corporal was standing there, drawing back the hobnailed boot he had kicked with.

He felt warm from all the pain of the lashing, and then he felt something tugging hotly through his body—and it was an orgasm from the pain. He lay limp.

The corporal's arm flung up with the whip and the lash came down across his groin and, Oh, God! he doubled up from the floor, and he'd thought he'd never move again. Doubled over into the deep-cutting pain in his crotch, he heard himself screaming.

One of the soldiers yelled: "Shame! You've damaged him!" And laughed.

Another slash cut across him. His brain seemed to explode, and there was blackness. No sound, nothing.

When he surfaced out of the deep black he was face down, feeling two of them dragging at him, one straining on each ankle, pulling his legs apart, and another one was on top of him, forcing and plunging into him.

He heard someone call. It was the Bey. The men tossed

77

water on him and cleaned him. Then they carried him, now heaving and sobbing, back to the bedroom.

"God's mercy!" The Bey sat back from him, on the edge of the bed. "What is this thing? Nothing is left of the pig!" He brushed a hand to the door. "Take him out! Take him away! Quickly! Quickly!"

They carried him out, down the stairs, and out across the yard behind the house, into a wooden shed. As he lay on the floor he was aware of someone, a man, washing and bandaging his bloody back by lamplight.

One of the Turkish soldiers crouched beside him and laid a hand on his shoulder. "It is what happens when a man does not heed an officer's wishes. He must pay, as you have."

Lawrence did not look at him.

"We will leave you here," the soldier said, and whispered: "The door over there is not locked."

Lawrence looked across the floor and saw a rough-looking wooden door on the other side of the room.

The soldiers walked out with their lamp, and he lay in the dark, feeling cold. His head ached, the pain thrumming into his eyes. He lay thinking about what had happened until bright light from the rising sun cut in narrow shafts between the planks of the shed. A train whistled in the station, not far away.

He felt very thirsty. He had to find water. There was no pain from all the cuts. It was unbelievable. No pain at all. Had he drugged himself against it, from trying so hard not to feel it for all the years when he was a boy?

Carefully he pushed himself up and—Lord! Oh, Lord!— as he came into a crouch, stretching and reopening the tightened slashes across his back, deep-ripping pain flashed through him and he felt sweat break on his forehead. For a moment he stayed crouched, until the hot pain faded. He got to his feet, pushed open the door on the other side of the room, and walked into a dispensary.

A suit of old clothes hung on a hook behind the door. Dark broadcloth. He pulled on the trousers, then gently eased his arms into the jacket. When the cloth touched his back he sucked in his breath. Then he braced himself against the weight of rough cloth on the open cuts, and he knew he would be all right now.

He climbed through a window into an alley and walked out to the road that led into the center of Deraa. Few people were out so early in the morning, but every step he took he felt that someone would grab him and take him back to that house. A soldier laughed behind him, and he looked around, startled, and saw the man had laughed at something another one had said.

At the side of the road men and women were standing around the town wells, washing and drawing water, laughing and talking. He walked among them, to a trough, and drank, then slapped water into his face.

Slowly he walked away from the town, moving south, toward where the Bedouin would be waiting. He turned into a valley, out of sight of Deraa, and as he walked down it he saw it would give safe access to an attacking force. Moving up this valley, they could come out close enough to Deraa to launch an assault before the Turks knew they were there.

In the bathroom of his cottage he dried himself with a rough white towel. In *The Seven Pillars* he'd written of what happened at Deraa, but he hadn't told of the discovery he'd made there about himself, and he'd never write of what had been happening for so many years since. That must never be known to any but the small group of men who were part of his secret life, and would never tell.

He'd done well. No one could say he hadn't. For a long time he'd resisted the terrible temptation to feel again all he'd felt that night in Deraa. For more than five years he'd resisted it. But at last, early in twenty-three, when he was in the Tank Corps, just a mile or so from this cottage, at Bovington Camp, he'd given way. The army life had been so terrible, not at all like the air force, and he'd been under the other awful strain then, revising the Deraa chapter for *The Seven Pillars,* and reliving it had been too much for him. For five nights he'd had nightmares while he rewrote that scene. And at last he'd had to experience the pain and pleasure of it again, so he paid Bruce to thrash him with a birch, on the buttocks. First with his trousers on, but that hadn't satisfied, so he'd asked for more, with his trousers off. And that had done it—he'd felt the terrible, beautiful pain remembered from Deraa, and at the center of the pain the delicious feeling of relief, all tension flowing away.

After that he hadn't been able to control his need for it. It had gone on, over the years. He hated himself for never being strong enough to resist the force that drew him to those beatings, from Bruce and sometimes others, and the flagellation parties in Chelsea that he'd attended years ago. Perhaps he would overcome this thing yet. It was almost six months since the last time. There was hope, wasn't there? But those journalists outside would give him no mercy if they knew that he could get sexual release only from being flogged by another man.

9

The Orient Express rumbled out of the Simplon Tunnel into sunlight, and Selim Shaalan, sitting at the window of a sleeping compartment, turned his face from the sudden glare on the glass.

In a few hours he would be in Paris—and soon, he hoped, he would see Lawrence again. Surely there would be no difficulty. Lawrence would agree to see him. It was many years, eighteen now, since they had been together in the desert. How much would Lawrence have changed? He could not imagine Lawrence ever being different from the man he had known in the desert. But much else had changed. Feisal, who had commanded the Arab army, was two years dead now. He had never made a reality of his dream of an independent Arab nation in Syria, because the French had driven him out of there, out of Damascus, less than two years after the war. And though the British had tried to save his pride by making him ruler of Iraq, he had never recovered from his humiliation at the hands of the French. Feisal's older brother, Abdullah, did rule an Arab nation, Transjordan, and he himself, Shaalan, was Abdullah's adviser, but even Transjordan might be in danger soon. Abdullah believed it, and because of his fear for

81

the future he had sent him on this secret mission.

It was more than two weeks since he'd left Amman, traveling slowly up through Iraq and across Turkey, to board the Simplon-Orient at Istanbul. On the journey he had stayed away from large towns, where he might have been seen by someone who knew him, doing all he could to keep the secret of his mission. Yet the secret was out. Days ago he'd learned that, before he'd even left Transjordan. Just outside Mafrak, in a caravanserai, he'd heard that Lawrence was coming again to lead the Arabs—this time against the Jews. It had surprised him to hear it. Well, he knew how difficult it was to keep a secret among Arabs. Secrets spread easily among his people, and of course they took different shapes as they spread. But it had surprised him that that story had traveled so quickly. Only Abdullah and he had known of it, he had thought; certainly it had been their conversation alone. But it was good that, in the spreading, the story had suffered distortion, so that now it was being told that Lawrence was coming—actually on his way. Perhaps that would confuse the British, if they heard it—and before long, with all their spies through Palestine and Transjordan, they surely would. When it reached them, they would perhaps laugh at the story and ignore it, knowing that Lawrence had only two months ago left the Royal Air Force as a common man in the ranks. They would, he hoped, treat it as just another of the strange stories that so often were told about Lawrence. He'd read most of them himself in the English press—some of them lately, since the end of February, when Lawrence became a civilian. Lawrence was a man who grasped the imagination of the press. Pray to God that this latest story would be taken as more work of the imagination.

And it would be, if it were also told that it was the Emir Abdullah of Transjordan who had invited Lawrence, because the knowledgeable British, the ones who knew Abdullah, would be aware that during the war he had not liked Lawrence. It had often been said. He himself had heard it during the war. So it had surprised him, a month ago, when Abdullah called him to his chamber and spoke of Lawrence, of whom he had just read in one of the newspapers from London.

Abdullah, with his round, dark face and pointed beard, said: "You have great regard for Lawrence, from your knowledge of him during the war."

"Yes, Your Highness." Shaalan could not guess at the reason for Abdullah's sudden interest in Lawrence.

"You know well that I did not trust him. I believed that he was using us for the British, and was never sincere whenever he spoke of wanting independence for us."

"Yes, I know it."

"I still believe I was right to doubt him. However, I think now that he suffered from his conscience for deceiving us. I believe he honestly regretted that he had not worked wholeheartedly for the Arab cause."

"I believe that his first loyalty was to Britain, but he was also convinced that Britain would deal fairly and justly with the Arabs. I believe he suffered great disappointment when he saw that it was otherwise."

"Perhaps." Abdullah, stroking down the side of his beard, looked as though he thought it was possible. "But what of the Jews? What do you believe were his feelings for them? When he was with Feisal at the meetings with Weizmann, do you think his loyalty was with the Arabs or the Zionists? Was he working with the British and the Zionists against us, do you think? Could it be that one of his desires was to see a Jewish state over there in Palestine?" He brushed a hand to a window, west toward the Jordan and Palestine.

"I am sure that it was as he always told Emir Feisal, that he wanted us to accept money and guidance from the Zionists, to help us create an independent state in Syria and make it impossible for the French to claim that they would have to take control there, to provide stability. It was the French that Lawrence wanted to exclude. He thought it would be safe for us to accept help from the Zionists because we outnumbered them and would never have been endangered by them. I am convinced he sincerely believed that. Never will I believe he was plotting with the Zionists against us. He wanted to make use of them to our favor."

Abdullah sat studying him, thinking. "This I believe. Yes, though I am certain he was with the British against us, I believe just as surely that he was with us against the Zionists."

"I have no doubt of it."

"And how would you say he feels now?"

"I believe he is not a man to change his views easily."

"Do you believe he would help the Arabs against the Jews now?" Abdullah asked it carefully.

"That is impossible to say, Your Highness." Shaalan was not sure what Abdullah meant. "What manner of help?"

"In an armed revolt," Abdullah said. "In Palestine."

Shaalan said nothing. He could not imagine what Lawrence would say to this.

"It must come," Abdullah said. "Years past, when he described to Feisal the advantages of Arabs cooperating with Jews in Palestine, Lawrence must have truly believed both could live together. Perhaps Feisal and Weizmann believed it too. But in the fifteen years that have passed, it has become clear that the Jews will never be content with merely a place in Palestine where they can live in peace and speak their tongue. They take more and more Arab land there, and if they are not stopped they will take it all—not just there across the Jordan, but here too."

"Yes. We know this is a danger." They had spoken of this before. Shaalan knew Abdullah was convinced that the Jews wanted a state whose borders would be not just Palestine as it now was, but all of old Palestine, which included a large area east of the Jordan, in what was now Abdullah's country. There was suspicion of the Jews here in Transjordan too, not just among the Palestinian Arabs, but Abdullah was completely trusted by the British as an Arab leader who supported their Palestine policy. And though Shaalan well knew how Abdullah resented the British control of Transjordan, seeing himself as their puppet, this was the first time he had heard him speak of taking arms. So far

84

all the fighting had been done by their brothers in Palestine. "And you are thinking of helping them in Palestine against the Jews?"

"The fight of the Arabs there is certainly our fight too," Abdullah said.

"Most certainly it is."

"What do you think Lawrence would say to this? Would he help us? When it was explained to him how far the Arabs have fallen from the condition he saw for them during the war—with the Jews—would he help?"

"That is impossible to know, Your Highness." What would Lawrence say to that? It was daring and it might attract him.

"It would mean fighting the British. We know this. They have pledged themselves to keep Arab and Jew from conflict, and when our people in Palestine attack Jews, they have to fight the British too. What would Lawrence say to the prospect of fighting his own people?"

"I believe Lawrence has no people but those he decides should command his loyalty. If he believed a thing strongly and it meant fighting the British for his belief, he would certainly do it."

Abdullah sat nodding. "I think this too, from all I know of him. And he would know that in helping us he would not be fighting against British policy. The British are working to reduce the Jewish presence in Palestine, but they must be cautious and diplomatic. If our people took strong action that the British saw they could not curb without great expense in lives and money, it would allow them to stand aside and let us solve this problem—for us and for them. Helping us, Lawrence would be serving his own country."

"Yes." It was as Abdullah said. Lawrence would be doing what his government secretly wished but could never admit. The British lacked the courage to act firmly in Palestine because they did not want to offend world Zionism.

"Do you think he would agree to come?" Abdullah said.

"I think it is possible."

"Will you go to England and ask him?"

"Yes. I would be honored to do it."

"Good." Abdullah smiled. "Good, Selim. I will give you a letter for him, telling him of my desire for his help."

"When do you wish me to go?"

"As soon as possible—but there must be the utmost secrecy in this, and you must make plans to go to England by a route that will ensure you are not seen. No one must know of it."

"It will take some time to arrange."

"Yes. Begin your preparations now, Selim. I will compose the letter for you to take to Lawrence."

"Yes, Your Highness."

Abdullah watched him back out of the room, pulling the door shut. He hoped Selim would succeed in persuading Lawrence. Yesterday he had told the two who had come to see him that he was certain it could be done.

One of them had come from the Grand Mufti of Jerusalem, Haj Amin el Husseini, the Palestinian nationalist leader; the other from Fawzi Kawakji, the Syrian guerrilla, who was training men in his country to go and fight soon in Palestine. The great uprising was coming, the two emissaries had said, to throw the Jews into the sea.

"And we wish your help, Your Highness," the Syrian said.

"What manner of help?"

"We want to have an Englishman with us in the uprising. We believe you can obtain him."

"Why an Englishman? Are Arabs not competent to lead Arabs?" And Abdullah wondered why they thought he could procure an Englishman. Did they believe he had Englishmen to do his bidding? It was the other way: Twelve years ago the British had separated Transjordan from Palestine, recognized him as ruler here, and agreed to supply money for government—but everything of meaning that he did had first to be approved by the British. But these two men must have a reason for wanting an Englishman— and for coming to ask him for help.

"Yes, there are competent Arabs—but the Englishman is necessary, Your Highness."

"Why?"

The Palestinian said: "For a plan that we have, Your Highness."

"Explain it."

"Yes. The British favor our people against the Jews in Palestine but cannot admit it openly. You know this and we know it. Our wish is to compel them to acknowledge their support for us, to make their position so clear that the Jews will be completely split from them—all Jews, even Weizmann and the moderate Zionists. Then the British will no longer feel the obligation to protect the Jews—and we will be free to deal with them."

"How would you compel the British to admit they favor us?"

"It is for this that we need the Englishman, Your Highness—one of such name and prestige that if he were with us the world would soon know of it and would believe without question that he was an agent of the British government, sent to help us against the Jews. It would be impossible for the British to convince anyone that they had not sent him. The world would see them as openly supporting us. The pretense would be ended." The Palestinian smiled. "And we would finish the Jews."

It sounded to Abdullah like a plot that could not fail. But who was the Englishman who would come to Palestine? "This Englishman—have you decided who he should be?"

"Yes, Your Highness."

"Who?"

"Lawrence. Colonel Lawrence."

"Lawrence?"

"Yes. He is in England, recently retired from the Royal Air Force."

"I know this." Abdullah smoothed his beard. This began to sound interesting. These men—or the ones who had sent them—had thought carefully on this. "But why do you believe I could bring Lawrence to Palestine?"

"He was a friend of your family, greatly respected by your brother Feisal."

"By Feisal, yes, not by me. He was no friend of mine—

87

and he knows it. I distrusted Lawrence and he always knew it. I distrust him still."

"You could tell him you have changed your estimation, Your Highness. It must be possible for you to convince him that you have."

Abdullah thought he might be able to persuade Lawrence—if he flattered him enough, if he spoke carefully enough. "It might be possible. But you are asking me to involve myself deeply—and this is not Palestine. The problem with the Jews is not mine."

"Not yet," the Palestinian said. "But in time, if they are not checked in my country, it will be your problem too. You must know this."

"I do not doubt it." Abdullah nodded. He had been playing with the man. He knew that, unchecked, the Jews would be his problem one day. "Yes, it is our fight—mine as well as yours."

"And you agree to help us with Lawrence?"

"I will try to persuade him."

"We are grateful."

"Now answer a question."

"What is it, Your Highness?"

"How will you ensure that, if Lawrence comes, his presence with you will become known—known widely enough to compromise the British government?"

"It will be done. This will not be difficult."

Abdullah nodded. "No, not difficult. With Lawrence, little remains secret for long. If he comes, he certainly will make it known to the world."

The Palestinian smiled. "This is true."

"Another thing." Abdullah held up a hand, a caution. "There is a condition to my own part in this."

"What is it?"

"It must not be known that I am involved. My part in your rebellion must be secret—and I have no need to explain this, I know. My value to the Arab cause will be much greater so long as the British believe me to be compliant and unquestioning of their policy."

"We understand this, of course, Your Highness, and we agree with you completely."

Abdullah nodded, satisfied. If this uprising should fail in Palestine, he would still be secure on the throne of Transjordan, so long as the British did not know he had been a party to it—and they would never know.

But he told none of that to Shaalan when he sent him to Lawrence. He told him nothing of the two men or their true reason for wanting Lawrence to come, because he knew of Shaalan's deep regard for Lawrence and of the great self-gratification he derived from the knowledge that such a famous man as Lawrence was his friend.

The Simplon-Orient drew into Paris, into the Gare de Lyon, and Shaalan climbed down to the platform. Before he left Amman he had decided that he would not go with the other passengers on the train to Calais, and across to Dover, but would stay in Paris for a day, perhaps two, then make his own way to London. It would take longer, but he would be less conspicuous.

10

The Imperial Airways flight from Palestine, a big Hannibal biplane, went into its descent at Croydon airport, south of London. The big wheels of its fixed undercarriage touched down and it trundled up to the terminal building, its four propellers slowing and stopping.

A man and a woman were the first two passengers to walk down the short flight of steps to the tarmac. They were listed on the manifest as Aaron Bergmann and Mrs. Sarah Bergmann, and during the flight they had told other passengers that they were just married and flying to London for their honeymoon.

As they strolled toward the terminal building, Bergmann limping slightly with a stiff-looking left leg, a big man came out of the Hannibal, ducking his head in the doorway, and stepped down behind three other passengers. He watched Mr. and Mrs. Bergmann walk into the terminal building and crossed the tarmac after them, not quickly enough for anyone to notice he was following them, but being careful not to lose them.

When Mr. and Mrs. Bergmann went through customs, the man was immediately behind them, but when they walked through the concourse toward the exit he hurried ahead of them with his bag, waving with his free hand to two men standing beside the doors.

The men saw him. The older one smiled, and they both came forward to meet him.

"How are you, old boy?" The older man shook the passenger's hand.

"Couldn't be better." Smiling, the passenger set down his bag as he shook hands. "It's good of you to come."

Mr. and Mrs. Bergmann passed them while the passenger was shaking hands with the younger man, and when they were a little way off, the passenger murmured: "Those are the two, Mr. and Mrs. Bergmann."

"Really?" The older man picked up the passenger's bag, turning to look at Mr. and Mrs. Bergmann, now close to the exit. "Let's go out to our car, shall we? On the way up to town you can tell us anything you know about them that wasn't in the message your people sent."

"Righto," the passenger said.

The three of them walked out of the terminal, casually, but in time to pass Mr. and Mrs. Bergmann waiting at the curb for a car that was pulling in toward them.

The passenger walked with the two men to their car, and as they climbed in, the younger man behind the wheel, the older one said: "The woman is with the Irgun too, is she?"

"Yes," the passenger said. "And her real name's Sarah Alexander. She's not married to Bergmann."

They shut their doors, the younger man switching on the engine. Sitting beside him, the older man said: "She's a damn good-looking woman. Why would a woman who looks like that join the bloody Irgun?"

"A lot of them look like that," the passenger said from the back. "A good friend of mine was killed last year by a woman who looked like that."

"God, what a bloody business."

The passenger said nothing, thinking of his dead friend as he watched the man and woman now climbing into the car that had come to meet them. He was a Palestine Police sergeant, Wilcox, a plainclothesman, and he had followed

91

the two Irgun agents on the Imperial Airways flight so that he could identify them to the MI-5 men who would be waiting, as the Palestine Police had requested in a message three days before. So there would be no confusion, MI-5, in their reply, had described the two officers they would send to meet the flight and had named them: Napier, the older officer, and Rawlins.

Napier said: "D'you recognize the chap driving that car, Michael?"

"Davidson, isn't it?" Rawlins said.

"Yes. Thought it was." Napier glanced back at Wilcox. "We're in your debt already, old boy. We've had a couple of reports from Scotland Yard on that chap. Name's Maurice Davidson. He's a militant Zionist and makes no secret of it—but we thought he was also working with the Irgun. Hadn't been able to confirm that, though—till now."

Wilcox watched the car as it pulled away from the front of the terminal building. The driver was a blond, heavy-looking man, about thirty. "I suppose there are plenty here like him, aren't there?"

"Oh, any number." Napier nodded briskly, watching Davidson's car, a black Morris, about one hundred yards ahead of them, up the road to London. "Your two Irgun beauties will be able to call on all the help they need here, I'm afraid."

"And drop out of sight, if they want to," Wilcox said.

"We'll try not to let them do that, old boy. Isn't that so, Michael?"

Rawlins nodded, watching a low, open MG that roared past them and swung in ahead, between them and Davidson's car. But they could still see the black Morris ahead, over the top of it.

Sitting beside Davidson in the front of the Morris, Bergmann told him they had been sent to London to organize a watch on Lawrence.

"Just that?" Davidson glanced back at Sarah Alexander. "Just watch him?"

"That's all, Maurice." Her accent was American, from

92

the eastern seaboard. "Just to see if he meets any Arabs." She saw the muscle flexing at the side of Bergmann's jaw, and knew how angry Davidson had just made him with that nervous little gesture, asking her to confirm what he'd just been told. Davidson was only trying to impress with his efficiency, but Aaron would hate the implication that anything he said had to be confirmed, that he wasn't in charge.

"For the moment, that's all," Bergmann said. "When we know definitely that he's working with the Arabs, we might have to do more."

Sarah Alexander wondered what he meant by that, but she said nothing.

"Even just to watch him, you'll need several people— to watch him all the time," Davidson said.

"You can find them for us, can't you?" Bergmann said. He was tall and thin, with wavy black hair and horn-rimmed glasses.

"Yes, yes. That'll be easy. We'll be pleased to get the people who can do that." Davidson thought he sounded businesslike. He hoped so. He wanted to impress Bergmann. He'd sensed something in Bergmann as soon as he stepped into the car. Though he looked like nothing, thin and wearing those glasses, Davidson had felt the confidence that came from him. And the thought that this man was actually a member of the Irgun, risking his life in Palestine for Zionism, a cause he himself had only talked and argued about— that thrilled Davidson. He'd never been to Palestine. Men like Bergmann were heroes to him. But he would have to try not to let Bergmann see any of that. If it came to it, he was probably as good as Bergmann. He just hadn't had the opportunity to prove it.

"Bring your people to me, when you've chosen them," Bergmann said. "I want to look them over and be sure of them."

"Yes, of course. One can't take anything for granted in a job like this. You have to know you can depend on the people you're working with." Davidson was sure he sounded as though he did things like this every day. He hoped he sounded like that to Bergmann.

Bergmann said nothing. He sat looking out the side window at the houses they were passing.

"Lawrence is down in Dorset now, I think," Davidson said. "He has a cottage down there. I've read that in the papers."

"They told us that before we left."

"I'll have someone confirm that he's there."

"No!" Bergmann jerked around, glaring through his horn rims. "Don't do anything till I tell you! When you've got the people and I've approved them, that'll be the time to start. It won't take you long to do that, will it?"

"To get the people? Oh, no. I'll have a dozen by this evening."

Bergmann nodded, looking out the window again.

For a moment Davidson watched him, to see if he would look at him and perhaps say something. Then he turned and watched the road, concentrating on his driving.

Sarah Alexander felt even more uncomfortable about Davidson now than she had in the first moments when she'd seen how hard he was working to impress Aaron. It was pathetic. She'd seen a lot of Jews like him. They talked a great deal about the homeland that should be created in Palestine, but they left the work—and soon, perhaps, the fighting—to the few who were there on the ground. You saw them most in the States. Many of her parents' friends in Philadelphia— and her own, for that matter—were like that. It seemed that the farther they were from Palestine, the louder they talked. The farther they were from the danger, the greater the need to sound like warriors. But they left it all to people like Aaron.

As for Aaron, sometimes he scared her. In the six months she'd known him, she'd seen, two or three times, a sign of cold-bloodedness that troubled her. And a lot of hatred. She didn't like the British, not at all, but she didn't hate them, as Aaron did. And it was an irrational hatred, which had been with him for three years. He'd told her when it began, on the day in thirty-two when his mother had been killed by a stray shot fired by Palestine Police in a gunfight with an Arab gang in Tel Aviv. He'd run out into the middle of the street, into the middle of it all, to try to save her, and was hit in the leg and crippled. She remembered how he'd looked when he told her about it. Terrible. Cold eyes behind those glasses. All the Jews in Palestine had good reason to dislike the British—but that hatred of Aaron's made her uneasy. Yet there was so much about him that was admirable. His dedication, for one thing—dedication to the ideal of a Jewish homeland in Palestine. She was sure he'd never stop until he saw that become a reality—or until something stopped him.

But there were a lot of them dedicated to that. Their methods were different, that was all. Simon, for instance. God, if Simon knew what she was doing now, with someone like Aaron—what the hell would he say? Much more than he'd said two years ago, when he'd driven her down this road from London to catch the plane for Palestine, to go to work for the Jewish Agency, the World Zionists' organization responsible for the development of the National Home.

"I don't understand it," Simon had said. "There's so much you could do here. Work for the Jewish Agency, yes, but you don't have to go out there to do it. Why the devil can't you do it here?"

"Because that's where the people will be going, the refugees. It's beginning now, and Hitler's only just taken power. They're starting to get out of Germany, and soon there'll be a flood of them. I can help in Palestine."

"But, dammit, Sarah—doesn't it mean anything that I don't want you to go?" He shook his head quickly, frustrated, watching the traffic ahead. "We've been married five years, and it's been damn good, hasn't it?" He glanced at her. "Hasn't it?"

"Yes." She brushed a hand on his arm. "You know it has. I just have to go. How many times must I say it?" She knew she couldn't make him understand it. There was so much about her that he couldn't understand. She didn't blame him for that; often she didn't understand herself. Sometimes there were things she just had to do, and she didn't know why. She was impulsive, that was all. Her father always smiled, shrugged, and gave up trying to reason with her. She wished Simon would just do that. It'd be so much easier.

Driving on, Simon said nothing. They'd talked about it long enough, but he still couldn't accept it. He didn't know why he was trying to change her mind now, in the last few minutes. But he simply couldn't stop himself.

"Why don't you come with me?" she said. "There's still time. You can just get on the plane with me."

"Please, Sarah"—he looked agonized—"don't say it again. You know I can't do anything of the kind. God knows I believe just as strongly in Zionism as you do, but . . ."

"God knows you've had longer to think about it." She smiled.

He chuckled quickly. He was forty-one, fourteen years older than she was, and she joked about it at times like this, when they got too serious.

"Yes, I have. And I think I can do more for Zionism here, in London, than in Palestine. Far more."

"I think you can too, Simon. You're right: You have to stay here and do all you can." And he did a great deal. As a very successful London barrister with a wide circle of friends, many of them in government, all of them influential, Simon worked hard for Zionism. But he did it his way, as a moderate Zionist, a friend of Chaim Weizmann, and she wasn't sure she believed any longer in Weizmann's way, the moderate, patient way. She'd said that, once or twice, when they'd talked about it, and Simon had tried to convince her it was the only way. Once she hadn't doubted it, but now she wasn't sure. That was something she hoped to resolve for herself in Palestine. Now, in their last couple of hours before she flew off, she didn't want to argue about it with Simon.

Sitting beside him, she looked at his left profile: his wavy brown hair, long, straight nose, and the black patch in place of the left eye that he'd lost in France during the war. The first time she had seen him, in Paris in twenty-seven, she'd thought him the most glamorous man she'd ever seen. She'd tried hard to be logical about it, telling herself it was the effect of being in Paris for the first time—on a European trip that was a gift from her father for her graduation from Vassar—but it had been much more than that. Two years later they were married in London, and she'd been very happy here ever since. But she had to do this, go and work in Palestine for a while. She only wished Simon could understand.

But he hadn't understood, she thought now, sitting behind Bergmann. They'd written to each other regularly—she'd written to him just before she boarded the plane to come here, without telling him she was coming, of course—but Simon still believed the moderate way with the British was the way they'd finally get their homeland. Perhaps if he'd been out there and seen how their people lived, never knowing when an Arab attack would come, he'd think differently. She'd certainly seen it—and when she'd been there four months she'd joined the Haganah. Then, six months ago, she'd decided that self-defense against the Arabs wasn't enough, and she joined the Irgun—ready to fight and take a land by force, if necessary. No, Simon would never understand the way she was now. It would be good to see him and talk about it—but that wasn't possible. Simon, of all people, would never understand why she'd come to do this job. He'd never approve. But it felt good to be back, traveling the road they'd driven down together. She sat looking out at it.

Rawlins held the MI-5 car about a hundred yards behind the black Morris all the way into London and followed it through the streets of the western districts to a block of flats in Baker Street. He drove slowly past as Bergmann and Sarah Alexander climbed out.

"Let me off at the corner, Michael," Napier said. "I'll keep an eye on the place while you phone and get some chaps over here to take up the watch." He looked back at Wilcox. "Then Michael will drive you somewhere so you can get some shut-eye, old boy. I expect you could do with it."

"I could," Wilcox said. He'd like to stay and find out why the Irgun had sent these two people here, but tomorrow he'd fly back to Palestine and leave all this to MI-5.

97

11

"Dear Lawrence," Shaalan had written, "It is important that I meet you and speak with you on a matter of great urgency, which I hope will interest you. It would also be a great pleasure for me to see you again after so many years. It is important to be discreet, so please say nothing of this letter to anyone."

Lawrence laid it on the wide arm of his chair. The envelope had a London postmark, dated the day before. Had Selim come to England only to see him? Something about the tone of the letter made him think so. If he had, why hadn't he come here to Clouds Hill, instead of writing from London? He stood up from the chair, picking up the letter and envelope. Because of the need for discretion, perhaps? Yes, that was probably why. Selim might've thought it would be difficult to come here without being spotted by the journalists who might be hanging about. He looked through the window. There were none out there now. Not for the moment. Since he punched the fellow a fortnight ago, there hadn't been so many of them here. And they weren't camping on his doorstep any more. They kept a polite distance and seemed content to watch, not troubling him with questions. It was more peaceful—but, on the other hand, the place seemed desolate without them. They'd all be back soon, he was sure. No, if Selim wanted secrecy for this meeting, he wouldn't want to come here. He'd given a London telephone number, so the only thing to do was ring him and see what it was all about—and that meant a ride into the post office at Bovington. There was no telephone closer.

From a side table he picked up his motorcycle goggles. Lately he'd decided that he could, after all, afford to ride the Brough Superior. It was his only real expense—he neither smoked nor drank—and riding it at speed on straight stretches was such great pleasure. The mile or so down the road to Bovington would give him some fresh air.

He went out to the Brough, wheeled it across the yard to the road, and swung into the saddle, tugging the goggles over his head and settling them comfortably on his eyes. He never wore a helmet, loving to feel the wind in his hair. He heaved up and kicked the pedal. The engine roared instantly, and he moved off down the road, the spreading blare of the engine held in by the trees on either side, the road speckled light and dark with sunlight and the shadows of leaves, all the sun and shadow flickering across his face as he rode, changing the gears up, gathering speed, swinging down through a gentle hollow in the road.

A black four-door Wolseley that had been parked at the top of the road, close to a T-junction, had moved out and was following him. Quint and Richmond were the two MI-5 men watching him this morning. In the past four weeks they had spent many hours watching, they and the other teams—sometimes parked on the road, where they could be taken for journalists, sometimes from the wooded land across from the cottage, watching through glasses.

Richmond, driving the Wolseley, accelerated as the Brough pulled farther away from them, Lawrence leaning forward into the wind, his hair flicking and tossing.

Now the Brough, in top gear, was moving fast down the road. Lawrence took it into another hollow, deeper than the first, and for a few moments was out of sight. Then he rode up again. Richmond drove down into the hollow,

99

and again they could not see Lawrence. Then they were out again and saw him speeding on toward Bovington.

He rode the Brough into a deeper hollow, and again he was out of sight. He rode out, and Richmond drove in.

"He should slow down, on a road like this," Quint said, as they came out of the hollow and saw Lawrence ahead, and down the road beyond him the buildings and shop fronts of Bovington.

Seeing the village now very near, thinking that soon he would be speaking to Selim, Lawrence remembered the last time they had been together, in late October of nineteen-seventeen.

In the force were some Indian army engineers, with two Vickers machine guns and blasting gelatine, and almost a hundred Bedouin, from the tribes of the Harith and the Howeitat. Leading them were Lawrence, Sherif Ali ibn el Hussein, with some of his Harith men, and Selim, with some warriors from the Howeitat.

They rode out of the base at Akaba, heading north into Turkish territory, careful always not to be sighted by enemy patrols. In ten days they saw in the distance the tops of the palms and a black smudge that was the basalt fortress at the oasis of Azrak, fifty miles east of Amman. It was where they would rest for a few hours, before they pushed on the last three days to their objective: one of the viaducts that carried the railway across the Yarmuk River.

The month before, Lawrence had been called down to the Suez Canal, to the headquarters of General Allenby, to take part in the planning of an offensive against the Turkish line between Gaza and Beersheba.

"London is insisting on a decisive breakthrough here," Allenby had said. "They want Turkey out of the war by the end of the year. It won't be enough for us to have Jerusalem by Christmas. The Turks must be knocked out, so that we can release men from this front for France. I expect more from your Arabs, Lawrence."

"I shall push them even harder, sir." It hurt Lawrence

deeply to hear anything but praise for the work he was doing with the Arabs, but he sensed that Allenby, with his experience of the murderous trench fighting against the Germans in France, was skeptical of the value of him and his Arab guerrillas.

"You must—but they'll have to do something more effective than blowing up bits of railway here and there, which the Turks can repair in a day or two. I want something done that will hurt them badly."

"Are you thinking of something specific, sir?" He didn't like it at all that Allenby was showing so much dissatisfaction with all he'd done this past year.

"Yes." Allenby stabbed a finger at the large-scale map that was hung on one wall. His fingertip was just west of Deraa, on the Yarmuk River. From Deraa the railway ran into Palestine along the Yarmuk gorge, crossing and recrossing the twisting river on high-arched bridges. "Here the railway into Palestine is most vulnerable to serious damage—here on the viaducts in the Yarmuk valley."

"I'm aware of it, sir."

As though he had not heard, Allenby said: "If one of those viaducts were destroyed, nothing would move down to the Turkish front." He cut with the side of his palm across the railway west of Deraa, with branches off to the south, supplying all the towns through Palestine as far down as Beersheba and Rafah. "It would take them two weeks to repair it—and with luck they'll be too late. With no supplies or reinforcements getting to their front, I see no way for them to hold back our offensive—or to escape from us." He stared at Lawrence. "The viaduct must be destroyed. And I want it done between the fifth and the eighth of November, to coincide with the opening of my offensive."

"I'll see to it, sir."

Riding toward the Azrak oasis now, Lawrence hoped nothing would go wrong. Blowing the Yarmuk viaduct was probably the greatest challenge he'd faced in the desert campaign. It wasn't just another stretch of track to be blown, something that he himself had selected, where no one but he would know of success or failure. No, this was an assignment from the army commander himself—and if he failed, Allenby would not forget it. His reputation, no matter what might be said about him by others in the future, would always be looked at with suspicion by that one powerful man. He remembered being introduced to Allenby in Cairo five months ago when the general had taken over the command, and the way Allenby had looked at him, sideways, assessing, clearly wondering if the reputation he'd been building in the desert was exaggerated. He still had to prove himself to Allenby.

And Allenby—The Bull, as they called him—was assuming his orders would be carried out and the viaduct would be blown. On their ride up from Akaba, they'd heard, faintly from the west, the rumble of British guns firing on Beersheba, preparing the way for the offensive. The job had to be done.

As they rode up to the oasis Lawrence looked across at Sherif Ali, riding beside him, and saw how excited he was, seeing the sun-gleaming springs of water among the meadows. Ali, the nineteen-year-old Bedouin leader, was seeing grass for the first time. They moved their camels forward at a trot, up to the old fort on a ridge above the palms, then sent them stepping carefully down the other side, among the rocks, to the springs and meadows.

"Grass!" Ali jumped down from the height of his saddle, dropping lightly on his feet and hands, bracing himself with his face down, smelling the rough grass. He pushed himself up, ripping off his headcloth, and ran out over the marsh, screaming the Harith war cry, vaulting over channels where reeds clogged the slow-flowing water, holding his cashmere robe high, his strong calves shining with the water he splashed up with his bare feet.

Lawrence sat in the saddle watching him. Ali, with his dark, cruel-looking face, was one of the handsomest young men he'd ever seen, and a beautiful athlete. He'd seen him run on bare feet for half a mile beside a trotting camel, carrying his rifle, then leap high into the saddle and ride. He was an incredible man, Lawrence thought, and he was pleased he'd been able to persuade Feisal to let

Ali come leading the Harith on this expedition.

"The sherif is happy here," Selim murmured. Smiling, he slipped from his saddle, rifle in both hands.

"It is a good place," Lawrence said. He felt excited here, sensing the presence of all who'd been here at the oasis before—back to the Romans who had served as garrison, guarding the water. Now he and the Bedouin were here, he thought, watching Ali running back, high-stepping through the grass.

The next morning they moved off, and for three days they rode hard. Then on the evening of the seventh of November, riding down a ridge, they heard a sighing, rushing sound from a long way off. They reined in their camels and sat listening in the gray night.

"It is the great waterfall below Tel el Shehab," Selim murmured.

Listening, Lawrence nodded. "Yes. Yes, we're close, Selim." He turned to Ali. "You hear it, Ali?"

"Of course I hear it! Why do we wait here?" Ali beat on his camel with his riding stick and went trotting forward.

They all followed.

Moving on in the grayness, they heard the rushing of the water louder and louder, and in a few minutes Ali pulled up on his camel and tapped on its head with his stick, urging it down on its knees, and jumped off. They all kneeled their camels. Lawrence jumped down and ran after Ali, hearing Selim close behind. They stopped together on a bank of grass near tumbled rocks, and in front of them was deep blackness, the rushing of the river now very loud below. They were at the edge of the Yarmuk gorge.

Lawrence looked down to the right and saw a frail yellow light on the far side of the gorge. It was a guard post on the other side of the bridge they were going to bring down. He looked through his glasses. The light was from a fire outside a guard tent.

They walked back to where the men were waiting. The Bedouin were in a group with their camels; the Indian troops were unloading their machine guns and explosives from the baggage animals.

103

Fifteen of the Bedouin took loads of explosives, the Indian gun teams picked up their two Vickers guns and boxes of ammunition, and they all moved forward, Selim and his Howeitat scouting ahead, all moving down a slope toward the bridge.

Earlier in the evening it had been raining, and the ground was still wet. To keep from slipping, the Bedouin dug in their bare toes, but the Indian troops in their nailed boots had to move carefully to stay on their feet.

They climbed down a steep stretch of the face of the gorge, where rocks jutted out, and below in the blackness of the valley the bridge was a strip of deeper black, stretched out above the river. The light Lawrence had seen from the top was at the end of it, close against the far side of the gorge.

Near where they were, they had been told, was an old construction path to the bridge abutment. They found it and moved down it in single file, their brown riding cloaks camouflaging them in the dimness against the stone of the gorge. They reached the abutment and crept forward on hands and knees until they were a few feet from the bridge girders. Sixty yards away, on the other side, they could see a Turkish sentry walking up and down past the fire outside the tent. Lawrence lay watching him.

Something metallic clattered behind. Lawrence jerked around. Someone was scrambling, falling on the path. An Indian soldier yelled, and there was still the clatter of him falling down the path, and rocks rolling and tumbling.

Someone shouted from across the gorge.

Lawrence snapped his head around and looked across there, at the muzzle-flash of a rifle, and then heard the snap of the shot above the sound of the rushing water. Men behind him began firing back, a clattering of rifle fire as the men in file up the path fired at the Turks' tent. In the firelight men were rushing out of the tent and firing back. A ripple of yellow muzzle-flashes broke along the far lip of the gorge.

Selim ran down and dropped flat beside him. "Do we

rush them across the bridge, Lawrence?"

He shook his head. It was finished. They could never do it now.

Ali flung himself down too. "Why not, Lawrence? There are but few of them over there. In this light, we could be on them before they killed many of us."

"We came to destroy the bridge. The alarm is out now. Even if we overwhelmed those guards, other Turks would come long before we could set our explosives." He got to his knees. "We must go."

Now the Turkish fire was heavier, and the fifteen men carrying the bags of explosives were shouting at one another, calling back along their file on the path. They knew what would happen if a bullet hit their explosives.

One of them tossed his bag out into the ravine. Two others tossed theirs, and then all the other, all the explosives dropping heavily

"There!" Lawrence pointed at the dropping bags of explosives. "It's finished! Get your men back up! Get to your camels!"

They ran back up the path, pushing the men standing and firing at the Turks, yelling to them to climb back up to their camels. Three Indian troops were kneeling on the path, working on the barrel and tripod of a Vickers gun, trying to assemble it and train it on the Turks.

"Get up!" Lawrence yelled at them. "Get your gun back up to the top! We're finished here!"

All of them, the long line of men on the path, scrambled back up to the lip of the gorge, firing wild shots across at the Turks as they went. The Turkish fire snapped at them all the way up.

At the top, when they mounted their camels, they saw that no men were missing. It was no consolation, Lawrence thought. If he could have blown the bridge, he would have been ready to lose half of them.

And that was the last time he had seen Selim, he thought, now riding into Bovington. After that failure at

105

the Yarmuk, Selim and his group of Howeitat had ridden back to Akaba. It would be so good to talk to him after all these years.

He stopped outside the post office, jerked the Brough up on its stand, and walked inside.

As he stepped through the doorway the black Wolseley drove slowly past, and Quint watched him through the side window.

"He goes too fast on that motorbike," he said. "One day he'll have a bloody accident."

"He rides very well, sir," Richmond said.

Quint said nothing. In the hours they'd been together watching Lawrence, he and Richmond had spent some time talking about him—but not much, because he'd found that Richmond had a sort of boyish hero worship for the man. He himself, on the other hand, thought Lawrence was a bloody little exhibitionist. And he didn't have the patience to talk much to Richmond, either; the fellow was a playboy and not very bright—and insisted on calling him sir, knowing it irritated him.

It amused Richmond, the way Quint talked about Lawrence. He couldn't understand why Quint was that way— except perhaps that he'd spent four years in France during the war and, so everyone said, had done some rather brave things, and he probably resented that Lawrence had become so famous for doing what was probably no more than he'd done himself. Whatever the reason, Quint was very impatient on the subject, and that made things even more difficult between them than they'd have been anyway, because he himself was frankly fascinated by Lawrence. For years, since he was at school, he'd read everything he could find to read about him. This surveillance was distasteful to him, though it was interesting actually to see Lawrence in person, if only at a distance. What had surprised him was that Lawrence was so short. He'd always imagined a much bigger man.

12

The day after Bergmann and Sarah Alexander arrived in London the men Davidson gathered had begun their watch on Lawrence. They had been watching him now for two days and had seen nothing suspicious. Lawrence had had no contact with an Arab or anyone else.

In the flat in Baker Street, Davidson reported to Bergmann.

"He hasn't noticed the people you've sent there, has he?" Bergmann said. He'd looked at the men Davidson had brought to him, and had approved them—but he didn't approve of Davidson. He saw that Davidson was trying hard to impress him, and he despised him for it. He'd seen others like Davidson, always talking of what they'd do to the Arabs if they ever got close to them, and always taking care never to get close.

"No, he hasn't noticed them," Davidson said. "There are quite a few people hanging about that cottage. Journalists come every day, just to see what he's doing."

"What does he do?"

"Nothing. Yesterday he rode his motorbike into the village near his cottage, and that's the only time he's been out in the two days our people've been . . ."

The doorbell rang, one long ring, and Bergmann's head snapped around to the foyer. Sarah Alexander sat with her hands in her lap.

It rang again: two short rings.

"It's one of our people," Davidson said, getting up. One long and two short rings was the signal they used when they came to this flat.

The two Irgun agents sat waiting in the living room while he walked out to the door. They heard him open it and say: "Hello, Arthur."

He walked back with a man named Gold, a small man with a full beard. They had met him on their first evening here. Now he looked excited.

"I've got some interesting news." Gold sat in a straight-back chair, leaning forward, tense. "Our people are watching a rather interesting Arab in London. He arrived yesterday."

"Who is he?" Bergmann said.

"His name's Selim Shaalan. Adviser to Abdullah of Transjordan."

"Yes. I've heard of him. What's he doing here?"

"We don't know yet. One of our people saw him come off the ferry at Dover yesterday morning, and he caught a London train. He went to a small hotel in Knightsbridge— that's not far from here. Obviously he wanted a quiet place, out of the way, so he could stay hidden—but we're watching it now." Gold looked satisfied with what they had done.

"Is there some reason to think this has anything to do with Lawrence?" Sarah Alexander said.

Gold opened his mouth, but Bergmann snapped: "Yes! I know something about this man. He knew Lawrence during the war." He nodded firmly. "Yes, he's come here to see Lawrence. There's no question about it."

"And d'you think he's been sent by Abdullah?" Davidson said. By now he was almost afraid to speak to Bergmann. Several times in the last three days Bergmann had snubbed him, and he made him feel ridiculous whenever he was with him, but he had to make it clear that he was here to participate.

"Of course he's been sent by Abdullah!" Irritated, Bergmann did not look at him. "Abdullah's in this too."

"Working with the British?" Sarah Alexander said.

"Yes." Bergmann sat nodding. To him it was all very clear. Abdullah, a tool of the British, was working for them—and for himself—in this. "Abdullah's sent his man secretly to England to invite Lawrence to go and help them—but he's doing it for the British government, and they're hiding behind him. If anything goes wrong—if we, the damn Jews, should find out about Lawrence—they can say it's Abdullah who's done it. The British would claim they didn't know anything about it."

"God! D'you really think it's that?" Gold said.

"Of course it is! Abdullah would never do anything like this on his own. He's never criticized the British policy in Palestine. You can be sure he doesn't like it, but he'd never say anything to embarrass the British—and he'd certainly never *do* anything. He'd never do this—not unless it was for the British."

The four of them sat looking at one another, thinking about this plot against their people in Palestine. The British and the Arabs against their people.

"But it won't help them," Bergmann said.

They looked at him.

"What won't?" Gold said.

"This damn Lawrence. What is he? What was he—ever—but a glory-hunting Englishman, always acting, posing for the camera? It won't help the Arabs, damn them, to have him helping them."

"I'm sorry," Gold said quietly. "I'm not so sure I agree with that, Aaron. Lawrence has a very powerful reputation. I'm sure his name still means a great deal among the Arabs. I think he'd be dangerous. I might be wrong." He really didn't want Bergmann to think he was arguing with him. "But I think he might be."

Bergmann did not look at him. He sat thinking.

"What d'you think we should do about this, Aaron?" Sarah Alexander said.

"Take this Arab—Shaalan." Bergmann sat staring at the floor.

"Take him?" Gold said.

Bergmann ignored him. "We'll kidnap him, Sarah, and make him tell us everything he knows—what Abdullah wants Lawrence to do and anything else he knows. He's very close to Abdullah. He'll know all about the British part in this."

"Yes. Yes, that's good. But they'll have to approve it in Jerusalem." She didn't want Aaron doing anything that wasn't approved.

"Yes. We'll send them a message—but they'll approve it."

"May I make a suggestion?" Gold said.

Bergmann glanced at him, not welcoming anything he had to say.

"Perhaps it would be better to wait till after the Arab's spoken to Lawrence," Gold said. "Then he could also tell you what Lawrence plans to do, whatever Lawrence has told him."

Bergmann said nothing. It made sense, but he didn't want to admit it.

"It's a good suggestion, Aaron," Sarah Alexander said.

Bergmann nodded. "That's when we'll do it. We'll get Shaalan when he leaves London, after he's seen Lawrence."

13

Coming up to the western outskirts of London, Lawrence throttled his motorcycle back. On the way up from Dorset he'd pushed it to eighty or a little better on stretches of good road. Oh, God, how he loved the speed, the feeling that the earth was coming alive and tossing back on each side of him, like a sea.

Riding fast through open country, he'd concentrated only on holding the Brough and on the feel of the speed, the vibrations of the earth coming to him through the bike. He'd been able to think of nothing else. Now, cruising through the quiet streets, he thought about soon seeing Selim, and again he wondered why Selim had come. Yesterday, when they'd spoken on the telephone, he'd given no hint of the reason.

He had called the number Selim had given, and it was a hotel, but he hadn't quite got the name when the woman answered.

Then a man had said: "Hello?"

"Selim?"

"Yes. Lawrence!" Selim had sounded so pleased.

"How are you?"

"Very well! Very well! And you?"

"I'm well. What are you doing in England?"

"I've come to see you."

"Really?" He wondered why, but he would not ask. Selim would tell him, when it was time.

"Yes. I must talk to you, Lawrence."

"I'd be delighted. Will you come down to my cottage?"

"I think not. There are journalists there, are there not?"

"Usually, yes."

"Then certainly I cannot come there. This is a matter of great confidentiality. Is it possible for you to come to London?"

"Yes, of course—but can't you tell me what it's about?" He hadn't wanted to ask, but he was growing more and more curious.

"I would rather tell you when I see you."

"Very well. I can run up to London tomorrow. How's that?"

"Excellent!"

"Where are you?"

Selim had given him the name of the hotel, in the Knightsbridge district, off Brompton Road.

Lawrence thought he must be very close to it now. Along Fulham Road he pulled out and passed a red double-decker, and the conductor, halfway up the outside staircase, leaned out, holding the rail, staring at the Brough, all its chrome and paint gleaming. Lawrence swung into Brompton Road, then into the street where Selim's hotel was, passing close beside a milk cart and making the horse jerk its head.

At the curb outside the hotel he tugged the Brough up on its stand and walked inside. There was a small lobby of dark wood and polished brass, with two sofas and three armchairs covered in chintz. A gray-haired woman was on a high stool behind the reception counter. It was probably mainly a residential hotel, Lawrence thought, where retired majors would live. It surprised him that they'd taken in Selim—they couldn't often have dark-skinned men staying here—but unless Selim had changed greatly, this little gray

112

woman wouldn't have dared refuse him. Certainly it was quiet here—and he wondered why Selim had wanted that. Why was he being so secretive?

The woman looked brittle when he asked for Selim's room number, and he suspected he'd been right: Selim was an inconvenience for them. One day, he hoped, such things would change.

The room was on the third floor, the top floor, and he walked up a wide, carpeted staircase that curved up from the side of the lobby. He felt certain they'd tucked Selim away somewhere out of sight.

They had, he found. The room was down a short corridor, at the back. He knocked.

"Yes?" Shaalan called softly.

With his face close to the door, he said into the wood: "Lawrence."

At once the door opened and Shaalan stood there looking just as he had eighteen years ago. Even the moustache and the neat line of beard around the jaw were unchanged. All that was different was his dress. He looked very western now, in a blue pinstripe suit. Very British.

Shaking hands, Shaalan drew him into the room. "Come in, Lawrence, come in." He shut the door. "You are still the same man. Unchanged."

"No." Lawrence shook his head. "I'm far from the same man. My hair's turning gray and my eyes are failing."

"You look very little different, Lawrence. Truly. Sit down, please."

Near the window was a chintz armchair, and beside the bed was a wooden chair. Lawrence sat beside the bed.

"It was a great surprise to hear from you, Selim. How has it been with you since we last saw each other?"

"Well. Very well." Shaalan crossed his legs. "I married, the year after the war ended. I have two sons now." He smiled, looking proud. "One is fifteen and one fourteen. Both are at school here, in England."

"That's wonderful! Where do you live?"

"In Amman."

113

"A long way from home." Lawrence smiled. The tribal area for the Howeitat was near Maan, in the south of Transjordan, toward Akaba.

Shaalan chuckled. "Yes. Several days' camel ride for us in times past."

"What do you do in Amman?"

"I am adviser to Emir Abdullah." Again Shaalan looked proud.

"It's a worthy post—and Abdullah's choice was wise." He wondered if Selim was here officially, from Abdullah. Why did he want this meeting?

"Thank you, Lawrence."

"Now you are here—and not to visit your sons but for this meeting with me. Is it true?"

"Yes. I have been sent by His Highness to speak with you."

"About what, might one ask?"

"To request your help." Shaalan leaned forward. "Lawrence, an Arab uprising is coming in Palestine—against the Jews—and the Emir wishes your help."

"Help? Help in what?" At once he was alert. He thought he could guess what help Abdullah wanted from him, and it excited him.

"To lead the Arabs."

Yes, it was what he'd guessed. Even so, it shocked him. And it was almost as great a shock that Abdullah was the one asking him. That was hard to understand. Impossible to understand.

"Abdullah is asking me? This is difficult to believe, Selim. We were never friends, Abdullah and I. Did you know that?"

"I know he distrusted you, yes." It embarrassed Shaalan to say it.

"And now?"

"Now he believes that, with time, there has been change." Shaalan reached inside his jacket.

Lawrence watched him draw out a long buff envelope. It was impossible to imagine what could have made Abdullah alter an opinion that had been so deeply held. "And

114

why is Abdullah concerning himself with the affairs of Palestine?"

"This letter will explain it." Shaalan handed him the envelope. "He wrote it for you."

The envelope was sealed with red wax. Lawrence broke the seal and pulled out the letter. It was three full pages of Arabic script:

Dear Colonel Lawrence,

Selim has by now explained why I have sent him to you. It is for me to explain why I have made this request, when you know well that once, when you were with my late brother Feisal, I was certain that you were no friend of the Arab people. I believed during the Great War that you were deceiving the Arabs, telling us that you were fighting for our freedom from the Turks and our independence, when all the time you were aware that at the end your country and the French would exchange Turkish domination over us for their own. However, I believe that you sincerely thought that your government would deal honorably with us, and when you saw it was otherwise you came to regret your behavior to us, and because of your feeling of guilt at the betrayal of the Arabs, especially of my late brother Feisal, who trusted you so strongly and for so long, you put yourself to serve as a common soldier in the ranks of the British army and the Royal Air Force. It was an act of penance for your disloyalty to us, I am certain. This belief strengthens me in the task of writing to you now.

In the years since the end of the Great War you have seen what has happened in Palestine. The Jews take more and more Arab land, and they enter Palestine in increasing numbers, especially since two years past, because of the events in Germany. Are the Arabs in Palestine to be victimized because of the misdeeds of the Germans, who persecute the Jews in their land and force them to look for refuge among us?

Do you ask, Colonel Lawrence, why I, Abdullah of Transjordan, concern myself with the plight of the Palestinian Arabs? It is because, as you know well, a threat to one Arab is a threat to all—but it is also because the Jews have made clear their intention to one day take the most fertile land of my country. You know well that they consider Palestine to include the area east of what was once the Hejaz Railway, wherein is the rainfall area of Transjordan; and they also count the Golan as part of Palestine, though it is recognized by all others to be in Syria. I tell you, Colonel Lawrence, I fear

115

their ambition. The Zionists plan to absorb the land of all of us.

So I am pledged to give all assistance to the Arabs in Palestine, and I ask for your help, for the memory of my late brother Feisal, whose friend you were. You will have an opportunity, Colonel Lawrence, to help the Arab people, to help some of them achieve that freedom which you once told Feisal you wished for them all. I trust in God that you will help us.

Abdullah of Transjordan

Lawrence looked at Shaalan over the top of the letter. It pleased him that Abdullah had written in this tone to him. At the end of nineteen-sixteen, when he was looking for a leader for the Arab revolt, an Arab who could command the respect of his people and yet be guided by Britain, he'd gone to see Abdullah and, not liking him, had decided on Feisal. He knew the dislike had been mutual. But now Abdullah thought enough of him to actually ask for his help. He couldn't deny that he was pleased and flattered.

"How does it seem to you?" Shaalan said.

"It surprises me. I'd expected nothing like this." The more he thought about it, the more overwhelming it became. "Do you know all that's in this?" He held up the letter.

"Yes."

Lawrence slipped the pages back into the envelope. "And Abdullah believes that the Jews threaten him—truly?"

"Of course, Lawrence. Did he not state it clearly? Consider." Shaalan leaned forward, hands on his knees. "At the end of nineteen-seventeen, at the time of the Balfour Declaration, there were fifty-five thousand Jews in Palestine." He stretched out a hand, beating it in the air for emphasis. "Fifty-five thousand only. Now we estimate there are three *hun*dred and fifty thousand. In only eighteen years they have increased sevenfold. And every year more and more enter. Should His Highness not believe they threaten him? Should all Arabs not wonder where it will end?"

Lawrence said nothing, but he could understand their nervousness.

"How does it seem to you, His Highness's letter? Does it persuade you, Lawrence?"

"It's a persuasive letter. But it still surprises me that he asks me, knowing how he distrusted me during the war."

"Were his suspicions just?"

"Do you believe they were, Selim?"

"I have always believed—and I told His Highness so—that your first loyalty was to Britain, but you believed too that Britain would deal fairly with the Arabs."

Lawrence nodded. "That is so. I was always a friend of the Arabs. But I was first a servant of my country, and I wanted it to assert its power in the Middle East—but with the Arabs as friends and allies."

"I told His Highness this—and I told him you were mortified when you saw how your country dealt with us after the war."

"It is true." Abdullah had described it accurately in his letter, writing of the guilt he'd felt at the treatment of the Arabs. He'd felt guilt for so many things.

"And I told him it was possible that you would help us now." Shaalan watched to see how he reacted.

Shaking his head gently, Lawrence smiled. "It's too late for that, Selim. The active part of life is over for me."

"This cannot be!" Shaalan slapped his hands on his knees. "There is much for you still to do! Much, Lawrence!"

"No. It's far too late."

"Lawrence, listen to me. If you truly felt guilt, as you say, for what was done to my people, then help us now. How better to wash away your guilt than to help us before it is too late? It is desperate. Truly."

Lawrence saw how anxious he looked. They really wanted him. Selim did, and Abdullah. It was really very flattering. Could he do this, lead them again? Of course he could do it, if he chose to—and it would be a repayment to them for his failure all those years ago. For the memory of Feisal, Abdullah had said. Poor Feisal. He'd felt so much guilt for Feisal and all of them. It would be the honorable thing to do this now. And it would be useful work—at a time when he'd begun to think there was nothing left for him. It really was an opportunity. And he wouldn't be working against Britain. On the contrary, for years Whitehall

117

had favored the Arabs. Nothing could be clearer than that, and of course it was only realistic. They had to ensure their base in Palestine. War was inevitable, sooner or later—and probably sooner—and to be certain of the security of Palestine they had to have the Arabs with them. Oh, no, he wouldn't be working against British interests.

"Will you do it?" Shaalan said.

He realized he was nodding slowly, and he saw Selim beginning to smile, looking very relieved.

"Yes," he said. "Yes, I'll help."

"Good!" Now Shaalan beamed. His teeth were very white and strong. "It is truly very good, Lawrence."

"But there must be a condition."

"Yes, yes. What is it?"

"There must be no killing—of British troops or Jews. No killing."

"What!" Shaalan's smile was gone. "How can this be— no killing? No killing of British troops—of course not, so far as it is within our power. But Jews? How can we not kill Jews?"

"It would be a campaign of economic and social dislocation. You would blow up railway lines, factories, warehouses, destroy Jewish crops. Do everything to make Palestine inhospitable to the Jews. But there must be no killing."

"I do not think Emir Abdullah could give such assurance. He is not in control of this. Obviously there are others. I don't know who, but clearly there must be Arab leaders in Palestine."

"Clearly. But Abdullah is the one who asked me. He is the one who must see to it that my condition is met. Believe me, Selim, it would be the most effective way, as I describe it. Wage a bloodless war and you will have sympathy and respect from many quarters in your struggle. Kill Jews and you will be accused of savagery against a weaker people, and the world will be against you."

"I believe there is much in what you say, Lawrence."

"Then tell Abdullah."

"I will do it."

"Good. When you have his response, tell me."

"I shall send you a telegram in a few days. As soon as I can, Lawrence."

"I shall be waiting." Yes, now he felt stimulated at the thought of this. It would be his chance to repay the Arabs for his failure so long ago. Never had he dreamed he would have such a chance.

14

Quint and Richmond watched Lawrence walk out of Shaalan's hotel and swing onto his motorcycle. They followed him out on the road back to Dorset. While he had been in the room on the third floor they had asked the woman at the reception desk where he had gone, and she had given them Shaalan's name and told them when he had registered. Now another team had arrived to watch Shaalan.

Later in the day, when MI-5 had gathered information on Shaalan, Harding went to the Home Secretary with a report.

Halfway through reading it, Gilmour glanced up, looking strained. "This is incredible. This man Shaalan is the adviser to Abdullah of Transjordan?"

Harding nodded.

"Incredible," Gilmour muttered, and went on reading.

Harding had thought it incredible too, but he felt relieved that at last they'd found an indication that Lawrence might be involved in something with the Arabs. These four weeks since Gilmour had given him the order to watch Lawrence, he'd been growing more and more uneasy with every day that his men found nothing suspicious. Every day he'd expected to hear that Lawrence had noticed he was being watched and had complained to one of the friends he had in Parliament. Now that they'd found something— though there wasn't anything yet but a meeting of old friends—he felt slightly easier.

"I'd give a great deal to know what those two talked about in that hotel room." Gilmour laid down the report.

"So would I, Minister. So would I."

"Shaalan's apparently taken pains to come here unobserved. That alone is fishy."

"Extremely." As soon as the report had come in, before lunch, Harding had sent an urgent message to an agent in Amman, and had been told that Shaalan had dropped out of sight three weeks ago, and no one knew where he had gone—and that was curious, because he was very prominent in the group at Abdullah's palace.

"Your people didn't actually ask about him in Amman, I trust?"

"No." Lord, what did Gilmour think he and his officers were—schoolboys?

Gilmour nodded. "Good. It wouldn't do to have them aware that we're interested in him—not at this stage."

"Quite so, Minister." Carefully, Harding stroked his gray moustache. "It's possible, after all, that he's come here for some perfectly innocent reason. He's got two sons at school here, and he might've come to see them. His talk with Lawrence might've been simply to renew old memories, nothing more."

"Has he visited his sons?"

"Not so far as we've been able to determine."

"Then it's not very likely he's come here for that, is it?"

"Frankly, no. It seems he's been careful to stay out of sight. The receptionist at his hotel says he hasn't been out. But at this stage we've no reason to believe he's up to mischief." There was every reason to suspect the worst, Harding had to admit, and very probably Shaalan's being here did mean trouble. But he was a professional, and he had to have something more substantial than intuition before he'd commit himself to Gilmour, who was, after all, a politician—and politicians were unreliable.

"I think we'd be rather naïve to assume that Shaalan's here for any other reason than to represent Abdullah, to talk to Lawrence for Abdullah."

"We might assume that, Minister, yes." There really wasn't much doubt of it. First there'd been the rumor that Lawrence was going out to Palestine. Now the adviser to the Emir of Transjordan was here secretly, talking to him. No, it was all too clear, Harding thought, despite the fact that they didn't yet have anything concrete.

"You'll have to watch Shaalan very carefully from now on."

Harding nodded. "Yes. If he and Lawrence meet again, we'll be there."

"Good. And what about those Jews—those Irgun people?"

"We're still watching them too, of course. They've been here five days now, and they haven't moved out of their flat, except for a walk every day—and they never talk to anyone or stop anywhere. They've been visited by a number of Zionists—people known to us as militant Zionists—but they've done nothing."

"Then why the devil are they here, Harding?"

"We shall have to wait and hope they show us, Minister."

"Strange, isn't it, that they and Shaalan have come at the same time?"

"Yes. That had occurred to me too."

"D'you suppose there might be a connection?"

"I think it's possible, Minister."

"My God," Gilmour said softly. "I sincerely hope not."

"Quite so."

"Be sure your people watch them carefully, Harding. If there's the slightest indication that they're here because of Shaalan, we might have to do something about them—before any unpleasantness begins. We couldn't tolerate Jews and Arabs bringing their troubles to Britain."

15

On the open roads west of London, with little traffic, Richmond sometimes had to push the black Wolseley close to its top speed to keep Lawrence in sight. The man was a wonderful rider, he thought, and he kept the Brough under perfect control always. On the way up he'd ridden it hard enough, at eighty for quite long stretches where the road was good, but now he was hardly slowing down at all, taking bends he hadn't dared on the way to London. It was as though he was exhilarated.

"The man must be mad," Quint muttered.

Lawrence, bent forward, was a small figure far down the road, rising and falling in smooth swoops as he put the Brough up and over the curves of the land.

"He's very good, sir." Richmond could almost feel Quint flinch when he called him that. All these weeks, he'd been enjoying doing that to Quint. He took the cigarette from his mouth and flicked the ash into the tray, feeling Quint watching him driving at this speed with one hand. That was something else Quint didn't approve: his constant smoking. And he approved even less the fact that he had his cigarettes made for him by a tobacconist in Jermyn Street. In addition to everything else, Quint clearly thought he was a playboy who didn't take his work seriously. But Quint was quite wrong about that; he took it very seriously indeed.

As a matter of fact, if there was anything about him Quint *did* approve, he hadn't mentioned it. But it didn't trouble him. Quint was a very tough, skeptical man, and if they stayed together long enough he'd probably learn quite a lot from him—except Quint's intolerance. He didn't want to learn that. Quint was a bitter man. Bitter and intolerant, and it made him rather difficult company.

Richmond held the car at speed around a long curve in the road. Still Lawrence was out far ahead. Even with Quint beside him, feeling the constant disapproval, these weeks watching Lawrence had been fascinating. In spite of all that Quint had said about Lawrence—that he was a poseur and a parasite who'd become famous through the work of better men—he still thought Lawrence was one of the most interesting men he'd ever see. He'd like very much to be able to walk into that little cottage and actually meet him and talk to him. It was frustrating to have to sit outside and just watch him. He'd give a great deal to know too what Lawrence and the Arab had talked about in that hotel. Something had changed him. It wasn't the same man riding that Brough.

Lawrence felt the wind billowing and rippling through his jacket and trousers, making the sleeves and legs bellow, pulling at him, tossing his hair, and he felt alive, more alive than he'd felt for years. Now what had happened in London was beginning to settle itself clearly in his head. He must have been slightly shocked when Selim had asked him and he'd agreed. It was unbelievable. Unbelievable! After so many years—years when he'd assumed that every Arab who'd ever heard his name was convinced he'd betrayed them—they'd come to him and asked him to lead them again. To lead them again! When he'd spoken to Selim on the telephone yesterday, he'd never, never imagined that this would happen. And to think it had happened now, when he'd become convinced that he'd never again do any useful work, that the valuable part of his life was over and all the rest was meaningless, a few years of pointless existence until his curtain fell—and he'd even begun to look forward to that curtain quite impatiently. Now everything had changed.

Leaning with the motion of the machine, he took the Brough smoothly around a bend. And, of all Arabs, Abdullah was the one who'd asked for his help. That was perhaps the most incredible part of this incredible thing that had happened to him. He'd always assumed that Abdullah had never forgiven him for passing over him for his younger brother, Feisal, as leader of the Arab revolt.

In the middle of October, nineteen-sixteen, then an army captain, Lawrence sailed down the Red Sea from Suez aboard the *Lama,* a merchantman converted for the Royal Navy. The Arab revolt had begun four months earlier when Hussein, the Grand Sherif of Mecca, had opened fire on the Turkish troops there, and since then it had been flickering through the Hejaz, the coastal region of the Arabian peninsula that was the Holy Land of Islam. But the revolt had a fragmented leadership, split among Hussein and his four sons. It was vital to find an Arab leader who would be effective, and yet not so effective that he might be difficult to rein in when the Turks were beaten. He would have to be a man who could be persuaded to accept British guidance. Lawrence had proposed this to the High Commissioner in Egypt, General Sir Reginald Wingate, and had been assigned to find the leader. Hussein would be too old, Lawrence had decided. The leader would have to be one of his sons, and because the first ship sailing down the Red Sea was this one to Jeddah, Abdullah's headquarters, he would be the first one to see.

The ship anchored off Jeddah, and Lawrence went ashore in a launch. Abdullah came to meet him at the British consulate on a white mare, surrounded by foot soldiers. As soon as he saw him, Lawrence was against him. Abdullah then was thirty-five and Lawrence thought him overweight. And when they talked through the morning he thought him too clever, a man who might not be easily controlled by the British. So he left Abdullah and sailed back north along the coast to Rabegh, and saw two more of Hussein's sons: Ali, the oldest, and Zeid, the youngest. Ali he decided was too much an intellectual to be a dynamic leader, too ready to take advice from whoever might be closest to him, and so not reliable. Zeid, perhaps nineteen or twenty, had too little enthusiasm for the revolt. That left Feisal. So from Rabegh, with an Arab cloak and headcloth over his army khaki, Lawrence moved inland by camel with an Arab guide, Tafas el Raashid. Feisal's camp was about a hundred miles across the desert, at Wadi Safra, near Medina.

On the first day out from Rabegh he and Tafas stopped to water at a well, where a few Bedouin were sitting in shade beside some broken stone walls and under palm-leaf shelters. Lawrence and Tafas did not speak to them. They watered their camels and then sat resting while they grazed.

Sitting in the shade of a wall, watching the desert around them, they saw two riders moving down from the north, trotting light and fast on thoroughbred camels. When they were closer Lawrence saw they were both young. One was wearing an embroidered silk headcloth and a cashmere robe. The other looked like his servant, in a red cotton headdress and a simple white robe.

The two trotted up to the well, and the man in the cashmere robe slipped down from the saddle before his camel had fully stopped, down from the height of the saddle without making it kneel.

He tossed the reins to the servant. "Water them while I rest," he said and sat against the wall beside Lawrence and Tafas. He looked at them very casually, showing how little they concerned him. The servant stood holding the camels, waiting for a man with a small herd to finish at the well.

Sitting watching his camel, the man in the cashmere robe rolled a cigarette, licked it, and offered it to Lawrence.

Bowing with his head, smiling, Lawrence said: "Thank you, no."

The man slipped the cigarette between his own lips. "You are from Syria?"

"Oh, we have been riding simply to look at the country, my friend and I." Lawrence had been warned in Rabegh to give no information to anyone he met. Many Arabs out in the desert did not support the revolt or the British. Many were Turkish sympathizers. "You are perhaps from Mecca?"

The man seemed not to have heard. "Have you seen Turks on your way here?"

"None," Lawrence said. "And you?"

"No." The man puffed quickly on the cigarette, tapping his riding stick on the ground and watching the sand it flicked up. He looked and saw his servant still holding the two camels, still waiting for the herd to finish at the well. "Why are you waiting, Mustafa? Water them at once!"

The servant came striding over, dragging the two camels. "Lord, they will not make a place for these two of ours."

"God's mercy!" The man jumped up, throwing down the cigarette, and lashed the servant with his riding stick, four times around the head and shoulders.

Lawrence watched the dark, strong arm rising and falling with the stick, the servant trying to protect himself with a hand up.

"Go and ask the herdsman to move his animals aside while you water these!" the master shouted.

The servant looked as though he would hit back. Lawrence saw how surprised and hurt he was. But he turned and ran with the camels to the well. The man watering the herd had watched the beating and, shocked and sympathetic, moved his camels aside so the servant could water his.

While the camels drank, the young master sat again with his back to the wall, puffing on the cigarette. Watching him, Lawrence thought he looked even more handsome than before. The excitement of beating the servant had put something else into his face. It was a cruel face, but unquestionably handsome.

The two camels were watered, and the man rose in one smooth curve from beside the wall and strode to the one that the servant held for him, his robe swirling as he walked. Not making the camel kneel, he leaped into the saddle and tapped its neck with his stick to turn it around, tapping until it had turned completely around to face the south. He raised his stick to Lawrence, saluting, and rode off fast, the servant galloping after him.

Tafas began to chuckle quietly. Lawrence could feel him shaking.

"What is it, Tafas?"

"Those two riders, Lord."

"The sherif and his servant?"

"Yes—except that they are both sherifs. The one who was beside you is Sherif Ali ibn el Hussein of Modhig. The other is his cousin, Sherif Mohsin."

"Then why are they traveling so?"

"Because they are lords of the Harith tribe, blood enemies of the Masruh, whose land this is. They came riding so disguised because they feared they would be driven from the well if the men here knew who they were. That Ali is a devil. From the first day of battle against the Turks in Medina, he has been with Lord Feisal." Tafas chuckled again. "When there are two to go in disguise and one must be the servant, one the master, it will never be Ali who is the servant. Truly, he is a devil."

Lawrence looked out across the desert. The two riders were growing small now, blurred in the heat shimmer from the sand.

"We must ride on to Emir Feisal's camp." He rose, wondering if he would see Sherif Ali again. Something about the man had stayed with him.

On the next day they rode into Wadi Safra, through Wasta, the largest village of the thirteen in the valley. They rode up from it to Kharma, a small settlement in a palm grove, and behind it, in a valley of red and black rock, they saw Feisal's camp. Camel herds were grazing there, and some of his men were sitting smoking and talking.

As they rode down closer to the camp they passed small groups of men here and there among clumps of trees and in small caves in the sides of the valley. The men called out to Tafas, and he waved and called back to them.

They forded a stream and rode up a path between

low rock walls, and made their camels kneel by the entrance gate of a long house. A slave with a silver-hilted sword led Lawrence into an inner court, and on the other side of it, in a black-framed doorway, stood a figure in white, very tall and slim.

This would be the man to lead the revolt, Lawrence knew. As soon as he saw Feisal across the courtyard, he knew he was the man, with his slim, sensitive-looking hands crossed in front of him on the hilt of his dagger. But he was still thinking too about the man he had seen at the well, the young Sherif Ali. That man was still in his mind.

In the end, it had gone badly for Feisal and the Arabs. They had won the war and lost the peace. And he'd done nothing to help them in all those diplomatic negotiations in which they'd been deprived, little by little, of all they had believed they were fighting for. No, that wasn't true. Not true enough. It wasn't enough to say he'd done nothing to help them. Much of the time he'd actively worked against them, deceiving them. Then, because he'd tried so hard to make some recompense to them, and failed—tried so hard and seen it all crumble—he'd had to escape. The need to escape had been even more desperate because in those early years after the war, when he knew how badly he'd failed the Arabs, Lowell Thomas was giving his lectures and creating the myth of Lawrence of Arabia. It had been intolerable. It had seemed like a joke because only he had known how far from reality was the thing Thomas was presenting. Even now, thinking of it made him shrivel inside. He'd had to get away from it all. So he'd joined the air force, as the lowest there was, refusing all the offers of a commission, wanting only to find somewhere where he'd never have to think again, or be responsible for anyone but himself, and that only in the most undemanding way. He'd had to hide. And he'd done it for almost thirteen years—in the air force, the army, and then the air force again. And except for those terrible two years in the army it had been good. For years he'd been happy, and leaving it two months ago had been terrible. He'd never felt worse, never felt any loss more deeply than the loss of his refuge in the air force.

But now he had another chance. It would go well this time. This was an opportunity to exorcise his guilt and prove himself to the Arabs. He didn't deserve this, but it had been offered to him and he'd take it—and he'd give them restitution for all his failures so long ago.

16

In the Prime Minister's study Gilmour told MacDonald and Cunliffe-Lister about Lawrence's meeting with Shaalan.

"It's shocking," MacDonald said. "Abdullah's involved in a plot against us? It's incredible! Why? We give the man every consideration. He's virtually independent in Transjordan."

"We're not the people who concern him, apparently," Cunliffe-Lister said. "It's the Jews. They're convinced in Transjordan that the Jews intend at some time to take their land. That's been a preoccupation of theirs for years. It's not new."

"What *is* new is that Abdullah apparently intends to do something about it," Gilmour said. "I don't think there's much question about why he's sent this man of his to see Lawrence."

"None at all." Cunliffe-Lister shook his head. "They want him to go and help them."

"I simply can't believe Lawrence would consider doing such a thing," MacDonald said. He looked and sounded as though he was thinking about something else. "The man was a British officer, after all."

"The last time we spoke about this, I said I thought

he was capable of it," Gilmour said. "I still believe that. More than ever, in fact."

MacDonald sat nodding. Now that Gilmour mentioned it, yes, he did remember that. Gilmour had said it. "I've had a telephone call from Weizmann on this subject, too, it occurs to me."

"Oh?" Gilmour looked mildly curious. "What did he want, may one ask?"

"He'd heard the rumor that Lawrence is going to Palestine. I gathered that he thought we were sending him." MacDonald sat nodding to himself, recalling all he could of the conversation with the Zionist leader.

"And what did you tell him?" Gilmour said. Good God, was it really possible that Britain had this doddering old socialist as Prime Minister? In one of those abstracted periods of his—which were the rule rather than the exception, these days—he could make the devil's own mess for the country. It couldn't be allowed to go on.

"I said, as I remember, that we'd heard the rumor too, and couldn't imagine that anyone would take it seriously."

"And was he satisfied?" Gilmour said.

"Yes, I believe he was. He seemed to be." MacDonald's drooping white moustache made him appear uncertain. "I think it was the sort of reassurance he wanted. He hadn't wanted to believe the story."

"The next time he hears it, Lawrence might actually be out there," Cunliffe-Lister said. "Obviously it's now much more than a rumor."

"Of course it is," Gilmour said.

"We should do something, I suppose," MacDonald said.

Gilmour glanced at him very coldly. "Yes, I think that can safely be said."

MacDonald looked vaguely at him. Something was wrong. He could tell that from Gilmour's manner. But he couldn't say what it was.

"Could we take any sort of action against Abdullah?" Gilmour said it to Cunliffe-Lister. For the moment he had no patience for trying to discuss this intelligently with Mac-

Donald. "Couldn't we do something to discourage him before this goes too far?"

"That would be delicate, John." Cautiously, Cunliffe-Lister shook his head. "Very delicate indeed."

"You're not suggesting we sit still and watch this all move ahead, I hope?"

"No. Of course not. But I think we should be extremely careful—as Abdullah's obviously being. He's sent his man very secretly to see Lawrence, and at the moment that's all we know. Abdullah's a wily chap. I assume all this didn't originate with him. The principals are in Palestine, I imagine, and they've asked him to help them. But it could all quite possibly come to nothing—as so much Arab talk does— and if that happened, Abdullah would've lost nothing. I'm sure he won't come out and declare himself till he's satisfied that it's going to be successful—and that's probably quite a long way in the future. Till then, he's saying nothing— and I don't think we should do anything to force his hand. If we so much as spoke sternly to him about this, we *might* force his hand—and then his pride might compel him to declare himself." Cunliffe-Lister nodded to emphasize it. "We'd make an open enemy of him—and we'd have trouble in Transjordan as well as in Palestine."

"I suppose that's all true." Gilmour didn't want to agree with it, but it did seem that—for the moment, at least— there was probably nothing they could do about Abdullah. "I suppose we'll just have to keep a very close eye on him."

"Until he comes into the open, there's nothing more we can do, in my opinion," Cunliffe-Lister said. "Don't you agree, Prime Minister?"

"I do." MacDonald nodded. "I do agree." A moment ago he'd almost fallen asleep, he was sure. He hadn't heard everything Cunliffe-Lister had been saying to Gilmour. Or perhaps he had, but it had seemed to be coming from far away. He found it so hard to concentrate, these days. "And what about that Jewish couple, Gilmour?"

"The Irgun people?"

"Yes. What d'you propose to do about them?" Mac-

Donald was pleased with himself for contributing something to this discussion. They had to do something about that Jewish couple. Couldn't allow them to come into the country and do anything they pleased.

"MI-5 are watching them," Gilmour said. "There's nothing more they can do at the moment, just watch them. They haven't yet done anything to justify our taking any action against them."

"But you think their being here is connected with Shaalan, don't you, John?" Cunliffe-Lister said.

"I'm convinced of it."

"Then you'll have to watch them," MacDonald said. He was pleased with the decisiveness in his voice.

"We intend to," Gilmour said. "We'll watch them, Shaalan, and Lawrence."

"And hope they don't all come together," Cunliffe-Lister said.

"Quite."

MacDonald said nothing. He was thinking, now, of something else.

Bergmann was standing at the window, looking down into Baker Street. He looked so tense, Sarah Alexander thought. Partly it was because of their routine here, going out only once a day for a walk, for a mile or so. Aaron was so careful not to risk being seen. She thought so much caution was unnecessary—there couldn't be any danger for them here—but he'd take no chance. So most of the day they sat here, waiting for the telephone to ring or Davidson or Gold to come and tell them what was happening with Lawrence and Shaalan. The problem was, nothing was happening—but Aaron wasn't satisfied when they told him that. He had no confidence in Davidson or Gold, but especially Davidson. The boredom was affecting him. She was feeling it too, but she was a lot more controlled than Aaron. She could imagine how it was for him.

But there was more than just that strain. There was the problem of the two of them being here together. Aaron was attracted to her. She'd known that in Jerusalem. When-

134

ever they met, at a party or even a meeting of their Irgun group, she'd felt it. Whenever there was the flimsiest pretext, he couldn't keep himself from touching her: a hand on her elbow when he held a door open for her, brushing her hand or shoulder with his hand sometimes when he was talking to her. And in the five days in this flat, so close together, the tension had become drawn so tight that she'd felt it would choke her. She hoped they'd be able to leave here soon. If not, she didn't know what she'd do. So far she'd been able to pretend she hadn't noticed anything, but if they stayed here much longer he'd say something to her—she knew it, Aaron was like that—and she couldn't decide how to handle it. She wasn't attracted to him that way. She respected him for the job he was doing, but that was all. As a matter of fact, she was a little afraid of him; she could never guess what he might do. If he said something to her about the way he felt, and she told him she wasn't interested, she didn't know how he'd take it. It was just that Aaron was unpredictable. Very unpredictable.

Bergmann turned from the window. He had his horn-rimmed glasses in the breast pocket of his jacket. Lately he'd begun to keep them off as long as he could when they were alone together, because he wanted to be more attractive to her. It troubled her to see the effort he was making.

"I don't like sitting here and having to wait for that idiot Davidson to come and tell us what's happening," he said. He dropped into a soft armchair and shoved his legs full out as though he wanted to kick something.

"There's no choice, Aaron."

He looked disgusted. "There must be a choice. They must have someone better than Davidson. I don't like it." Quickly, nervously, he shook his head. "All the time we're sitting here, I'm feeling something's happening and he doesn't know about it."

She smiled. "It's just that you don't like delegating responsibility." It was pointless trying to joke with him. She knew that. He didn't have a sense of humor. But there was nothing else she could do.

135

"Ah, Sarah! Please!" He took a deep breath and let it slowly out.

The doorbell rang. One long ring.

Bergmann was out of the armchair with a push of his long legs, and stood listening.

Two short rings came, and he was striding out to the door, limping with his left leg, pushing his glasses on.

Sarah Alexander stood listening. She heard the door open, but there were no voices. Aaron never spoke when he opened the door to Davidson, and poor Davidson never knew what to say; so he said nothing either. He couldn't understand why Aaron was impatient with him.

They walked in together, and Davidson smiled at her. "Good afternoon, Sarah."

"Hello, Maurice."

Bergmann sprawled again in the armchair, not looking at Davidson.

"What's happening?" Sarah Alexander said.

Davidson glanced at Bergmann, wanting to know he had his attention. "Shaalan's still in his hotel. He's obviously not going to leave London yet."

Bergmann stared up at him. "So? What does that mean, d'you think?"

"Gold and I have discussed it, and we think it means he's going to see Lawrence again. We think he's asked for some instructions, and he's waiting for them before he talks to Lawrence again."

"You and Gold discussed it, did you? And that's what you think?"

Davidson flushed. "Yes. We think that's probably what's happened."

"What could Lawrence want from the Arabs? Did you and Gold decide that too?"

"No—but, Aaron, what other reason could there be for Shaalan to still be here, two days after he talked to Lawrence? Something still has to be agreed; that's the only explanation. He must be waiting to hear from Abdullah. Lawrence must've asked for something that Shaalan didn't have the authority to agree to. It must be that. It couldn't be

136

that Shaalan asked Lawrence for something; the Arabs are in no position to ask for anything from Lawrence or the British."

"I think what you and Gold decided together is as obvious as anything could be. I hope it didn't take you too long to reach this conclusion."

Davidson flushed again.

God, Sarah Alexander thought, why does he have to treat the poor man like this? It's pointless—cruel and pointless.

Bergmann turned from Davidson and said to her: "Obviously Lawrence wants something from them. Now Shaalan's waiting to hear Abdullah's answer—and when he hears it, he and Lawrence will meet again."

"Yes," she said.

"What could Lawrence want?" Bergmann sat back, thinking. "Could he be playing his old game—wanting something more from the Arabs for the British government?" Briskly, he shook his head, dismissing it. "It's not important. Whatever it is, Abdullah's not likely to refuse. He'll agree to it, and as soon as Shaalan tells Lawrence he has, Lawrence will go. Don't you think so?"

"Yes, I do, Aaron," she said.

He nodded, satisfied. "Then we'll wait before we take Shaalan. We'll wait till he has Abdullah's reply—then he'll be able to tell us everything."

17

When he received Shaalan's telegram telling of Lawrence's demand for no killing, Abdullah sent messages to the Grand Mufti in Jerusalem and Fawzi Kawakji at his camp in Syria, telling them to send their delegates to his palace to discuss a complication in their plan.

It took several days for his messages to be delivered, by a chain of underground couriers, and several more days for the Palestinian and the Syrian to reach Amman unseen by the British or any of their agents.

Abdullah met them in a small chamber in the east wing of his palace.

"The man I sent to England has spoken to Lawrence," he said.

"And does he agree to come, Your Highness?" the Palestinian said.

"He would come—but there is one condition, and unless we agree to it there is no possibility of drawing him here."

"What is the condition?"

"He insists that there be no killing—not of Jews or British."

"Ah!" The Palestinian slapped his hands silently together, smiling thinly at the absurdity of it.

The Syrian grunted, looking disgusted. "How would Lawrence propose we conduct a campaign against the Jews without killing them, Your Highness?"

"By destroying their crops and the railways and factories. To make Palestine unbearable for them."

"It sounds pretty, a war without bloodshed," the Palestinian said. "Does Lawrence believe it would discourage the Jews to destroy their crops? Does he think they would not plant fresh ones? Does he think anything less than death will drive them from our land?"

"Clearly he believes he alone knows the way," Abdullah said. "This was true of Lawrence when I first met him, almost twenty years ago. I see that he is unchanged."

"Could your emissary in London persuade him that the course he would have us take would win us nothing?" the Syrian said.

"With Lawrence it is not possible to exchange views and find a common course that all can accept. He sees the truth so"—Abdullah cut a straight line through the air with the side of his hand—"and that is the way it must be. His way and no other. He is at his best with people who have no ideas of their own."

"Then it cannot be," the Palestinian said simply. "Our plan for bringing Lawrence here and using him is not possible."

"I think it is," Abdullah said.

"It is not possible to fight the Jews as Lawrence says, Your Highness."

"Of course not—but it would be possible to *tell* Lawrence that we think it is," Abdullah said. "We could tell him that his proposal appears sound to us." He smiled. "We could even tell him that we were foolish not to have arrived at this plan ourselves, before he showed it to us in his wisdom."

"Would he believe that, if we told him, Your Highness?" the Palestinian said.

"Yes."

The Syrian said: "I must tell you, Your Highness, that

139

I would doubt it, if it were told to me that we would fight the Jews without killing them."

"But you are not Lawrence," Abdullah said. "We asked for his help, and he imposed a condition. His vanity would never allow him to suppose that we might refuse him. He would never doubt."

"Could this be so?" The Palestinian wanted to believe it.

"Yes," Abdullah said firmly. "Lawrence would never believe that the Arabs could use him as he once used them. If we tell him we would follow him without question, wherever he wants to lead, he will believe it."

"Then we should tell him that we agree to his condition," the Syrian said.

"Yes," the Palestinian said.

"Good." Abdullah smiled. "All we require is that Lawrence comes, of his own will."

"This is true," the Palestinian said. "When he is here, committed to us, and the world knows it, we shall have all we need. After that, Lawrence may do as he wishes."

By the following day the Irgun in Jerusalem had a report that Abdullah had sent a telegram to Shaalan, telling him that his friend's condition had been accepted. The Irgun could not guess what the condition was, but they were sure that the friend was Lawrence, and they met again in the house in the Nahlat Shimeon district.

"It's clear now," Yassky said. "There's no doubt about Lawrence. He'll be here to help them."

"I wonder why there's been a delay?" Ben-Joseph said. "What could he have wanted from Abdullah?"

"What difference does it make?" Matot hit the table with his wooden right hand. "The British want something from Abdullah in exchange for sending Lawrence—it makes no difference what it is. He's coming, and that's the fact we have to deal with now."

Ben-Joseph nodded, looking at the table. He'd hoped they could get through this meeting quietly, without any of Matot's outbursts. But he should have known. He said to Yassky: "What do you think we should do about it?"

"Tell Bergmann to go and kill Lawrence!" Matot snapped.

They both stared at him.

"No," Yassky said.

"Why not?" Matot snapped. "He's coming to help them kill us, isn't he? Tell Bergmann to kill him before he leaves England. Then he'll be no problem."

"We can't do that, Yehuda," Yassky said.

"And I asked you why not."

"Because it's dangerous. If it became known that Jews had killed him—no matter what the provocation, no matter how justified we might be—we'd not only incite the Arabs at once, we'd have all Britain against us."

"They're all against us now!"

Tiredly Yassky shook his head, smiling tightly at Ben-Joseph, asking him to have patience with Matot. "All right, Yehuda—not just Britain but the whole world would be against us if they found we'd killed him. Lawrence is a hero, a legend. He's a legend all over the world. If we killed him, we'd be outcasts. We could never prove that the British were going to send him to fight against us. Who would believe it?" He leaned over the table to Matot. "How could we prove it?"

Matot said nothing.

"No, my friend." Yassky sat back. "If we did it, we'd lose sympathy everywhere—including America." He raised a warning finger. "Including America. Our friends there wouldn't condone killing Lawrence. The man's a god, don't you understand?"

"He's a god," Matot said. "So we do nothing and let the god come and lead them to kill us."

"No. I think there's something we can do," Ben-Joseph said.

They both looked at him.

"If we killed Lawrence we'd be outcasts," he said. "Yes, you're right, Mordechai. We'd suffer a moral defeat. Isn't it so?"

Yassky nodded.

"But we can win a moral victory if we work carefully. Without firing a shot, we can gain a great advantage from the British."

"How?" Matot said.

"Bergmann proposes to kidnap Shaalan and make him tell everything of his talk with Lawrence. Let him do that— but instead of just using that information to help us prepare for the Arab attacks when they come, we'll take it to the British government and threaten to expose the whole plot unless they agree to concessions that we shall ask of them."

Yassky smiled. "I think this is something."

"Thank you. I think so too." Ben-Joseph was pleased with his plan. "If we told them in London that we'd expose all this to the press of the world, as proof of British bias against the Jews, they'd not only abandon this plot, they'd be ready to begin talking seriously with us about improvements for our position here."

"I wish I could believe it," Matot murmured.

"Believe it," Yassky said softly, looking at Ben-Joseph, thinking about it all. "Jacob's right. This is the way. The British couldn't afford to have us publicize such a statement from Shaalan, implicating them. Think what it would do to them in American public opinion. They couldn't afford to have such a story known! They'd be villains in America— and they're very anxious to have nothing but friendly relations there. They want allies in America, not people who think they're persecuting Jews. They don't want to be thought of as Germans." Smiling, he nodded. "Yes, this is our way. We'll tell Bergmann to take Shaalan and get such a statement from him—in writing. A written statement, signed, fingerprinted, and whatever else is needed to prove its authenticity. And he should get it without delay!"

In London MI-5 intercepted Abdullah's telegram to Shaalan and copied it, and at once Harding went to the Home Secretary with the copy.

Gilmour read it:

TELL YOUR FRIEND THAT HIS CONDITION HAS BEEN
ACCEPTED.

Leaning forward in his chair, he flicked it onto his desk.
"You let the original go through to Shaalan, did you?"
"Oh, yes," Harding said.
Gilmour sat gazing at the copy on his desk. "Obviously
the friend is Lawrence and obviously he agreed to go out
and help the Arabs—but with some sort of proviso. And
now Abdullah's agreed to it."
"Unquestionably."
"What the devil could the condition be? What could
he have asked them for, d'you suppose?"
"I can't begin to imagine, Minister."
"It's academic, in any event." Gilmour sat back. "It
seems clear now that Lawrence will go."
"That's certain, I'd say." Harding had not wanted to
believe Lawrence would go to Palestine, and now that it
looked as though he would he couldn't understand what
had made him decide to do it. He wondered if Lawrence
might be mentally unbalanced. Certainly he had a very
personal sense of reality. Or perhaps Lawrence was right
and the rest of them were wrong. But he couldn't afford
to let himself become philosophical. Lawrence was a man
whose actions would create a serious complication for the
government and the country—and that was all he could
allow himself to think about.
"And what about those Irgun people?" Gilmour said.
"Have they done anything that looks curious?"
"No. They still take their daily walk, and that's all."
"Why are they here, Harding? Why the devil are they
here?"
"I don't know, Minister—but they're certainly here for
some sort of mischief. They've been well-behaved for a long
time now, but they're waiting for something. Sooner or
later they'll try to do whatever it is they've come for."
"When that happens, I hope your people will be there
to stop them."

143

"They will be, Minister."

"But our most immediate concern is what to do about Lawrence."

"He and Shaalan will have to communicate with each other again. Either they'll meet or Shaalan will send him a letter or telegram. Lawrence has no telephone. We'll watch for what happens when he tells Lawrence that they've agreed to his condition, whatever it is—and I'm sure he'll tell him that very soon."

"I'll go and talk to the Prime Minister," Gilmour said. "We'll have to decide what our action should be."

18

Lawrence carried his sleeping bag out of the cottage and laid it in the sun to air. A car drove slowly past on the road and he thought it looked like journalists watching him. Would they never leave him in peace? And what would he do if they ever did?

He stepped back inside, into the kitchen. His breakfast and lunch dishes were still there to be washed, stacked on a sloping brick counter at the sink. He poured boiling water over them and left them standing to dry. To save time, he tried to reduce the work here to the minimum. He had no beds to make. There was just his sleeping bag, and a spare one that he kept for any friend who might stay. And there were very few dishes to wash; whenever he could, he ate his food straight from tins. What he wanted was as much free time as possible, to spend on important work.

But was there going to be any important work? Now it was twelve days since he'd spoken to Selim, and he'd heard no more. It could only mean that Abdullah had refused to consider his stipulation that there be no killing. He should have expected it. He'd been foolish to let himself begin thinking that there could be another chance for him.

When he'd left Selim he was so confident about it all, feeling lighter and more optimistic than he'd felt for years. More optimistic than he'd felt since the war, as a matter of fact, because it had seemed he'd have a chance to make good all that he'd failed to do for the Arabs. And now it seemed that they didn't want him. Abdullah, at least, didn't want him. He probably had been presumptuous, expecting Abdullah to accept his condition for helping them.

What surprised him most, though, was that Abdullah had asked him at all. Abdullah, of all Arabs. Abdullah, he'd always felt, understood him well, and sensed much of the truth of him, from that first time they'd met, in October, nineteen-sixteen.

From the launch that had brought him in from the *Lama*, Lawrence stepped onto the dockside at Jeddah with Storrs, the Oriental secretary to the High Commissioner in Egypt, and they walked together up through the town, toward the British consulate. The Red Sea heat, heavy and humid, was like a steam bath, and he felt the sweat running all over his body, staining dark his khaki drill uniform. Storrs' white suit was dyed red down the back from sitting in the heat in the scarlet leather armchairs aboard the *Lama* for four days down from Suez, and now, as he walked and sweated, the sweat began to glow through the red-tinted back of his jacket.

When they walked through the food market, swarms of flies around the meat and dates on the stalls looked like clouds of great dust specks in the shafts of sunlight that broke down into the narrow alleys through the torn sackcloth awnings over the booths.

At the consulate they were led into a big, high-ceilinged room, to Colonel Wilson, the British representative to the new Arab state of Jeddah that had been proclaimed in the summer when the revolt began. The louvered shutters were open at every window, for the breeze off the water—but for three days there had been no breeze. Lawrence felt dirty and sticky in his wet khaki drill, which had been starched and now was limp and heavy-feeling. He hated

146

to sit down in the clamminess of the uniform, but he had to. They sat in the hot, still air in the room, waiting for Abdullah.

Then they heard the clacking of a horse's hooves and the soft padding of barefoot men, and through the windows they saw Abdullah ride into the courtyard on a white mare, with his guard around him.

He was shown into the room where they stood to welcome him, and four men came with him. He introduced them as the closest of his bodyguards, but Lawrence saw how young and handsome they all were, and how Abdullah looked at them when he introduced them. Lawrence felt something, seeing the young men—boys, really—and Abdullah with them. He wanted to get out of the room and away from the consulate, but he had to stay and make an assessment of Abdullah as a possible leader of the Arab revolt. But he'd already decided. As soon as Abdullah walked in—short, smiling, slightly fleshy—he'd decided that this would not be the man to lead the Arab army. But most of all, he had to confess, he was troubled by the young men. Abdullah's young men.

Abdullah spoke no English or French, and Lawrence and Storrs spoke for hours with him in Arabic on the administration of the new state of Jeddah and on the way he thought the campaign should be fought against the Turks.

Lawrence had heard of Abdullah's reputation among the Arabs. They thought him a wise statesman and a shrewd politician; the second of Hussein's four sons, he was said to be the brain behind Hussein and the Arab revolt. As they talked, Lawrence could see how ambitious he was. Abdullah wanted Arab independence from the Turks, and he wanted to build Arab nations. He was ready to accept British help against the Turks, but Lawrence wondered how much direction he would take when he felt confident enough to refuse it.

They talked of the new Arab government that had replaced Turkish rule in the towns of the new state, especially Mecca and Jeddah.

"Public opinion in these places is against an Arab state,"

Abdullah said. "Most of the citizens are foreigners—Egyptians, Indians, Africans, Javanese. They have no sympathy with Arab aspirations—especially when it is a Bedouin like myself who speaks of them." He smiled, and the young men around him smiled.

"Could these foreigners be an impediment to the progress of the Arab revolt?" Lawrence said.

"No. They are the majority, it is true—but in the Bedouin is the strength. My father depends on the Bedouin alone. He provides them with free arms, feeds their families while they are away fighting, and hires their transport camels for the troops in the field. To obtain the money for all this, there are taxes on the people in the cities—so the countryside, where the Bedouin spend their money, becomes prosperous, while the towns feel deprived. It is causing a split between the townsmen and the Bedouin, but it will not cause harm to the revolt because the Bedouin are the only fighting men." Abdullah looked content.

"Is that the only source of complaint in the towns?" Lawrence said. "If so, we can remove it easily, by supplying money so that you can afford to reduce taxes."

"No, it is not all. Since we chased away the Turks from these parts we have also abolished their civil code and returned to the laws of the Koran." Abdullah smiled. "Perhaps in time we shall discover in the Koran such judgments as might be suitable for such necessary commercial functions as banking. Until we do, the businessmen of the towns will be discontented."

"That might be a serious problem, Your Highness. Certainly it would hinder the improvement of the economy of the state."

"Yes—but that improvement is for the future, when the war is won. Now our strength must be concentrated on winning. For that, we Bedouin are the ones—and the removal of Turkish law pleases the Bedouin people. My father has restored the old system of tribal law, so that a man who has been wronged may take his case to the lawman of his tribe, as in olden times. It pleases the Bedouin to have it so."

"Good that it pleases the Bedouin," Lawrence said. "Much is being done to please him, it sounds to me: He is paid to fight, his family is being fed, the return of the old system of law is to his liking. What is he returning for all this? How goes the war here, Your Highness?"

Abdullah murmured something quickly to one of the young men standing beside his chair, and the young man giggled, watching Lawrence.

It irritated Lawrence and made him uncomfortable. He didn't like the way Abdullah had been looking at him— or the way the young men watched him.

Still looking amused, Abdullah said: "The war would go better if you British would take more of a part."

"Specifically—what, Your Highness?"

"To specify on one matter alone: Because you have not seen fit to cut the Hejaz Railway, the Turks have been able to send reinforcements down to Medina, and these have enabled them to drive back my brother Feisal from there. Now they are even preparing a mobile column to advance on my brother Ali, at Rabegh. All this because the railway functions without interruption."

"That is not an oversight of ours, Your Highness. Your father has asked us not to cut the line, because he will need it for his final advance against the Turks into Syria."

"So you say."

"Your father will confirm it, if you ask him."

"I shall. Meantime, there is the need for supplies for Feisal. He would impede the Turks' advance on Rabegh, but he is too weak in machine guns and artillery to hold them long."

"These weapons will be supplied," Lawrence said. He felt more and more uncomfortable, with Abdullah's young men staring at him and always smiling.

"When? Why have they not come before?"

"Because Emir Feisal has not asked us for them."

"I find that difficult to believe."

"Nevertheless, it is true."

Abdullah murmured something to his young men. They all giggled softly. "There is more we need than weapons.

149

There is a problem of manpower here. All Bedouin are not for the revolt. The tribe of the Masruh Harb has joined the Turks, and if that Turkish column advances from Medina against Rabegh, another tribe, the Harb, will join them. If that happens, it will go badly for us. My father will have no choice but to barricade himself in Mecca and die fighting there, on the walls of the Holy City."

"That cannot be allowed to happen," Lawrence said.

"You British can prevent it."

"How?"

"Be ready with troops. A British brigade—of Moslem troops—should be held at Suez, with ships ready to rush them to Rabegh as soon as the Turks begin to move out from Medina in that direction. How does the proposal please you?"

"It is not an easy one to comment on, Your Highness." Yes, he could see Abdullah was ambitious. Now he wanted nothing less than a brigade of British troops to help him— but Moslem troops, because he wanted to take no risk with the presence of white Christian troops, who might undermine his influence. He wanted Moslem—which meant native—troops, who would be no threat. Yes, the stories about Abdullah had been right: He was shrewd. "There are several complications. First, ships are precious, and it would be impossible for us to hold empty transports indefinitely at Suez. Second, we have no Moslem units in our army. Third, the Rabegh position is a large one, and a brigade would hardly be strong enough to hold it; the most they could do would be to defend the beach under a ship's guns— and the ship could do that as well, without the brigade of troops."

"Ships do not inspire confidence in my men. Since your navy tried and failed to force the Dardanelles against the Turks, we have no belief in the power of your warships. We must have troops, so that my men can see they are not alone in this war against the Turks."

"I can tell you, Your Highness, that my commander-in-chief would be most reluctant to spare troops from the defense of Egypt—though this is not to say that Egypt or the canal is in any danger from the Turks—but I will present your views in Cairo."

Again Abdullah muttered something in very rapid Arabic to the young men. By now Lawrence dreaded seeing him turn to them with one of his remarks. He hated being in this room with them. And he didn't like Abdullah. It was true, too, that the man was much too shrewd for the Arab leader he was looking for. Above all, the British wanted a man who could be steered to follow the course they set for the Middle East. Lawrence could see Abdullah would not be easy to steer—not by him, at least. Abdullah was not at all overawed by him.

As the conference went on, it became worse. From time to time Abdullah even corrected Lawrence's Arabic, and whenever Lawrence began to condescend to him, as a British officer with the authority to select a leader for the Arab revolt, Abdullah made one of those quick comments of his to his young men, and they giggled softly, always looking at Lawrence as though they could see something through his limp khaki uniform.

Now, carrying his sleeping bag inside, he remembered how relieved he had been to leave Abdullah after that uncomfortable meeting, to go to Rabegh and then ride out into the cleanness and harshness of the desert for Feisal's camp. And on the way he'd had the meeting at the well with Sherif Ali.

Yes, Abdullah had always, from that first time, seemed to understand things in him. Because Abdullah had seen so much, and because he himself had known it—wasn't that the real reason he'd rejected Abdullah in favor of Feisal? Yes, of course. There had been no other reason.

If Abdullah had seen through him so well, it wasn't difficult to understand why he might not, after all, want him to help now. More difficult to answer was why he'd wanted him in the first place.

19

When the message came from Yassky in Jerusalem, Bergmann and Sarah Alexander had just come in from a walk
through Regent's Park to the zoo, the farthest they had
been from Baker Street in the days since their arrival. The
doorbell rang, one long and two short, and Sarah Alexander
walked out and opened it. It was Davidson.

"Good morning, Sarah." He smiled at her, uncertain.
Because she was so much more pleasant to him than Bergmann was, he was always uncertain with her, never knowing
when she'd change. With Bergmann, he knew what to
expect.

"Hello, Maurice." This man irritated her at least as
much as he did Aaron, she was sure, but she worked hard
not to show it. She wished Aaron would try too, before
he made a nervous wreck of Davidson, who, with his wide
hips and bulging belly, walking flat-footed, always tried so
hard to please.

As they walked out to the living room Davidson took
a white envelope from inside his jacket.

Bergmann said nothing when he saw him. He just
looked at him, sitting gently rubbing the calf of his left
leg. Sometimes when he walked too far the wounded leg
gave him pain.

"Shalom, Aaron," Davidson said.

Bergmann nodded. "Good morning."

"I have a message for you, from Jerusalem." Davidson held out the envelope.

Bergmann put out a hand. Davidson stepped forward and handed it to him. He ripped open the envelope, took his horn-rimmed glasses from his pocket, and sat reading.

Sarah Alexander stood waiting to hear what it was.

"Abdullah's sent a telegram to Shaalan." Bergmann looked up at her. "He's told him to tell Lawrence they agree to his condition."

"Does it say what the condition is?"

"No. But Yassky assumes Lawrence wanted the Arabs to agree to something before he'd go, and now they've agreed."

"What could it have been?" she said.

"Who can say? The British wanted something—some kind of assurance from the Arabs, to keep them from getting out of control, probably—and told Lawrence to ask for it." Bergmann waved the telegram. "Now they have it."

"What does Yassky want us to do?"

"We're still to take Shaalan. But now we're to make him give us a statement in writing, telling all he knows of this plot, involving all of them—Abdullah, Lawrence, and the British government. Everything. Then we're going to use it against the British."

"Use it?"

"Yes. We're going to tell them we'll expose it unless they begin treating us fairly in Palestine." Bergmann smiled. "I like the sound of it. We're going to use their own plot against them."

"I like it too."

"It's brilliant, Aaron," Davidson said quickly. "A brilliant idea."

"It's not mine," Bergmann said.

"No, but it's very clever."

Bergmann said to Sarah Alexander: "We'll have to decide how we'll get Shaalan."

"Yes. When do they want us to do it?"

"As soon as possible."

153

"Before he sees Lawrence again? He'll have to do that, to tell him Abdullah's agreed. And they'll have to make some arrangements for Lawrence to go out there."

"Yassky says we're to get Shaalan as soon as possible and make him talk. That means now. There's no need for him to talk to Lawrence again—no need for us to wait for that. Lawrence is going to Palestine—that's obvious and it's all we need to know."

"Yes, I suppose so." But she wasn't eager to go rushing into anything. She hadn't really thought it might come to something like this, where a man might be hurt.

"You'll have to tell us everything about that hotel where Shaalan's staying," Bergmann said to Davidson. "You say he doesn't come outside—so we'll have to go in and get him. We'll have to know where his room is, and how to get to it and out again with him."

"I'll get all that information, Aaron." Davidson was pleased that Bergmann needed him now.

"By this evening. No later. I want to get Shaalan tomorrow. No later than that."

"You'll definitely have it by this evening. Definitely, Aaron."

Bergmann was already talking to Sarah Alexander. "We'll bring him here and keep him till he's given us everything in a signed statement."

She nodded. What might have to be done to make Shaalan give them that statement? It probably wouldn't be easy to force him. She didn't want to think about that. Aaron would do it. But if he wanted her to help, she'd have to. It would be hard, but she'd have to. She had come here with him as part of his cover, as Mrs. Bergmann, because it was safer for him to travel that way, but she should've known she might have to do something unpleasant. That was always a possibility. In Palestine she was ready to fight the Arabs eye for eye, tooth for tooth, for the homeland—but the thought of what they might have to do to get the statement from Shaalan wasn't quite the same. She didn't like it, but it might have to be done. She couldn't leave Aaron to do it alone.

"After that, I'll take care of Lawrence," Bergmann said. Davidson looked puzzled.

"What d'you mean?" Sarah Alexander said.

"He won't get away with it, wanting to fight against us." Bergmann's face was tense and hard-looking. "I'll have him for it."

"What d'you mean, Aaron?" she said quietly.

"When we're finished with Shaalan, I'll go down to his cottage and kill him."

"Does Yassky want that?" She nodded at the message in Bergmann's hand.

He sat looking at her.

"Does he, Aaron?"

"Of course he does."

"May I see that?" She held out her hand for the message.

For a moment it looked as though he would not let her see it. Then he jerked his hand out with it.

She took it and read it. "He says nothing about touching Lawrence. Just for us to get the statement from Shaalan."

"Lawrence is my idea." Bergmann was sullen.

"You mustn't do it, Aaron." This was serious. It would be pointless murder, but she didn't want to say that. She knew that was the wrong thing to say to him. Pointless murder wouldn't trouble him, and it came to her now that she'd felt this about him since she first met him. "There's no need to kill Lawrence."

"No need? He's ready to fight us, and he could be a danger to us. I say there's a need to make sure he's no threat. That's the need."

"You can't kill everyone who might want to side with the Arabs, Aaron." She could feel Davidson watching her, standing in the middle of the room and not knowing what to say.

"I can kill Lawrence."

"But it's dangerous!" God, he was going to do it. He really meant to do it!

"Dangerous? He's one man. What's dangerous?"

"The consequences could be dangerous. If we were

155

blamed for it—if Jews were blamed for it. Don't you understand what that man's reputation is? You can't just go and kill a man like that, Aaron. My God, we'd never be forgiven for it."

He looked at her as though he could not hear her, his eyes very steady.

She could see how much he wanted to do it. "Yassky won't approve it," she said.

"I won't ask him."

"But I'll tell him. I'll send a message to him right now, Aaron. Don't do this crazy thing."

He sat staring at her through his horn-rimmed glasses. Then he nodded, resigned. "All right, all right. Perhaps I was wrong. I'll forget Lawrence. Damn him, I'll forget him." He waved a hand, sweeping Lawrence away from him.

Watching his face, she wasn't sure. She was uneasy, but there was nothing more she could say. He'd said he would forget Lawrence, and she'd have to leave it at that. But she didn't like it, knowing there was nothing she could do to control him.

"I should move along," Davidson said. His throat was dry and he coughed to clear it. "I'll have to tell our people what information you need on Shaalan's hotel." With all the tension in the room, he was uncomfortable, and he wanted to get out.

"Tell them to hurry with it," Bergmann said. "But tell them it must be completely accurate. I want no mistakes."

"Of course," Davidson said, one professional to another. "I'll see you this evening, with the information."

Bergmann ignored him.

"Shalom, Sarah," Davidson said.

"I'll see you out, Maurice."

She walked with him out to the foyer and opened the front door.

"I'll be back this evening," he said.

"Yes." She stepped outside with him, drawing the door closed behind her, and whispered: "Maurice, I think there might be a problem here."

He looked as though he didn't understand.

156

"With Aaron," she said. "He wants to kill Lawrence. He's serious about it. I know."

"But he said he's not going to. He agreed it'd be a mistake."

"I know he said it—but I'm not sure he means it."

"Of course he does." He patted her shoulder. "Anyway, what difference would it make if he did it? Lawrence is asking for it, isn't he?"

"Don't you understand?" Why was she talking to this man? He'd probably be thrilled at the thought of killing Lawrence—so long as someone else did it. It would give him one of those surges of power he seemed to get from thinking of all the risks other Jews were running in Palestine. "Didn't you hear anything I said to him in there? It'd be stupid and pointless, for one thing. And it could hurt us all."

Smiling gently to soothe her, Davidson shook his head. "Don't worry about it, Sarah. Aaron's all right. He won't do anything that'll make trouble for us."

"You don't know him."

"Oh, yes. I understand him very well. He's a man of action. He's very impetuous. But you mustn't be frightened, Sarah."

"Oh, for God's sake don't be a bloody fool!" she hissed. "I tell you I think he's capable of doing it."

Davidson said nothing, but now he was not smiling.

"If he asks you to help him with anything—anything to do with Lawrence—if he wants you to take him down to Lawrence's cottage or anything at all, don't do it."

Davidson looked unsure.

At once she knew she shouldn't have asked him that. This damn man wouldn't be able to refuse Aaron anything he asked. She should have known. "I'll have to do something to make sure he doesn't touch Lawrence."

"What will you do?"

"I don't know yet. You'd better go, Maurice."

"But what will you do?"

She shook her head. "I'm not sure."

"You mustn't do anything rash." Now Davidson looked concerned.

She said nothing. What did he think she was going to do?

"I think you're being dramatic about this, aren't you, Sarah?"

"No. You'd better go."

"Yes, all right." But Davidson did not move. "Don't do anything silly. Don't do anything that'll cause trouble for Aaron."

She stepped back into the doorway. "Goodbye, Maurice." Firmly she shut the door. She wished she hadn't talked to him.

Bergmann did not look at her when she walked back into the living room. He hadn't taken off his glasses, and he sat reading the morning paper. She knew he wasn't going to talk to her. What was he thinking?

But she couldn't trust him. She couldn't believe he'd stopped thinking about killing Lawrence. He didn't give up that easily. But he had to reassure her when he realized how strongly she opposed him on this. Had he really imagined she wouldn't? Yes, of course he had. To him, killing Lawrence because he was ready to help the Arabs was the most natural thing, and he couldn't understand anyone who didn't agree. It couldn't happen, though. She couldn't let it happen. But what could she do to stop him? She couldn't do anything that would harm Aaron. What they'd been sent here to do was too important for anything to happen to him. But she had to make sure he didn't touch Lawrence. How could she do that? Telephone the police, maybe? Anonymously? They'd never take it seriously. She'd make her anonymous telephone call and say someone she wouldn't name was talking about killing Lawrence of Arabia, and she wouldn't even be able to tell them why, because the last thing she wanted—the thing she wanted to avoid most of all—was any hint that Jews wanted Lawrence dead. No, she couldn't warn the police. And she couldn't do anything that would cause Aaron to be hurt or captured—but she had to make sure he didn't do this thing that she knew was still in his mind.

20

Gilmour sat in an armchair at the front of the Prime Minister's desk, watching him read the copy of Abdullah's telegram. Reading just those few words seemed to take a great effort of concentration from MacDonald, and Gilmour wondered how much longer things could go on this way. It seemed that he was asking himself that question more and more often lately. MacDonald's age and poor health were making him unfit to hold his office—or any other, for that matter. And it wasn't that he was so old. Sixty-eight was only ten years older than he himself was, after all, and he hated to think that in ten years he might be like this. No, MacDonald had been unfit for a long time. He should've retired years ago.

MacDonald looked up from the telegram, gazing at Gilmour over the tops of his horn-rimmed glasses. "And you believe that this means Lawrence was willing to go to Palestine but imposed some sort of qualification, and now this has been accommodated?"

"I think it's fairly obvious, don't you?"

"I suppose it is." MacDonald could think of nothing else to say. He didn't know how he tolerated it when this man Gilmour condescended to him so, but he seemed unable to defend himself against it or to do anything to discourage it. When he was younger he would never have accepted it, but these days very little was worth the effort of objecting. "And I suppose this means that Lawrence will go."

"Precisely. If we allow him."

"Can we prevent him? He's no longer in the service, Gilmour. He's a civilian, perfectly free to go wherever he wishes. There's nothing we can do, so far as I can see."

Gilmour remembered a few weeks ago, when they'd first discussed the rumor that Lawrence was going to Palestine, MacDonald had suggested preventing him from leaving the country and he himself had pointed out that that was legally impossible. There was no point in reminding MacDonald of that; at least he grasped it now: There was nothing they could do to stop Lawrence. Legally, nothing. What MacDonald didn't understand now was that they might have to consider other means. But it was too early to discuss that—and one hoped it wouldn't be necessary. There had to be something else they could try before considering last resorts. There had to be.

"Where's Abdullah's man now?" MacDonald said.

"Still here. Still at his hotel. MI-5 are watching him. Harding rang me just before I left my office and said the chap's sent off a telegram to Lawrence, telling him his condition has been agreed to and asking when they can meet."

"Oh, dear. Then they'll decide how Lawrence will make his way to Palestine, I suppose. There'll be only the details still to be decided."

"I imagine so, yes." Gilmour could see MacDonald was beginning to drift away again. In a few minutes he'd be losing the thread of the discussion.

"It's unfortunate, perhaps, that Abdullah's man wasn't prevented from sending the telegram—or it wasn't kept from reaching Lawrence."

"Possibly they'd have found some other means of communicating." Gilmour said very heavily, but he thought MacDonald had not noticed his irony.

"Yes. I suppose that's true." MacDonald thought Gilmour was condescending to him again. The man was impos-

160

sible. "But we'll have to do something. We'll have to. This can't be allowed to happen. Lawrence can't go out to Palestine and cause trouble and embarrassment for us. It'll have to be stopped." He sounded very decisive, he thought.

"Have to be stopped? It's a desirable objective, I grant you. But how? What d'you propose we do, Prime Minister?" It gave Gilmour some amusement to address MacDonald that way. He rarely did it. One hand on the edge of the desk, he leaned forward in his chair, gazing into MacDonald's thin, tired face. "What d'you propose?"

MacDonald lifted off his glasses and laid them on his desk, rubbing his eyes.

Gilmour felt some sudden sympathy for him. The man looked so fragile and vulnerable. He shouldn't be here, forced to make decisions on matters that were so important to the country and possibly the rest of the world.

"I really don't know." MacDonald lifted his glasses on again. "Do you have anything to suggest?"

"No. I don't know either. I confess I don't. I wonder if it might do any good to have a talk with Lawrence."

"A talk?"

"Yes. Have him in and explain how delicate all this is. I doubt very much that he realizes that if he goes out there it'll be assumed, as soon as his presence is known, that he's acting for the government—and that it'll cause the devil of a row. I really don't think even Lawrence would be irresponsible enough to do something like that if he understood what the repercussions would be."

"Do you think he'd reconsider, if this were explained, Gilmour?"

"It should be tried, I believe."

MacDonald sat thinking. "Yes. I could have the man come here and explain it all to him. D'you think I should do that?"

There might be a danger in it, Gilmour thought now. Having Lawrence come here for a talk might be risky. "Perhaps not. The press would hear of it immediately, and there'd be no end of speculation. Anything Lawrence does causes the press to speculate for days. If he were seen com-

161

ing here to Ten Downing Street, who can say what they'd print? No, perhaps it wouldn't be wise to have him here. Something more discreet, perhaps. And perhaps it would be the wrong psychology for you to talk to him. It might inflate his sense of self-importance, and might very well make him more difficult to deal with."

"Do you think so?"

"I think it might very well. He's a difficult little man, I'm convinced."

It was clear to MacDonald that Gilmour didn't like this man Lawrence. In the times they'd discussed him, over the past few weeks, that had become more and more clear. "What do you suggest?"

"Someone else should talk to him. Someone less prominent than yourself, but senior enough to carry authority."

"Who?"

"Cunliffe-Lister, I think. Palestine's his responsibility, and it'd be perfectly logical for him to talk to Lawrence about it."

MacDonald nodded as he considered it. Yes, Cunliffe-Lister could do it very well—and then he himself wouldn't have to talk to Lawrence. He doubted that he could have done that. How could he possibly have explained to Lawrence all the reasons why he shouldn't go to Palestine? "Yes, I agree. I'll ask him to invite Lawrence up next week and have a talk."

"I don't think it should wait until next week, frankly. It should be done as soon as possible. Lawrence and Abdullah's man might meet again at any time—and Lawrence could leave for Palestine immediately after, for all we know. We shouldn't delay this. And Lawrence shouldn't be invited to London at all; he might be seen by the press, and it's vital that they get no hint of this. That would be disastrous. In no time they'd be printing articles saying that we were arranging to send him." Gilmour shook his head. "No, no. We can't risk having this become known."

"No, certainly not. But what should we do?"

"I suggest you have Cunliffe-Lister go down to see Lawrence at his place in Dorset."

"Do you think that would be best?"

"Yes. And I think he should go as soon as possible—over the weekend. And go inconspicuously."

"Yes. All right, Gilmour. Do you think he might persuade Lawrence not to go?" MacDonald hoped so. It would be such a relief not to have to give any more attention to this.

"I certainly think he might. He has as much hope as anyone else."

"I'll telephone him at once, and tell him."

"Excellent. Tell him to impress upon Lawrence that this is nineteen thirty-five, not nineteen-seventeen, and he can't any longer go riding about in the desert on a damn camel and blowing up railway lines. The world's a much more complicated place now."

MacDonald nodded, trying to be sure he would remember all that and tell it to Cunliffe-Lister. "I hope Lawrence listens. I hope he'll be persuaded."

"He'll have to be persuaded. I think he's every kind of a damn fool and totally irresponsible, but I think he'll understand how serious this it."

"Let us hope so," MacDonald said.

21

Davidson had been sitting in his car for almost two hours when he saw Sarah Alexander walk out to the street and stand at the curb. He had been waiting there, parked down Baker Street, since he left the flat, and now that he saw her he couldn't decide whether he was pleased or disappointed.

He eased himself lower in the seat, behind the wheel, watching her. When he'd left her at the door of the flat, after all she'd said about Aaron, he had a feeling she might really do something. He hadn't thought it was just talk. She'd been so upset. He had to stay here, to see what might happen, so he'd just hurried to the telephone box down the road, called Gold, and told him what information Aaron wanted them to get for him. Then he'd sat here, waiting, just in case. Now she was here.

Short of killing Aaron or putting him out of action some other way—and he didn't think she'd do anything to harm him—all she could do was warn someone that Lawrence was in danger. And he decided she'd have to come out to do that, because she couldn't use the telephone in the flat, with Aaron sitting there. Now she was here, standing at the curb as though she was waiting for a taxi. It meant something. She'd never been out alone before. Always with Aaron—and only once a day. She must've told Aaron she was going out for something.

Now she raised a hand to a taxi moving down the street, and it stopped in front of her. Davidson watched her climb into it.

It moved down into Oxford Street and turned east. Davidson followed it in the traffic, staying about fifty yards back, but closing up to keep it in sight when it crossed Oxford Circus. Farther along, it slowed down while a big coal wagon drawn by a pair of Clydesdales turned in front of it into Tottenham Court Road. Davidson followed it on, still moving east. He couldn't guess where she was going, but he felt more and more certain that her ride had something to do with Aaron's threat against Lawrence, and he was afraid that it might mean trouble.

The taxi swung down Kingsway and he followed it, around the end of a high red tramcar. It turned off into the quiet square of Lincoln's Inn Fields, and Davidson followed it in, careful now in case it stopped and he might have to pass it. The last thing he wanted was that she should see him.

Around the square the terraces of big houses, four or five stories, were mostly offices for law firms and insurance brokers. Davidson wondered what she could want here. In the center was a wide square of shrubs and trees, and when the taxi turned around the end of the square it went out of sight behind them. Davidson drove down beside the trees, and as he turned the corner he saw the taxi driving in through the old arched gateway to Lincoln's Inn, a smaller square. Carefully he drove in. This was the only entrance and exit for cars.

Lincoln's Inn was one of the four Inns of Court, the societies that admitted all British lawyers to the bar. In the terraces of houses around this square were only the offices of law firms and the apartments of some lawyers and judges. Along one side was an old chapel, and Davidson drove beside it now, wondering why Sarah Alexander wanted a lawyer.

The taxi stopped outside one of the houses near the end of the terrace on the far side of the square. Davidson stopped at the other end, near the chapel, and watched her step down and pay the fare. As the taxi pulled away, circling the square to the exit, she stood looking up at the house. It was a five-story red-brick. She walked through the gateway in the black iron railing, up the steps, and inside. Davidson drove slowly down the side of the square, and when he passed the house he looked up through the open front doorway. She was not in the foyer. He drove to the end of the terrace, turned past an arched pedestrian walkway out to a street, and stopped his car beside a terrace of houses along the end of the square.

Davidson walked back to the house Sarah Alexander had gone into, up four stone steps and into the narrow foyer. The walls were whitewashed and there was a bare stone floor. Beside the open front door was a white-painted board with the names of the five law firms in the house, in black copperplate, one firm on each floor. On the third floor the name was Simon Alexander. Davidson walked back out to his car. He'd heard of Simon Alexander; the man was a Weizmann supporter, a Zionist who believed everything would come to the Jews in Palestine if they were patient and cooperated with the British. Gold had told him that Sarah Alexander was married to him. He thought Aaron should know that she'd gone to him now.

Her husband's secretary showed her into his office, and at once he was up and striding around his desk, smiling, arms out to her.

"Sarah! What . . . ?" Beaming, he took her by the shoulders and kissed her. "I don't know what to say. I can't believe it! When did you arrive?"

"A few days ago, Simon." On the way here she'd tried to decide what to tell him, and she still didn't know. But she couldn't lie and tell him she'd just arrived.

He looked puzzled. "Really? Why didn't you let me know?"

"I've been busy. I wanted to call you, but I've been

166

very tied up. I'd like to talk to you now, if you've got time."

"Time? Of course I've got time, darling. Sit down." He laid a hand on the back of a brown leather armchair in front of the desk, patting it. "Sit down. Would you like a drink?"

"No, thank you."

He watched her as he moved back around his desk to his chair, wondering why she was here—in London and suddenly in his office. "You look very well. Very fit."

"Thank you."

"What're you doing here—in London?" He looked hopeful. "Are you back from Palestine—have you decided to come home?"

"No, Simon." She wished she could say yes, to please him.

"Oh." He sat back in his chair.

She knew how disappointed and hurt he was, but he showed nothing and she respected him for that. Behind him on the wall, in a dark wood frame, were the decorations and medals he had won in France in four years as an infantry officer: Distinguished Service Order, Military Cross and Bar, and the campaign medals, all hung on red velvet. She knew how proud he was of them, and even of his wounds, his lost eye. He was proud that he'd been able to give so much for England. What would he think if she told him Aaron might kill another man who'd done so much, an Englishman who was a legend and a national hero? She couldn't do it. She couldn't tell him about Aaron.

"How long are you going to be here?" he said. After two years, it was as though he was seeing her for the first time, and he felt unsure. He knew he should be able to ask her frankly why she was in London and how long she'd been here, but he was nervous. He was afraid something had happened to keep her from ever coming back, and now she'd come to tell him.

"I'm not sure, Simon."

"But you're not going to stay." He hoped he didn't sound too disappointed. He wouldn't want his disappointment to influence any decision she might make. He didn't

167

think it would—Sarah was too honest for that—but he didn't want to show how he felt.

"No, not yet. There's more I'd like to see done out there, before I come back."

He nodded. "How is it? Do you tell me everything in your letters?"

"No. No, it's much worse than I've written, Simon. Our people are in a great deal of danger there, all the time. If you're a Jew there, you never know when an Arab will shoot you or throw a bomb into your shop or your house. Oh, Simon, people shouldn't have to live like that, under that kind of strain, every day."

"No. It will improve, though, Sarah."

"When?"

"One day. What more can anyone say? One day it will improve. I hope for that—and I believe it. They'll have a better life."

"God, I hope so."

"But I understand the Arabs' side too. They have some understandable fears, and it's not hard to sympathize with them."

"It's hard for me, Simon. If you lived there for a while, I think it'd be hard for you too."

"Perhaps. I'm sure you're right. It's easy to be objective, sitting here. But I believe I can be more effective—and help our people more—if I maintain some objectivity. You know that."

"Yes." She knew how he believed that his English friends—in government and the others with influence— were impressed more by quiet, reasoned discussion than emotion. At more than one of their dinner parties she'd learned that. "And before I went there I wasn't sure whether you were right or not. I only knew I didn't agree with you. That's why I had to go and see for myself. Now I believe you're wrong, Simon. I think we'll have to fight for it if we want a homeland in Palestine."

"And you're prepared to do that?" he said carefully.
"Yes."

"I'm not speaking of self-defense, Sarah. I'm speaking

of actually fighting the Arabs for a place in Palestine. Are you prepared to do that?"

"Yes."

He sat studying her. "You're much more militant that you were two years ago."

"I know it, Simon. I told you: I've seen what's happening."

Nodding, looking thoughtful, he said: "But you're still working for the Jewish Agency, aren't you?"

"Yes."

"Do they know how you feel? Surely they couldn't approve."

"I haven't spoken to anyone there about it. There's no reason for them to know. There's no conflict between the work I do for them and the way I feel, Simon. I went out there to work for them because I wanted to help. Now I feel we'd all be helped a lot more if we began fighting back against the Arabs. One's an extension of the other."

"No, Sarah, one's a contradiction of the other. We've got to win the respect of the world through reason—convince them of the rightness of our case through our intellectual and moral strength. That must be our way. We can never win by turning to violence. There are too few of us for that. If we use violence—no matter how we rationalize it—it will only bring more violence back against us. And in the end we'll lose."

"I know that's what you believe."

"I've believed it for a long time."

"But things are changing, Simon. The world's changing. If you were there, seeing Jews killed and wounded by Arabs, and the British seeming unconcerned, I can't believe you'd be content to do nothing but watch. We've got to make a stand. And it's not just for a place in Palestine. Look at what's happening in Germany now—and no one's making a protest, Simon. Not the Jews or anyone else. We've got to begin to fight for our place, so the things they're doing to our people in Germany won't be allowed to happen anywhere else—not without a struggle."

169

"I'm not sure about the world, Sarah, but you've certainly changed."

"I don't think I have. Things have become clearer to me, that's all."

"Clearer? I don't know. Perhaps you've been too close to it all. It doesn't necessarily make things clearer. On the contrary."

"I don't think we can discuss this, Simon. Our experiences are different. If you were in Palestine, I don't think you'd say we shouldn't use force. I don't say we should use it unless we're provoked—but, by God, we've been provoked."

"And now you're ready to use force."

"I've said it, Simon: Yes!"

Carefully he said: "Then why aren't you in Palestine?"

She sat looking at him.

"Why are you in London, Sarah?"

"Don't ask me that, Simon." She didn't know what to say. She wanted to tell him, but she couldn't. She needed his help, but there was very little she could tell him.

He could see how nervous she was. Something was troubling her and he wished he knew what it was. Gently he said: "If you don't want to tell me why you've come to London, surely you can tell me why you've come to see me. Is that too much to ask?"

"No. I'm sorry, Simon—I'm not being reasonable at all—but it's not easy for me." She didn't know how she could tell him.

He sat waiting.

"I need your help," she said.

"You know I'll help you in anything, if I can. What is it?"

"I think someone might be going to kill T. E. Lawrence."

"T. E. Lawrence?" He sat very still. "Lawrence of Arabia?"

"Yes."

"Why? Why would anyone want to do that?"

She shook her head, impatient with him for asking,

170

and afraid he might want her to tell him more than she wanted to. "I can't say any more. I think it might happen, that's all—and I came to you because I thought you might be able to warn someone and prevent it."

He was watching her closely, looking for all she was not telling him. "Who's going to kill him?"

She was uneasy, with him staring at her. "Don't try to make me tell you any more, Simon. Please."

"I'm afraid I must ask you to, darling. If I pass along this warning to anyone, they'll want to know more than you've told me. How d'you know about this, Sarah?"

She said nothing.

"Have you been sent to do it—you and someone else?"

"Simon! No! What d'you mean?" But he was close. She and Aaron had, after all, been sent to watch Lawrence— but she'd never have come to kill him. Could Simon really believe she would? Did he really think she'd changed so much? "How can you say that?"

"You've been talking very angrily here, my dear. You sound quite violent. You tell me you've been in England for a few days. Since I didn't know until now that you were here, you obviously didn't come to see me. You've stayed out of sight somewhere—and the fact that you've been so secretive leads me to suspect that you've come for some purpose that might not be lawful." He was very anxious and he was trying hard to control it. "Will you tell me why you've come, Sarah?"

"No," she whispered. "I can't tell you."

"You haven't come to do anything for the Jewish Agency, have you?" Now he was questioning her as a lawyer with a hostile witness.

She shook her head.

"But for someone else?"

"Yes," she said quietly. Simon had always been able to make her say more than she meant to—just as her father always had. "I was sent to do something."

"Who sent you?"

"The Irgun."

It shocked him. He'd heard that Haganah B, the mili-

171

tants, had begun calling themselves the Irgun Zvai Leumi, but that was all. The Irgun was nothing but an organization he'd heard of—and disapproved of. It had all been so far away. Now his wife was here, telling him she was one of them. He couldn't grasp it.

"What have they sent you to do, Sarah?"

"To watch someone, that's all."

"Lawrence?"

She said nothing. There was nothing more she could tell him. She'd already said too much.

"You've been sent to watch Lawrence, haven't you?"

Frantically she shook her head. "Simon, I can't say. Please don't ask again. Please!"

Yes, of course she'd been sent to watch Lawrence. But why? He couldn't imagine why. "Did you come alone?"

She shook her head.

"How many of you are there?"

"One other."

"A man, Sarah?"

"Yes."

He watched her sitting in the armchair with her head down, staring at the front edge of his desk, not wanting to look at him. She seemed to him very young and immature. And she was immature. Immature and emotional. He wondered about the man who'd come with her from Palestine. He didn't like to think about that. He felt something like jealousy, and he'd thought that was something he'd never have reason to feel with Sarah.

"Is he the one who's going to kill Lawrence?"

Her head jerked up.

"Is he, Sarah?"

"I'm afraid he might."

"Why is he?"

"I can't say, Simon. There isn't a reason. There's no logical reason for it, but I think he might do it."

It pleased him that she was here telling him this about the man she was with. It made him much easier, knowing that her loyalty to this man wasn't limitless. "Why have you come to tell me about it? Why not the police?"

172

"Because . . ." She didn't want to tell him it was safer this way. It would sound as though she'd come here just to use him. It wasn't like that—but she couldn't explain it all.

"Because they'd have wanted to know more than you were prepared to tell them?"

She nodded. "You can do something, can't you?"

"I suppose I can—but, Sarah, I'd like to know more about all this. Can't you tell me what it is you're involved in? It's worrying me, you know."

"I know it is, Simon, and I'm sorry." She leaned to him over the edge of the desk. "I wouldn't have come to you if I could've thought of any other way. I didn't want you to worry."

"You're in England with a man who wants to kill Lawrence of Arabia, and you don't want me to worry?" Smiling, he shook his head at her.

"So long as you warn someone who can see he's protected, nothing will happen—and certainly nothing will happen to me." With her hands on the arms of the chair, she began to get up.

"Are you going?"

"Yes." It was almost two hours since she'd left the flat. Aaron would be wondering where she was—and she didn't want that.

"I don't like it, Sarah." He was up and moving around the desk to her. "You're going back to this man, aren't you?"

"Yes. We're in the same flat—but there's nothing going on. There's no reason for you to be . . ."

"That's not what I mean." But he was relieved to hear her say that. It had been troubling him. "The man sounds dangerous. I don't know why the Irgun are interested in Lawrence and I won't ask you again—but, darling, I don't think you should be with this man."

"I must go back." She laid a hand on his arm. "I'll be all right, Simon. Don't worry—no one will be hurt—but warn someone about this."

"Yes, yes, I'll do it. But please don't go."

"Oh, Simon." She hated to hear him say please. She

hated it that she'd made him do that. "Don't make it hard, for God's sake." She had to go. Not so much for the assignment now—Aaron and the others could get Shaalan and do the rest very easily without her—but to see that Aaron didn't even try to go after Lawrence. She'd tell him she'd given this warning and he'd have to stay clear. She had to go back for that, if nothing else. But she wished she could stay here. It did feel safe. "I've got to go." She felt guilty about what she'd done too, and she didn't want to hide from Aaron now.

"All right." He stood away from her. "If you want to go, there's nothing I can do."

"I'll be back—before too long. Will that be all right?"

"You know it will."

She kissed him.

"I'll come downstairs with you," he said.

"No. You stay here. Bye, Simon."

"Goodbye, Sarah."

He shut the door behind her and walked back to his chair. He wondered whom he should tell about this threat to Lawrence. Someone at the Home Office. Perhaps Gilmour himself. He certainly knew him well enough. Yes, it would save a lot of time, and he'd be certain that the warning had gone to the man who could act on it.

But why hadn't he tried harder to keep Sarah from going back to this madman she was with? He could have stopped her, if he'd really wanted to. If no other way had been possible, he could've called the police and had her held until she told everything and they could question this man. Instead, he'd let her go, when he had the distinct feeling that it might be dangerous for her. Why had he? Did he, after all, resent her for leaving him and going to Palestine? Was there some bitterness that he wasn't conscious of? He hoped not, because if this man was seriously thinking of killing Lawrence—for whatever reason—he was unstable, and she wouldn't be safe.

22

When she got back to the flat and walked into the living room she saw at once that something was wrong. Bergmann sat staring at her through his horn-rimmed glasses.

"Where have you been?" he said.

"Out for a walk."

"It was a long walk."

"I like long walks." She hadn't expected he'd be like this—but since he was, she couldn't tell him what she'd done. It wasn't the right time.

"Why did you go to your husband?" Slowly he got to his feet.

"Why the hell shouldn't I?" How did he know where she'd been? He couldn't have followed her. He'd been in the bathroom when she went out. How did he know? "I don't have to explain it to you."

"You do, when it concerns me."

"Why d'you think it does?"

"You told him I'm going to kill Lawrence." He stood staring at her.

It was that damn Davidson! He must've followed her. Of course! After she talked to him outside, he'd gone down and watched to see what she'd do—and he'd followed her to Simon's office, and telephoned Aaron right away. Oh, God!

"Yes, Aaron. All right, yes, I did tell him that." She could sense he was jealous because she'd gone to Simon. There was more than that, but there was jealousy too.

"Why?"

"To ask him to give a warning. He knows people in the government, and he'll tell someone who won't ask many questions. They'll be watching Lawrence—so don't go near him, Aaron."

The back of his hand was swinging up very fast, and she tried to jerk her head away, but the knuckles caught her across the cheekbone. She staggered back. Her face felt numb. She couldn't believe it had happened. No one had ever hit her before. Never.

"Why did you do it?" Bergmann's face was very white, and his voice was low and stifled. He could hardly speak.

"To keep you away from Lawrence." Now she was scared. She hadn't expected this. She had expected to explain it to him quietly. That way it would've been all right, she was sure. But Davidson, wanting his approval, had done this.

"You've betrayed me!"

"No, I haven't, Aaron. Dammit, what d'you think I am? I told my husband there might be danger for Lawrence. That's all. I didn't name you and I said nothing about anything else. I haven't done anything that'll harm you, only to keep you from Lawrence."

"Why?"

"I told you this morning—killing Lawrence could do nothing but harm to us. Dammit, Aaron, what's *wrong* with you? Can't you understand?"

"Did you tell your husband anything of our plan to take Shaalan?"

"No."

"Why not? Since you're such a humanitarian, why didn't you tell him I plan to take that Arab? D'you think I'll make him give us what we want without hurting him?"

"Shaalan's here to work against us, and he has to take

his chance. I don't like what we have to do, but it must be done. I said nothing about it to my husband. Only about Lawrence."

"You expect me to believe your husband sat and listened to what you wanted to tell him and asked no questions?"

"No. He asked questions. He wanted to know why I was in England."

"And you told him?"

"Of course not. I told you: I said nothing else."

"You expect me to believe that? You've been away from him for two years. The man wouldn't have let you walk in and tell him your story of Lawrence and go again without wanting to know why you were here. Is he an idiot?"

"No, he's not. Of course he wanted to know why I was here. But I didn't tell him. I told him I was with the Irgun—that's all."

"You told him that?" Bergmann's right hand went to his side, resting on something under his jacket.

"Yes—but that's all." What was he going to do? He looked crazy!

"Why did you tell him?"

"We talked. I had to tell him something."

"And do you think he'll be content with that? Do you think he'll be satisfied with warning the British about this danger to Lawrence? Don't you understand that people like him—like all Weizmann's supporters—are our enemies just as much as the Arabs and the British? Don't you realize that people like your husband and Weizmann will soon lose any hope of a homeland for us in Palestine?"

"What are you saying—that my husband will betray us?"

"Of course he'll betray us! And you've betrayed me! Damn you!" Bergmann's right hand swept in under his jacket, reaching for the butt of a big British revolver, a Webley, jutting from a holster on his right hip.

"Aaron!" She stared at it. She could try to grab it or turn and run, and she didn't know what to do. "Aaron!"

177

She was turning, running for the front door.

There was an explosion in the room and something punched her in the back, harder than anything she'd ever felt in her life. She was on the floor. Face down on the floor and she couldn't understand how it had happened. What had happened to her? She couldn't move. She had no strength. She couldn't get up.

From a long way off she heard Bergmann say: "You bitch! You filthy bitch!"

Then there was another explosion, very close behind her head. An enormous explosion. And suddenly nothing.

Gilmour ate a long lunch, and it was after three o'clock when he walked back into his office. His secretary told him that Simon Alexander had telephoned at half past two, and had said he'd try again at three.

The call came in as Gilmour sat down behind his desk.

"How are you, Simon?" he said.

"Very well, thank you, John. How are you?"

"Very well. Sorry I was out when you telephoned the first time."

"Don't mention it—though, actually, I want to talk to you about something that might be rather urgent."

"Oh? What?"

"I've been told that someone might be intending to kill T. E. Lawrence. Lawrence of Arabia."

"What! You don't say so?" Gilmour wondered who'd told Alexander this.

"Yes. 'Fraid so, John."

"D'you mind telling me who told you?"

"Sorry. I'm not at liberty to say."

"I see." Who could it have been? Gilmour wondered. "Who wants to kill Lawrence—can you tell me that much?"

"I don't know, John. I was told nothing more than that someone might try to kill him. I know nothing of why or who."

"Why were you told about this, Simon? Why didn't your informant simply telephone the police?"

"Because it was assumed that the police wouldn't treat

the warning seriously—not without considerable detail, which my informant was unwilling or unable to give."

"I see. But your informant is reliable, in your opinion?"

"Completely."

"And you suggest I take this seriously?"

"I urge you to, John."

"Yes, well—I shall. Thank you for telling me this. I'll see that it's given attention at once."

Gilmour called his secretary and said he wanted to see Harding in his office as soon as possible.

Harding was there in half an hour, and Gilmour told him about Alexander's telephone call.

"I know this chap Alexander," Gilmour said. "He's a Jew, but quite a decent chap. Very English in his ways, and lays it on a bit thick sometimes, but he had a damn good war record—lost an eye and was well decorated. A sound chap, really. I believe this information he's given us should be taken seriously."

"So do I, Minister. I intend to treat it very seriously."

"Oh?" Gilmour had expected some skepticism from Harding.

"Yes. I believe I know who Alexander's informant is."

"Really? Who?"

"His wife."

"What!"

"Yes. She's one of the Irgun agents we've been watching."

"What! Alexander's wife?"

Harding nodded. "I'd have mentioned the name as soon as we had it if I'd thought you knew her."

"Yes, well, there's no reason why you should've thought it'd be significant to me. Fact is, I've met her only three or four times, as I remember. She's quite a bit younger than he is—an American."

"That's correct, Minister. She's American. One of my people followed her this morning from the flat in Baker Street to Lincoln's Inn, to the address where Alexander has his office. We didn't know conclusively where she'd gone in the house, but my officer assumed it was to her husband's office. Obviously she's the one who told him about the danger to Lawrence."

"Yes. Yes, obviously. What the devil can that mean?"

"It means, for one thing, that at last we know why these Irgun people are here—because they've heard about Lawrence and they want to stop him before he gets to Palestine. I think it's safe to assume that."

"I'm not so sure, Harding. If that were so, why would Mrs. Alexander have given her husband the warning?"

"Um. You make an excellent point, Minister. Then why were they sent?" Harding stroked his gray moustache. "The only other possible reason is that the Irgun heard the story about Lawrence and sent them here to find out more about it."

"I should think that might be it."

"Yes. Now they've confirmed the story, and the order to kill Lawrence has come from Palestine—or it's her partner's idea. He's a bad case, the Palestine Police tell us—a man named Bergmann. Whichever it is, apparently Mrs. Alexander has balked."

Gilmour nodded. "From what I know of her, she certainly would do that. She's an emotional young woman—in many ways immature, I think, and extremely passionate on the subject of a Jewish place in Palestine—but I can't believe she'd involve herself in a cold-blooded killing."

"Apparently she doesn't intend to. But Bergmann presumably does."

"Yes. It's an untidy business. This man Bergmann will have to be stopped, Harding."

"He will be, Minister."

23

Lawrence stood at the window in his downstairs room, staring out into the dark. He thought he must have been standing there twenty minutes, perhaps longer, still trying to decide what to do.

He walked back to the big armchair in front of the brick fireplace and sat staring at the telegram on the wide arm. It had come late in the afternoon from Selim, and by now he knew it by heart:

YOUR CONDITION ACCEPTED. PLEASE ADVISE
WHEN AND WHERE WE MAY MEET TO DISCUSS FINAL
ARRANGEMENTS FOR YOUR JOURNEY.

It had shaken him when he opened it. After all the time—two weeks now—since they'd met and he'd heard nothing from Selim, he'd felt certain that Abdullah had refused to consider his demand that there be no killing. He'd been sure of it. It had seemed unreasonable, even to him, when he'd thought about it in the days since he met Selim. Now Abdullah had agreed.

But now he wasn't certain what he wanted to do. He'd had too much time to think. In the first excitement of it, for a few hours after he left Selim, he'd been so sure that he wanted to go. It had made him feel useful again, as though he still had the ability to accomplish great things, the spirit to meet any challenge. Now he doubted. He'd become convinced that he'd overestimated his value in trying to bargain with Abdullah. Waiting so long for Abdullah's reply—the long wait that had convinced him he'd been rejected—had weakened his confidence in himself. It would take him time to rebuild it—if he could rebuild it at all. Sitting here now, alone, with the dark outside, he didn't feel at all confident. Now that there was no impediment and he could go to Palestine on his own terms, he felt almost—yes, he had to admit it—almost afraid to go. He knew how weak he was capable of being. Few others knew it— most of them, millions of them, believed all they'd read and heard about him—but he knew how far he'd often fallen from that heroic ideal. It could happen again. What if he should go to Palestine and, because of his weakness, there should be another loss of control, as he'd lost control of himself at Tafas and given that terrible order? If something like that happened again, it would be disastrous for him, his reputation, and possibly for the future of the Arabs in Palestine.

Near the end of the war, in September, nineteen-eighteen, the British army was pushing the Turks north into Syria, and east of the main fighting the Arabs were attacking Turkish columns as the troops pulled out of towns and villages to keep abreast of the line of their army's withdrawal.

On the morning of the twenty-seventh Lawrence was north of Deraa with part of the Arab army, sitting with some of the leaders—Auda abu Tayi, Sherif Nasir, and Sheikh Talal—all on horseback, watching from the top of a ridge as a party of their men came riding back from an attack on a Turkish formation that had been retreating up the Damascus road.

Through his glasses Lawrence saw, beyond the Arab horsemen, a white line moving up the road, shimmering and blurred in the heat haze. Carefully he tried to focus the glasses to bring the moving thing in more sharply.

"The Turks look much less formidable without their uniforms, Lawrence," Auda said, gazing out across the desert without even shielding his eyes with his hand.

"Much," he said, still trying to focus more sharply. That was what the moving white column was—Turkish troops, stripped. There had been sounds of firing when the Bedouin rode in on the Turks. That had been the officers and a few tough veterans putting up a fight and being shot down. The rest had been disarmed and stripped, and sent on their way to get to the next village and be fed by their own people, who were already suffering from shortage of rations because of the constant demolition of sections of the rail line and the destruction of supply trains from the north. Every unarmed, useless Turk left to be fed put a greater strain on their army.

They sat watching the men come riding back.

"Smoke!" someone called behind them. "A fire!"

They looked around. Down the reverse slope of the ridge their men were sitting in groups, resting, their horses tethered in strings, and some of the men were staring across the plain to the south.

Heavy smoke was rising behind the hill between them and Deraa, drifting high in the still air.

"A rider!" someone shouted.

Lawrence glanced down the ridge at the man who had shouted, and he was standing pointing across the plain. He looked where the man was pointing and saw a rider coming in fast. He held the glasses on him and saw the little spurts of sand kicked up by his horse's hooves and his checkered red and white headcloth fluttering in the wind of his ride. He was one of Talal's men.

The rider came on, putting his horse to the ridge, skirting the packed circle of men sitting there, and reined in close to Lawrence and the others, swinging down and rushing to them, one hand steadying his rifle slung on his shoulder, one holding out a folded piece of paper to Talal.

Talal took it and opened it.

"The Turks are making ready to evacuate Deraa." Talal glanced at the smoke on the horizon. "What we see is from

183

the fire that the German airmen and engineers are making. They are burning their airplanes and stores."

"What do you think we should do, Lawrence?" Auda said.

"What I should like to do is attack them when they march out," Lawrence said. "But that might be too ambitious for our numbers. Before we think seriously about it, we must know what the Turkish strength is in Deraa. We must send out scouts."

The leaders began calling for scouts to come to them and get their orders.

Watching the smoke, hearing the men scrambling up the ridge, calling to ask why they were needed, Lawrence saw a shape in the sky, flying across from Deraa.

"Wait!" he shouted, and held up a hand, watching the plane. He pointed at it. "Be ready to scatter and take cover. The Germans might not have burned all their airplanes in Deraa."

He focused his glasses on the plane. It was flying straight for them, aiming for the top of the ridge, and he could not tell from its head-on silhouette whether it was German or British. Then its wings tipped up and it went into a circle. He saw the British roundels on the wings and now saw it in profile: a Bristol fighter.

It circled low around them and the observer leaned over the side and dropped a pouch that landed softly in the sand near the group of leaders. One of the men around them snatched it up and handed it to Lawrence.

He took the message from the pouch. It was from the officer commanding the British troops nearest them, to the west:

FOUR THOUSAND TURKISH TROOPS ARE RETREATING
TOWARD YOU FROM DERAA, ANOTHER TWO THOUSAND
FROM MEZERIB.

Lawrence told the others.

"Only four thousand from Deraa?" Auda said. "Is that all that remains of the Turks' Fourth Army?"

"And only two thousand of the Seventh," Talal said. "The British army has devastated them, Lawrence."

"Now let us finish those who remain!" Nasir shouted.

"If those are all that survive, yes, we could give them battle and end our work here," Lawrence said. "But we cannot be sure of that. We do not know with certainty that there are not more of them, and we cannot risk our force against these six thousand if there are more of them still capable of doing damage in the area."

"What is this?" Auda snapped. "Are you saying we should let these six thousand Turks pass unmolested?"

"Not all of them. We will attack the smaller force, the two thousand from Mezerib. That way we shall be able to hold a reserve to deal with any other Turks who might come our way."

Auda grunted. "For the moment it will suffice. We shall do battle with the two thousand from Mezerib."

Talal said nothing, but Lawrence saw how anxious he looked.

"We shall take half our force," Lawrence said, "and two pieces of artillery—two of the mountain guns. That should be enough strength."

"Lawrence," Talal said.

Lawrence turned to him.

"Let us move with all speed." Talal's fingers were flexing and unflexing on the hilt of his sword. "The march of these Turks from Mezerib will take them through Tafas." It was his own village. He was the sheikh of Tafas.

"As fast as we can," Lawrence said. "But the men and horses are tired, Talal. I will take my bodyguards on ahead and try to hold the Turks from Tafas until the rest of you join us."

"There is a ridge to the south of the village. If you seize it you will have a good position from which to hold the Turks."

"We will do it." Lawrence called to his own men to mount, and they galloped off toward Tafas.

Halfway there they met Arab horsemen driving a group of naked Turks up the road toward their camp. There were red weals across the prisoners' backs, where the Arabs had been whipping them.

Lawrence reined in his horse beside the Arabs and

185

shouted at their leader: "Why have these prisoners been mistreated?"

"These are not fighting soldiers, Lawrence. Not honorable men. They are from the police battalion that was at Deraa. For years they have been terrorizing the peasants hereabouts. They have been made to give a small payment for their many crimes."

Lawrence looked at the prisoners. The sight of their bloody backs made him think of ten months ago in Deraa, and what the Turks had done to him there.

"What news have you of the Turkish column moving toward Tafas?" he said to the Arab.

"Some of them are entering Tafas now, Lawrence— the vanguard, Jemal Pasha's lancers. We passed that way and saw them riding in."

Jerking around in the saddle, Lawrence waved at the men behind him. "Quickly! Ride for Tafas and spare no horse!"

They galloped on, but when they got within sight of the village they saw thin pillars of white smoke rising from it, and there were groups of figures standing out in the rough grass that circled it. Lawrence signaled his men to stop, and as he reined in he grabbed up his glasses and focused them. The figures outside Tafas were Turkish troops, some of them cavalry. Now and then there was a single shot from the village, very thin and brittle-sounding as it came to them across the distance. The Turks were finishing off some of the villagers.

"Let us rush them in there, Lawrence!" one of the Arabs called.

"Be not foolish! We would be trampled under by them. We will wait for the rest of our force. Then we will deal with the Turks. Whatever they have done in Tafas is done now. We can save no one. But we will deal with the Turks."

They sat out of range of the Turks, and Lawrence watched them forming up behind the houses of the village. At last the column began moving. He looked back for the rest of the Arab force, but they were still not in sight. Again he trained his glasses on the Turks. At the head and rear of the column were lancers, and between them the massed files of infantry were formed up, with machine guns in carts set out as flank guard. In the center of the column were transport and field guns. He saw that the Turks would pass out from behind the village and into full view, section by section.

"We will move up to rifle range and snipe at the head of the column," he said. "It might delay them slightly. We must try to slow them and give our main force time to reach here, so that we may finish with the Turks."

They galloped closer to the village as the head of the Turkish column marched out from behind it, into the open country. Lawrence and his men slipped down from their horses, dropped on their bellies, and opened fire on the lancers and the first sections of infantry.

The Turks did not stop. Lawrence saw some of the lancers hit, and two fall from the saddle, and some of the marching infantry drop. But the troops kept moving. Then two gun teams galloped out from the center of the column. The drivers swung their horses and guns around in an arc and stopped with the guns aimed at Lawrence and his men, and as the horses were jerked to a stop the crew jumped down from their seats on the guns and limbers and opened fire. The shells passed over and burst in the sand fifty yards behind them, scattering shrapnel. Lawrence's men kept firing and one of the gunners dropped.

Now the rear of the column was clear of the village, the long brown line of men moving away, a wide dust cloud hanging over them. The pair of Turkish guns fired four more shells, then the crews hitched up to the limbers and they galloped off after the column, and through his glasses Lawrence watched them swing back into their place in the center.

"Lawrence! Here come ours!"

He looked around and there was a wide dust cloud moving fast toward them. Too late, he thought. Too late to save the village, but not too late to make the Turks pay for it. The first riders were in sight at the base of the dust, and he trained the glasses on them. Talal was in the lead, bending along his horse's neck.

Lawrence turned back. The lancers of the Turkish rearguard were almost a mile from Tafas now. It was quiet in the village. There were only the white smoke clouds rising. He rode slowly down toward the village, his men following, and when he was close to it he heard the fast-drumming hoofbeats of the main force behind. He glanced back and they were less than half a mile away, closing up fast on him.

He rode on at a canter and heard them galloping up behind, now very close, the thunder of them smothering the sound of his own men. He glanced back again. The great surge of horsemen, Talal in the lead, with Auda and Nasir half a length behind, was only a few yards behind his men, and he saw they were not going to slow down but would ride on past him for Tafas.

"Come on!" Standing in the stirrups, he swung an arm, waving his men on, kicking in his heels and sending his horse forward as Talal drew abreast of him. He looked at Talal's face and saw how terrible it was. They rode on knee to knee, their horses straining, and the mass of Bedouin behind, a great dust cloud rising above them.

Close to the first houses they saw some low mounds in the long grass, some in colored robes, some in white. All women. From the middle of one stuck a long Turkish bayonet. Talal looked more strained when he saw them, but they were all lying very still and he did not stop.

Outside the first houses of the village stood a small group of old men and women, and a few children. Very few children, Lawrence thought. He and Talal reined roughly and jumped down beside them.

"What happened, Shakir?" Talal called to one of the old men. "Tell me how bad it is."

"The Turks have finished us, Sheikh. They have violated and killed the women, even the girl children. They killed and burned." Tears were running down the old man's creased brown face, but he had no expression. "All the young men they killed—my two sons. We are finished, Sheikh."

"No! By God, no!" Talal did not want to be told what had happened here. He did not want to believe it.

He stood looking back and forth along the streets of the village. Bodies lay between the smoking, crackling houses: men shot and bayoneted, face down and crumpled against the walls and doorways of their houses, women and girls spread on their backs with their robes dragged up over their heads, but all dead now too. From between two smoking houses a girl of four or five staggered, her gray-white smock stained rusty down the left side with blood that still ran from a wide lance thrust into the side of her neck.

The main body of men came riding in, and the child stopped, turning to look at them, then turned away, eyes wide, screamed once, and dropped, twitched, then lay still.

The mass of horses stopped among the first houses and the men swung down, staring at what the Turks had done. A low, quivering moan went up from Talal's men, and they ran among the houses, looking for their wives and families. Lawrence and Talal stood watching them, hearing the higher screaming moans when they found them.

Lawrence and Talal mounted and walked their horses through the village, past the bodies. They did not know how many were in the burning houses. On the other side of the village were the low mud walls of sheep pens. Something red and white was folded across one of them. They rode closer and it was the body of a pregnant woman, her robe tugged around her hips, nailed bottom-up to the top of the wall with a saw-edged Turkish bayonet.

They sat looking. From the other end of the village now came the sharp cracks of their two mountain guns firing at the Turks as they moved slowly out of range.

"Merciful God," Talal murmured, staring at the woman's body. "Merciful God, Lawrence."

Lawrence said nothing. He could think of nothing but the Turks—what they'd done here and what they'd done to him at Deraa. They must be made to pay. He could think of nothing but that: They must be made to pay.

They rode beyond the last of the village buildings and sat looking out across the plain where the Turkish column had marched. In groups the men rode up and halted behind

189

them. Auda and Nasir rode up beside them.

"I want to go after them, Lawrence," Talal murmured. "Now!"

"Yes," Lawrence said. "Yes, Talal." He turned, rising in the stirrups, and yelled: "The best of you brings me the most dead Turks! No prisoners!" They had to kill all the Turks, for Talal and for him—for what they'd done to him at Deraa.

"No prisoners!" Auda and Nasir called, dragging out their swords and waving them high. "No prisoners!"

"No prisoners!" came in a roar from the ranks of men. "No prisoners!"

They trotted out across the plain, down the dusty road the Turks had taken. Not far from the village they saw a Turkish infantryman sitting beside the road, back resting against his big pack, legs straight out, mouth hanging open.

"Water!" he called.

As they rode up Talal unslung his rifle, swung the muzzle down from the saddle, and shot the man in the head, slamming him back against his pack and knocking it over.

Farther down the road, one after another, they found more exhausted Turks who had fallen out of the march, and Talal or his men shot them as they rode by.

They walked their horses up a rise, and from the top of it they saw the two thousand Turks less than a mile away. Talal stopped his horse and sat staring out at the long brown column. Lawrence saw he was trembling: his hands on the reins, his chin, his whole body. He knew what Talal was thinking, watching the Turks, and he kneed his horse gently forward to him, to say something that might help, but Auda laid a hand on his arm and murmured: "Leave him with his thoughts, Lawrence. No one can share this with him."

Lawrence reined his horse.

Still staring at the Turks, Talal carefully pulled the drape of his headcloth across his face, covering everything but his eyes. He kicked his heels into his horse's sides and he was gone, galloping down the slope and out across the flat toward the Turks, drawing his sword and bending low in the saddle.

Lawrence, Auda, and all the men sat their horses in long, silent ranks along the ridge, watching Talal ride.

The Turkish column had halted and formed up to receive a cavalry charge, the infantry and dismounted cavalry standing and kneeling in ranks, ready to fire, machine-gun crews crouched at their weapons. Their field guns were manned at the center of the line.

Between the Bedouin on the ridge and the waiting Turkish column there was no sound but the drumming of Talal's horse. Then, very close to the Turks now, Talal sat straight in the saddle, waving his sword, and screamed his war cry: "Talal! Talal!"

Instantly the Turks opened fire. Lawrence saw the muzzle-flashes of rifles and machine guns flickering along the column and then heard the crackle of the firing. Talal and his horse were stopped dead and blasted into the ground.

Softly Auda said: "God be merciful to him. We will take his price from them."

He urged his horse down the slope at a walk, Lawrence and Nasir close beside, and the long ranks of horsemen following. At the foot of the slope they broke into a canter and then, across the plain, into a full gallop, now all screaming and yelling their battle cries.

Lawrence saw the muzzle-flashes as the Turks opened fire, but he could not hear the sound over the thunder of hundreds of hooves. Men and horses were falling. From the corner of his eye he saw a man drop from the saddle. He glanced to see if Nasir had gone, but he was still riding.

Now the Turkish column was moving again, but to try to escape the charging Bedouin they had turned across a stretch of rough, broken ground where it was hard for them to keep formation, and the infantry were becoming separated from the cavalry. With the lancers in the rearguard Lawrence saw three cars with machine guns mounted, and the crews were in German uniform. They were slightly behind the main column, and the Bedouin were riding into the gap to cut them off and surround them. But the Germans kept up a continuous fire with their heavy Spandau guns, clearing a wide circle around the rearguard. The rest of the column moved away from them, the infantry double-timing to keep up with the cavalry.

Concentrating on the rearguard, wanting to finish them before they moved on to attack the rest of the column, the Arabs charged in on them again and again, but they were always stopped by the German fire before they could get close enough to overwhelm them. All around the small group of cars and lancers, the ground was thick with Arab dead, men and horses.

Lawrence sat with Auda and Nasir, watching another attack go in against the rearguard, seeing the men and horses falling as the fire from the machine guns lashed across them. He looked away with his glasses at the retreating column, and the last of the infantry were almost out of sight, still double-timing, their big packs bobbing on their backs.

"This rearguard is dying too hard," he said. "I think we should leave them and go for the others. If we stay here we will lose many against these German machine guns, and their main strength will escape."

Watching the men riding back from the Spandau fire, Auda nodded. "I do not like to leave this unfinished—but neither do I like to see so many Turks escape."

"Then let us go, Auda. These will be finished too. The British will come with armored cars and take them."

"Yes." Auda called to the men, waving his sword. "Leave it here! Follow the Turks! No prisoners!"

The Bedouin wheeled away from the rearguard and streamed out over the plain, after the column. The Turks kept moving, not looking back. Now peasants were running in from villages around. They had heard of the massacre at Tafas and they all wanted to kill Turks.

With Lawrence, Auda, and Nasir leading, the Arab troops split into two as they overtook the rear of the Turks, swinging out wide on either flank and riding in again in a pincer to hit the center and split the column in two, surrounding the rear half, riding in on them, firing and hacking with their swords.

In small groups the Turks stood and died, the peasants who cut at them with swords and knives grabbing up their rifles as they went down. Lawrence was in among the Turks, firing into them with his rifle until it was empty, then slinging it on his back and firing with his revolver.

A Turk rushed at him, thrusting with a long bayonet on the end of his rifle, and Lawrence shot him in the face and rode over him as he dropped. In all the pressing clamor of firing and screaming, deafening as if it were all under a low roof, he was aware of someone shouting and screaming very close, and then he realized it was himself, swearing and yelling as he fired. Still riding back and forth, he broke open his revolver and grabbed cartridges from his belt, fingers trembling, dropping some, shoving some into the cylinder, snapping it shut, and firing again.

Around a field gun a small group of Turks still stood shoulder to shoulder, firing into the Arabs who rushed in against them on foot and horseback. For a few moments they held the rush, and then they went under. Others broke out in small groups, fives and tens, and tried to run and catch up with the first half of the column, still moving away, but they were shot or cut down. Dead men and horses were all across the plain, and now the Arabs were firing at the dead bodies.

Auda went riding out after the rest of the Turkish column, yelling for the others, and they rode after him. Lawrence saw them going and kneed his horse, galloping with them.

Still hoping to escape, the Turks did not stop until the Bedouin were riding into them, and then they turned and began firing. But the horsemen broke into them, firing and hacking.

The battle went on over the plain, Turks standing in small groups here and there, for a while holding the Arabs off. But by sunset the column was finished.

Lawrence felt weak, sitting his horse and looking

around at the humped dead. He could feel his body running with sweat. His robe was sticking to him and to the saddle.

An Arab rode up to him, sweating and breathing hard. "Lawrence, there are Turkish prisoners," pointing back across the plain.

"I ordered none to be taken."

"Yes. But these were taken by the reserve company, who did not hear the order."

He swung his horse around to where the man had pointed. "Take me to them."

They rode back and he saw the prisoners in a close group, sitting on the ground, bulky-looking in their rough uniforms. There must be two hundred of them, he thought. All around them Bedouin stood with rifles leveled.

He sat looking at them. The battle was over and he was cooling. And there had been killing all day. Nothing but killing. Perhaps these two hundred could be left alive, free to go and tell other Turks what would come to them if they did what these had done to women and children in another village like Tafas.

Then somewhere behind the Turks a man screamed something in Arabic. A Bedouin galloped up. "Come, Lawrence! Look at this!"

They galloped past the circle of prisoners. On the far side of them some of the Bedouin were standing around a man lying on the ground. Lawrence swung off his horse and pushed through. It was a wounded Bedouin. He had been shot in the left thigh, and the earth beside him was stained deep with blood, but the Turks had caught him and not left him to die in peace; they had nailed him to the ground with bayonets hammered through his shoulders and right leg. He was still conscious.

"Hassan, who did this?" one of the Arabs said.

The man could not speak, but weakly he turned his head to the group of prisoners, all standing now, watching him, knowing what was going to happen. Slowly Lawrence rose from beside him and mounted his horse. He glanced at the prisoners, then at the Arabs who circled them with their rifles. He nodded and at once the Arabs began firing into the brown mass. The Turks made no sound and none of them tried to break out and run. They stood and let themselves be shot down in rows, and in a few minutes there was only a mound of dead and moaning wounded. The Arabs moved in among them, firing into the bodies until nothing moved.

When there was no more sound, the last shot fired, Lawrence turned his horse and walked it away. It was the first time in his two years with the Arabs that they'd taken no prisoners. The first time. But he felt satisfied. All the Turks lying across the plain looked harmless now. Not like the ones who'd held him at Deraa. At last he'd repaid them for that.

He pushed himself up out of the armchair. It was still so clear, all that had happened at Tafas. Until then he'd always thought he was cool and in control of his emotions, but what had happened there had shown him a weakness in himself that he'd tried ever since to forget. He couldn't. It was always there. It had been revenge for Deraa, and perhaps most men would think it pardonable, but he should have been able to control himself. He should have been capable of something better.

But what if something like that happened again—with Jews next time, instead of Turks? At Tafas it had been war, and though there'd been criticism from British officers who heard of it, there had never been any general condemnation. They'd been Turks, after all, known for their bloody atrocities, and he'd been Lawrence, with his reputation already assured—not yet made legendary but even then beyond question. But could his reputation, massive as it was now, survive another Tafas—against Jews in Palestine? And not in a war but in an Arab uprising? No. He'd be called a bloody murderer. And the Arabs would lose a great deal of sympathy for their cause.

But it wouldn't happen. Why should anything like that happen again? It never would. He was sure of it. There'd be no more weakness. No loss of control. It would all be disciplined and clean. It would be.

195

24

Cunliffe-Lister was pleasantly surprised that there was very little traffic on the road southwest from London. On a bright May Saturday morning like this, he'd expected to have to share the road with a lot of people driving down to the coast for the weekend, to Bournemouth or some such place. But there were very few of them. With things as they were, so many people affected by the Depression, there probably weren't terribly many who felt they could afford to spend money on a weekend at the coast. Whatever the reason, he was pleased to have so much room on the road. Moving into a long, straight stretch, he eased his foot down and sent his Bentley on a little faster. With luck, he could be back in London by early afternoon.

Back in London and able to report success, he hoped. But he wasn't at all certain of that. After MacDonald called him in yesterday and asked him to drive down and talk to Lawrence, he'd felt there was hardly any chance that he'd be able to persuade Lawrence to change his mind. But that had probably been the effect of MacDonald's apathy and tiredness. It had all sounded so hopeless. But after Gilmour dropped in and said he'd proposed him to MacDonald as the one who should go, and they'd talked about it for a bit, and Gilmour said he thought Lawrence would be a damned fool if he didn't pay attention, he'd felt there might, after all, be some chance. If Gilmour, impatient as he was with Lawrence, thought it might work, it might. He sincerely hoped so. If it didn't, they'd have a very ticklish problem. Very ticklish indeed.

He passed north of Bournemouth and in a few minutes drove through a small town, Bere Regis. Outside it he stopped and looked at his map. Now he was very close. Another couple of miles and he would turn off along the secondary road that would take him down to this cottage of Lawrence's. He drove off again, looking for the road. He hoped there weren't any journalists there today. From all accounts, they'd spent a great deal of time camped there, watching Lawrence and his visitors. If any were there, he could only hope that they didn't recognize him. Fortunately the Colonial Secretary's wasn't the best-known face in the Cabinet. He could only hope. It was vital that the press not begin to speculate. They had a way of creating the most fantastic stories about Lawrence.

At the secondary road he turned off and drove south, looking for the place where he'd been told to turn off again. It was about three miles down the road, and he turned left. On this road he had to drive about a mile and a half, then turn right, and Lawrence's cottage was just below a T-junction. It was a quiet road. No traffic at all. But he drove very carefully, looking for the junction. He saw it, and swung the Bentley around the bend.

Just below the junction he passed a car parked at the side of the road, with two men in it. He had a feeling that they were MI-5, some of Harding's men. They looked a bit too neat to be journalists. They paid very close attention to him as he drove past, but he saw no sign of a camera. Yes, he was satisfied that they weren't journalists.

He saw no one else down the road, and just ahead of him, on the left, he saw through the trees the sun on a brick chimney above the whitewashed wall of Lawrence's cottage. In front of him was a wide bar of sunlight across the road, shining through the open entrance to the cottage

197

garden. Carefully he turned the Bentley in. He hoped Lawrence was here. It would've been more convenient if he could have sent word that he was coming, but they thought it best not to do that. Gilmour had thought Lawrence might tell the press and they'd all be there waiting.

A motorcycle was standing near the wall at one end of the cottage, close to the front door. From all accounts, Lawrence didn't go out except on that. It was a good sign that it was here. He switched off the engine, and as he stepped out the cottage door opened and a small man in shirt sleeves and baggy gray trousers stood watching him. From all the photographs he'd seen, Cunliffe-Lister recognized the large, well-shaped head and the face. But the man was smaller than he'd expected.

Not moving from the doorway, Lawrence called in his high voice: "I don't think I know you, do I?"

"No, Colonel Lawrence." Cunliffe-Lister walked over to him. The high, thin voice surprised him. He hadn't expected that. It wasn't a hero's voice. "But I should like a few words with you, if it's not inconvenient. Are you alone, may I ask?"

"Yes. But I'm afraid this isn't convenient."

"It's rather urgent. I'm Sir Philip Cunliffe-Lister." He thought Lawrence would recognize his name, though not his face, but just to be sure, he said: "The Colonial Secretary." He held out his hand. "I'm very pleased to meet you."

Cautiously Lawrence shook his hand. "How d'you do?"

"Are you sure we can't talk? It really is rather urgent."

For another moment Lawrence stood in the doorway, then stepped back, holding out a hand inside. "Please come in."

"Thank you." Cunliffe-Lister stepped in through the low doorway to a narrow hall with a strip of coconut matting on the floor. It wasn't as clean in the hall as he'd have liked. Lawrence was more of an eccentric than he'd thought, living here like this, in a place like this. It really might not be easy to make him see reason. Perhaps even Gilmour had underestimated the difficulty.

198

Just off the entrance was a room with bookshelves from floor to ceiling, all around the walls. Lawrence led him into it.

"Please sit down." Lawrence held out a hand to a big armchair drawn up beside the empty brick fireplace.

"Thank you." As he sat, Cunliffe-Lister wondered how he should begin. It wasn't going to be simple. He could feel that. This was a physically small, not particularly im-pressive-looking man—but there was something about the steadiness of his eyes, the way he had of looking at you as though he was seeing all the way through you.

Lawrence stood with his back to the fireplace, waiting for Cunliffe-Lister to begin. His heels were on the edge of the guard around the hearth, to give him more height.

"I've read a great deal about you," Cunliffe-Lister said.

Smiling with his lips tight, Lawrence inclined his head to acknowledge the interest. "A great deal has been written."

"Yes." Cunliffe-Lister smiled. "How are you spending your time, now that you're out of the air force?"

"Prodigally. I sit here reading. I'm thinking about writ-ing a book. But I've done very little but throw time away." Lawrence smiled shyly. "It's odd to feel laid aside and worn out, but that's how I feel. It's a lost sort of life."

"Yes. I suppose it is." Cunliffe-Lister couldn't decide whether Lawrence was serious or simply playing with him. He looked and sounded sincere enough—not at all like a man who was preparing to go to Palestine to lead an Arab uprising. Delicately he said: "I've heard you might be taking up some sort of employment in the Middle East."

"Oh?" Lawrence looked surprised. "Where, exactly?" So this was why the man was here. Inevitably, they'd heard Abdullah had invited him, and they wanted to know all about it. And, what was more, they'd sent no less than the Colonial Secretary to find out.

"Palestine."

"Ah!" Slowly Lawrence nodded, as though he under-stood it all now. "Yes, there has been an offer of some sort."

"Have you decided to accept, may I ask?"

"No, I haven't."

"I rather thought you had. My impression was that you'd decided to go."

"I'm considering it. Nothing more than that, at the moment."

Perhaps he was telling the truth; perhaps he wasn't. Cunliffe-Lister couldn't be certain. Perhaps he hadn't heard yet that Abdullah had agreed to his terms, whatever they were. "Colonel Lawrence, I must speak very frankly."

"Please do." Lawrence smiled the closed smile. "I think frank talk saves a great deal of time."

"Yes. Well, frankly, we've learned that Abdullah has invited you to go to Palestine and involve yourself in an uprising that the Arabs are planning against the Jews."

Lawrence stood smiling.

It wasn't going to be easy. More than ever Cunliffe-Lister thought that. Lawrence was enjoying it. He was enjoying getting this attention from a member of the government.

"Colonel Lawrence, I'm sure it's not necessary for me to point out to you how delicate the situation is in Palestine. It's extremely difficult for us to keep things from exploding there. The Arabs are convinced we're conspiring with the Zionists to take the country from them; the Jews are convinced that we wish the Balfour Declaration had never been written and have been trying ever since to annul it."

"It's the price that must be paid for compromising."

"Perhaps. But the issue we must deal with is the instability there. It must not be aggravated. You, of all people, Colonel Lawrence, know how vital it is for us to have a secure base in Palestine. As things are now, with the clear likelihood of a war at some time in the future—not too distant, perhaps—that base in Palestine must be kept secure."

"I couldn't be more in agreement with you, Sir Philip."

"I see." So far, so good, Cunliffe-Lister thought.

"I think it'll be a great deal more secure if the Arabs are satisfied that we're their friends and that no one will take their land from them. They're by no means sure of that now."

"Yes. But surely our policy's clear. Our bias is clear. We favor the Arabs. Virtually every pronouncement a British government has made on Palestine in the last fifteen years has made that clear—indirectly, perhaps, but clear nonetheless."

"Obviously not to the Arabs."

"It's been clear to the Jews—and it's caused no end of trouble with them."

"Yes. Again, the penalty for compromising. But the Arabs see hundreds of thousands of Jews in Palestine who weren't there eighteen years ago—and we've allowed them to immigrate. To the Arabs, that's hardly progress toward self-determination."

"But . . ." Cunliffe-Lister did not know what to say. Leaning to Lawrence from the chair, open hands out to him, looking for understanding, he said: "Surely they realize that it's very delicate for us? We can never consider the problem of Palestine in isolation; we must always see it in the context of the whole world, of our alliances and friendships in the rest of the world."

"I think that's asking too much of the Arabs—or anybody. They see their own problem as the most urgent one. They care nothing for the rest of the world, those of them who are aware of it at all. They want their land."

Trying very hard to be patient, to sound reasonable, Cunliffe-Lister said: "Surely the government's been doing all it can to assure them that we sympathize with that wish?"

"Not enough, I'd say, Sir Philip. The Arabs certainly don't think it's been enough—or there wouldn't be talk of this uprising that you mention."

"But surely they understand that we can't—don't want to—openly alienate the Zionists? Especially the American Zionists. I don't need to tell you, Colonel Lawrence, what an influence they have on their government. We can't afford to do anything that might cause the American Zionists to work against us in Washington. If and when war comes, having America as a strong ally will be almost as important as having a secure base in the Middle East."

"You and I understand all this. It means nothing to the Arabs. It's Britain's problem, not theirs."

"Britain's problem is yours, though, isn't it?"

"I suppose it is."

"Suppose? Is it uncertain?"

"It's a long time since I was called on to involve myself deeply in any of Britain's problems."

"You're apparently becoming involved in one now."

Lawrence smiled.

"I've come to ask you not to do it," Cunliffe-Lister said. "Tell Abdullah you won't consider going to Palestine."

"Why should I do that?"

"I thought I'd explained how vital it is for us to keep the goodwill of the Zionists."

"You did—but how is that relevant? If I were to go to Palestine—and I don't say that I am—it'd be as a private citizen, not a government representative."

"Who'd believe that, Colonel Lawrence? As soon as it was known that you were in Palestine, who'd believe you hadn't been sent by the government, to further a policy favoring the Arabs—in armed attack on the Jews?"

It was probably true. Lawrence hadn't thought of it. In all the time he'd spent thinking about it, this hadn't occurred to him. Of course it would be assumed that Whitehall had sent him. A fascinating thought.

"You do see, don't you?" Cunliffe-Lister was anxious. It seemed to him that he wasn't swaying Lawrence at all.

"Yes."

"And what do you say? Will you agree not to go?"

"I can't do that, Sir Philip. I must think about this. But even if it were as you say, and I were assumed to be acting for the government, that would be a factor only if it became known that I was in Palestine."

"If you were to go, Colonel Lawrence, I think it inevitable that your presence would become known to the world in very short order. You do, if I may say so, have a faculty for attracting publicity."

Lawrence smiled his thin smile. "I can't deny it."

"But you still won't tell me you won't go? Even though the risk is clear?"

"The risk is very far from clear, Sir Philip. If the Arabs

were to gain predominance in Palestine, and they had been helped—officially or unofficially—by Britain or someone representing it, you might depend on it that they'd be everlastingly grateful. The benefits to this country would be enormous. We'd never have to be concerned about a secure base in the Middle East. That you could be sure of. There's no risk about it."

"And the Zionists—the American Zionists?"

"If they should be displeased, the effects wouldn't be permanent. No single incident could permanently affect the relations between two countries like Britain and America. Even the influence of the American Zionists couldn't work forever against us. No. I understand your concern, but I'm not sure I agree with you on the assessment of the risk here."

"The Prime Minister agrees with me. You understand, don't you, Colonel Lawrence, that if you go to Palestine it'll be in defiance of the wish of the Prime Minister?"

"If I go, yes. I hadn't thought for a moment that you'd come here on your own authority, Sir Philip."

"I see." There was nothing more he could do, Cunliffe-Lister saw. Lawrence was playing with him. The man was impossible to reason with. He got up from the armchair. "I'll not take any more of your time."

Lawrence walked outside with him. There was no one on the road. That was the one thing Cunliffe-Lister was thankful for: He hadn't been seen by a journalist.

With a hand on his car door, he said: "You're quite certain you won't reconsider, Colonel Lawrence?" He hated himself for saying it. It sounded as though he was pleading with the man.

Smiling, looking schoolboyish and shy, Lawrence shook his head. "Any decision I make will have to be my own. It's a policy I try to follow always."

"I see." Cunliffe-Lister tugged open his car door. "Good day to you." He climbed in and slammed it.

Lawrence watched the Bentley drive out to the road. He walked into the cottage and stood looking at the chair Cunliffe-Lister had been sitting in. It was incredible that they'd sent the Colonial Secretary down here to try to persuade him not to go—and sent him very discreetly, driving his own car on a Saturday morning. They must certainly consider it important that he not go to Palestine. What must they have been saying about him up at Ten Downing Street?

He sat in the chair. All these days he'd been sitting here telling himself that his best years were gone and he was no longer able to do what Abdullah wanted him to do—and all the time the Prime Minister had been discussing him as a danger to British policy in Palestine. Obviously they considered him still capable of influencing the course of events. He was the one who underrated himself, not the politicians in London. He'd always underestimated his ability, and because of that he'd always driven himself so hard, to try to achieve the ideal that he set for himself. And of course he'd often achieved it. There'd been moments when he'd been able to see himself objectively, to recognize all he'd accomplished—and he could accomplish great things still. In spite of all his self-doubt, he was entirely capable of going to Palestine and leading the Arabs. The Prime Minister obviously didn't question his ability. It was nothing but his stupid, masochistic self-depreciation that had caused him to hesitate. But no more. He'd go. On Monday morning he'd ride into the post office at Bovington and send Selim a telegram. They'd have another talk and arrange whatever details there were—and then he'd go. Oh, it was exhilarating to have it decided. And of course he could do the job out there. He'd be magnificent there—as he'd been so long ago with the Arabs.

On his way back Cunliffe-Lister stopped at Bere Regis and telephoned the Prime Minister.

"I'm afraid Lawrence wouldn't be persuaded," he said.

"He insists on going?"

"He didn't actually admit he's going. He was altogether evasive. He didn't even admit he'd heard from Abdullah. Simply said he's had an offer to go to Palestine. His words, as I remember, were that he's had an offer of some sort. And he's considering it."

"Considering it. Perhaps he's no intention of going."
Surely Lawrence wouldn't go? MacDonald thought. How
simple it would all be if he decided not to go.

"I fancy he will."

"But he didn't say so?" MacDonald didn't want to believe it.

"No—but he's obviously sympathetic to the Arabs."

"So are we all—but doesn't he understand the need
for delicacy? We can't antagonize the Zionists. Surely he
understands that?"

"He minimized the difficulty that might come from
that. He favors direct action that would leave the Arabs
in no doubt of their position in Palestine."

"He favors it! Does he understand that we don't?"

"I made that perfectly clear to him, of course, but it
didn't move him. He's a very difficult man to reason with."

"I see." MacDonald didn't know what else they could
do now. "D'you think it might be useful to have him come
here, so that we could all talk to him—you and I and Gilmour, all together?"

"I doubt very much that that would be more effective."
Cunliffe-Lister didn't care for the implication that Mac-
Donald or even Gilmour would be more persuasive than
he had been.

"No, well, perhaps not. We'll have to wait and see.
Perhaps he won't go." MacDonald wanted to forget all about
it. He wanted nothing more than to simply forget it.

"Perhaps." But Cunliffe-Lister couldn't convince himself.

25

In the afternoon Bergmann and Davidson walked out of the flat in Baker Street and climbed into Davidson's car. Parked up the street behind them in their black Wolseley, Quint and Richmond watched, and when the car moved south toward Oxford Street they followed. Another car with two more MI-5 men in it stayed parked, watching the flat in case Sarah Alexander came out or any of the known Zionists went in. The evening before, Harding had grouped into one team all the officers watching Lawrence, Shaalan, and the Irgun agents, and ordered action against the Irgun agents at the first sign of trouble. Quint and Richmond had joined the men watching the flat because Quint wanted to be there when it happened. And now all the MI-5 men were armed. Harding had ordered that too, after he heard that Bergmann meant to kill Lawrence. They all carried Browning .32 pistols in belt holsters under their jackets. Quint liked the feel of it; it reminded him of the old days, during the war. Richmond found it strange, the solid weight on his hip, and wondered how he would be if he ever had to use it. He'd always done well at range practice, but he'd never fired at a man. He couldn't believe it would ever happen. The clumsy belt holster got in his way when he was driving. His elbow jogged against it when he turned the Wolseley west along Oxford Street, following Davidson's car.

"I wonder why the Alexander woman didn't come with them, sir," he said. The officers who had been watching Baker Street from the beginning had reported that Bergmann and Sarah Alexander always went out together, except for yesterday, when she'd gone to Lincoln's Inn.

"God knows. Perhaps they're on their way to Dorset now, to that bloody little exhibitionist, and don't want to involve her in any of that unpleasantness."

"Possibly." By now Richmond was used to the way Quint spoke about Lawrence. From the beginning of this surveillance he'd never called him by name. Always "that little man" or "that bloody little exhibitionist." For the first few days it had seemed amusingly cantankerous, but not now. Now it was tiresome. Once he'd asked Quint why he disliked Lawrence so strongly, and Quint had spoken of all the men he'd known in France during the war who'd done so much more than Lawrence and were unknown. He thought Lawrence had done nothing but happen to be in the right place at the right time—and that he'd exploited his luck shamelessly. Richmond had stopped talking to him about it—or much else. No one, Quint least of all, would ever convince him that Lawrence was anything but exceptional: part genius, part mystic, completely heroic. He'd come to find Quint's skepticism—about Lawrence and everything else—distasteful, and he looked forward to the time when this assignment was finished and they no longer had to work together.

They were moving down Park Lane, and over in Hyde Park all the trees were deep green in the sunlight, making wide, cool-looking shadows on the grass. As they turned Hyde Park Corner, into Knightsbridge, there were two couples riding along the side of the park, down Rotten Row, the horses and the riders' boots gleaming in the sunlight.

Then Davidson's car swung off into Brompton Road.

"Christ!" Quint sat up straighter. "They're going to Shaalan's hotel!"

207

Richmond followed Davidson's car down past the intersection with Cromwell Road, and they saw it turn off along a side street.

"Yes!" Quint snapped. "That's it!" He unbuttoned his jacket and it swung open, showing the polished leather of his pistol holster.

There were only two or three cars parked along the street. Quint recognized an MI-5 car on the side across from Shaalan's hotel and a few yards from it, up toward the corner they had just turned.

"Stop behind our car there," he said.

As Richmond swung in, braking, he saw Davidson stop down the street, at the curb outside the hotel.

"I'll go and have a word with them." Quint nodded at the two men sitting in the car ahead of them.

"Very well," Richmond said, watching Davidson's car. No one had left it yet.

Quint strolled forward and bent down to the window of the other MI-5 car, one foot on the running board. "Is Shaalan in the hotel?"

"Yes," one of the MI-5 men, Sainsbury, said. He had thin blond hair and was smoking a Dunhill pipe. "We've been here since midday and haven't seen him. The chaps we relieved hadn't seem him either."

"Keep your eyes open now," Quint said. "Bergmann and Davidson are in the car that just stopped outside the hotel. I've a feeling it means trouble."

"Oh." Sainsbury unbuttoned his jacket, glancing at the man beside him. "D'you want us to stay put?"

"For the moment," Quint said. "We won't move till we see what they're up to. But if we do anything, it might be very fast, so be ready to follow Richmond and me at once. Understood?"

"Perfectly," Sainsbury said.

Quint walked back.

Bergmann and Davidson sat looking at the front door of the hotel, up two low stone steps. It had been converted from a big house, and there were wide bay windows on either side of the front door. It looked quiet inside. Bergmann was sure he'd have no trouble getting Shaalan out of there.

"All I want you to do is stay here and wait," he said. "When I come out with him, start your engine. As soon as I get into the back with him, drive off. No delay. I don't want him to try to call out."

"I'll be ready, Aaron. Don't you worry, old man." Davidson sat very stiffly behind the wheel. He was sure he looked as though he did this kind of thing every day, and he was trying very hard not to think of Sarah Alexander's body back at the flat.

Bergmann looked at him and said nothing. He climbed out of the car and limped up the steps into the hotel. There was no one in the lobby. Only a gray-haired woman receptionist behind the counter.

"Yes?" She looked at Bergmann as though she did not approve of him. "Is there something I can do for you?"

"No, thank you." She was like all the English, Bergmann thought: stupid and condescending—and pathetic because they didn't know how stupid they were. "I'm going to see Mr. Shaalan."

She looked as though she did not approve of Shaalan either. "Do you know which room it is?"

"Yes." Bergmann walked to the stairs.

From the car Davidson saw him leave the reception desk and limp across the lobby. So far, it was all right. Not that he expected anything to go wrong. Aaron would take care of it, all right. Nothing would stop him. But who'd have thought he'd kill the woman? Yes, she'd been a traitor and deserved to be punished—no argument about that— but when he told Aaron about her yesterday he'd expected him to frighten her a bit, perhaps even hit her, knowing his temper. He never dreamed he'd kill her. Never. He must've gone mad, for a minute, to do that. Good God, he'd never forget seeing her body on the floor when he went back to the flat last night. What a terrible bloody mess! Aaron hadn't even tried to hide it. For Aaron it was just as though she'd never existed. A strange man. And, yes, even a bit frightening, perhaps, to a lot of people. He, of

209

course, understood Aaron perfectly, and he'd been completely justified in shooting her. They were fighting a sort of war, and traitors had to be punished. He'd be ready to do his part, whatever he had to do. He felt the big pistol tucked awkwardly into the waistband of his trousers: a big German pistol, a Mauser, with a box magazine, that his father had brought back from the war, off a dead German officer. He wasn't sure he'd remember how to fire it, if he had to. It was a few years since he had, and only three or four times then, at a tree. But Aaron had insisted he bring it. Oh, of course he'd remember how to fire it, if he had to. He'd never let Aaron down.

Bergmann climbed to the third floor and found the corridor Davidson had told him about. At the end of it, at the back of the hotel, was Shaalan's room.

He felt under his jacket and eased the big Webley revolver in his belt. He knocked on the door.

"Mr. Shaalan?"

"Yes!" Shaalan called. "Who is it?"

"I have a telegram for you."

There were footsteps in the room, and then the sound of the door being unlocked. It opened and a man of about forty stood there, with a black moustache and a neat beard. He was fully dressed, in a three-piece blue pinstripe suit.

"Yes?" Shaalan looked puzzled. He had expected someone in a uniform.

Tugging out the Webley, Bergmann stepped inside the room and slammed the door. He rammed the muzzle into Shaalan's belly.

"Who are you?" Shaalan looked down at the revolver pointing into him.

"I'm with the Irgun. I want you to come with me."

"Irgun? What is the Irgun?" Shaalan could see this man was a Jew, and he felt uneasy.

"Irgun Zvai Leumi. The military organization of the Jews in Palestine."

"This is England, not Palestine. And I am not a Palestinian. I should like you to leave my room at once."

Bergmann held the Webley tight into him. "I want information from you."

"About what?"

"I want to know everything you and Lawrence have talked about. I want from you a signed statement of all that you Arabs want Lawrence to do for you in Palestine. I want to know everything, including the British government's part in your plot."

"British government?" Shaalan wondered if the Jew knew something he didn't. No. The Jew was foolish, that was all. "What do you mean? What is this about the British government?"

Still holding the gun into him, Bergmann hit him hard across the mouth with the back of his left hand. "You filth! Don't play with me!"

Shaalan tasted blood in his mouth and felt the sting in his face. He moved to take a step forward, but the gun muzzle dug deeper and he saw Bergmann's eyes and the hardness of his mouth. He knew he could die here. It was not the place or the time; he didn't want to die uselessly. Whatever the Jew did, he would not allow himself to be provoked.

"I don't know what you're talking about, Jew," he said quietly.

Bergmann hit him again. "I don't like your tone of voice. Be very, very careful. I want information from you, but don't make the mistake of thinking I'll allow you to speak to me as you wish. If you annoy me, I'll kill you." He nodded firmly. "Yes. Whether I've got the information or not, I'll kill you. So be very careful with me."

Shaalan said nothing. Yes, he would be careful now. But when the moment came, he would kill this Jew.

"Sit down and write the statement," Bergmann said.

"I will write nothing." As soon as he had written it, this Jew would kill him, Shaalan was sure. The longer he held out against him, the longer he would live—and as long as he lived there was hope for revenge.

"Yes." Bergmann nodded. "Yes, you will write. But not

here. Here I can do nothing to compel you. We'll go to a more private place—and there you'll give me what I want." He prodded him with the gun muzzle. "Come on!"

Shaalan did not move."I demand to know where I am going."

"I told you—to a more private place." Bergmann hit him across the face. "Move!" He stood back, motioning with the Webley to the door. "Now!"

Shaalan walked to the door and Bergmann stepped close behind him, holding the gun in his back. "One moment!"

Shaalan stopped with his hand on the doorknob.

"We'll walk down the stairs and through the lobby side by side—and I'll be holding this gun against you all the time. Don't speak to the woman in the lobby. Don't say anything. Just walk outside and down to the car that's waiting. Do you understand?"

Shaalan nodded.

"Don't make any mistake. If you do, you'll die. Now open the door."

They walked out, down the corridor to the stairs.

In their car, Quint and Richmond sat watching the hotel and Davidson's car at the curb in front of it.

"If Bergmann's doing anything in there—anything to Shaalan—oughtn't we to go in and stop it, sir?" Richmond said. He didn't like the waiting. It was more than ten minutes since Bergmann had gone in.

"We can't!" Quint snapped. "We've no reason to go in. Just sit and watch that bloody hotel." He was beginning to feel edgy, he had to admit. That bloody man Bergmann could be doing anything in that hotel. He felt useless, sitting here, but they had no legal right to go in.

"There!" Richmond hissed.

Someone had come out of the hotel. It was Shaalan. Bergmann was close behind him. They walked together to the steps down to the street.

"Get down there!" Quint snapped. "Drive the damn car down there in front of theirs!" Richmond was already moving the car. "Stop them! Don't let them drive off!"

As they passed the other MI-5 car Richmond saw it was moving too, following them. He sent the Wolseley surging down the street.

Limping down the hotel steps, his gun muzzle hard into Shaalan's side, Bergmann glanced at the two speeding black cars, the first one now very close, and then it was braking hard, swinging into the curb in front of Davidson's, and he knew it was trouble.

"Shoot!" he yelled at Davidson.

Davidson stared at him through the car window, his mouth slightly open.

Swinging up the Webley, aiming at the first black car, Bergmann shouted: "Shoot at them, Davidson! Damn you!" But before he could fire Shaalan grabbed at his gun and they fell struggling against the black iron railing at the side of the steps.

Quint and Richmond jumped out of their Wolseley as Davidson shoved open his car door, tugging at the bolt of his big Mauser to cock it. There was a shot on the hotel steps and Shaalan fell away. Bergmann kicked at him as he fell, to get clear of him, swinging his Webley on to the men running from the black cars.

Standing on the curb Davidson aimed over the top of his open car door at Quint.

"Look out, sir!" Richmond shouted, and fired twice. Glass shattered in Davidson's door and he dropped back along the curb.

From the steps Bergmann aimed carefully at Richmond and shot him in the head.

Quint fired twice and Bergmann dropped against the black iron railing, his big Webley clattering on the stone steps. Aiming carefully, arm out, sighting as if he were on the range, Quint fired again, and whispered: "Take that, you bastard."

Sainsbury and the other MI-5 men were there, pistols out. Now it was very quiet on the street. At the far end a red double-decker bus passed along Brompton Road.

213

Sainsbury looked at Richmond's body, lying across the curb, at the blood that soaked the blond hair, and murmured: "Oh, God."

"Yes. Poor devil," Quint said. "If it hadn't been for him, this one would've had me." He nodded at Davidson, down in the gutter beside his car. Both Richmond's shots had hit him in the heart.

The gray-haired receptionist was standing behind the hotel door, staring down through the glass.

Quint waved her back, and snapped at Sainsbury: "Go in and tell that woman to say nothing about this, nothing to anyone. And telephone the police!"

Sainsbury jumped up the steps.

"And get an ambulance for this one!" Quint called. He knelt beside Shaalan.

"Right!" Sainsbury rushed into the hotel.

Shaalan had been hit in the right thigh. He was sitting up against the railing, sick-looking, his right leg hanging limply down the steps, blood soaking the stone.

"There'll be a doctor very soon," Quint said.

"Yes. Thank you. Are you police?"

"No."

"I don't believe my leg is broken." Shaalan tried to make it move and sucked in sharply with the pain.

"You'd better keep still."

"No. I have things to do. I must be able to move." If this man was not police, he must be security. Shaalan wondered how much they knew about him—and Lawrence.

"Just wait for the doctor," Quint said. "You won't be going anywhere for at least a few days with that leg, broken or not. Just sit still, old man. And we'll have to know what this was all about—why those two were trying to take you out of here."

Shaalan stared at him.

Yes, Quint thought. You don't want to talk about it. But you will. You'll tell us all you know about it.

As soon as Shaalan had been taken to hospital and the bodies moved, Quint reported to Harding.

214

"Shaalan's not seriously hurt, is he?" Harding said.

"No, sir. He'll be all right. He's comfortable in the hospital and I've got two men watching his room."

"How soon can you begin interrogating him?"

"Not until late this evening, the doctor says. Perhaps not until the morning."

"You'll have to be very careful, Quint. He's an influential visitor from a friendly country—ostensibly friendly, at least—and it's important to maintain the appearance of friendliness. Abdullah's playing fast and loose with us, but if this damn plot falls through, we'll all have to behave as though nothing ever happened."

"I'll do the best I can." Quint knew he sounded short but, great Christ, after all that'd happened old Harding was becoming nervous. Richmond dead—and those two bastards—and the Arab in hospital, and now Harding wanted it gentle. "But surely what's most vital is to get all the information Shaalan can give? Without that, we're going nowhere."

Harding brushed a fingertip along his gray moustache. "Yes, yes, you're absolutely right, of course. But be very delicate, Miles, for God's sake."

"Of course." Now it was first names. That was a bloody bad sign. Whenever Harding really felt the pinch, it came to first names, because misery loved company. The poor devil was growing too old for it. Too old, anyway, for a job as vicious as the one they had now. And he'd been good once.

"What about the rest of it? Everything cleared up?"

"Yes."

"Damn bad luck about young Richmond." Harding looked worried. He hadn't decided how he'd explain it to Richmond's parents.

"Yes. He was very good at the end too. Probably saved my bloody life."

"Really?"

"Yes."

"Might some sort of award be possible?"

"Many've had them for less."

215

"Very well. That's a first-rate suggestion, Miles. Let me have it all in writing, will you?"

"Yes."

"And I'll recommend it. His parents'd certainly like it."

Quint said nothing.

"What about the woman at the hotel—the receptionist? She saw it all, you think?"

"She saw a street that looked like a butcher's shop; I know that."

"My God," Harding muttered.

"There wasn't any bloody way to avoid it, sir. The woman ran to the door and saw it. But she won't talk. I explained it all to the police who came, and impressed on them that she mustn't tell anyone what she'd seen. Then I spoke to the Special Branch, and had them go to the hotel and make sure she understood. It'll be all right." The Special Branch of Scotland Yard worked closely with MI-5. They knew the importance of secrecy.

"Did anyone else see it?"

"God knows. I saw no one in the street, and that's all I can be sure of. It was all over in a few seconds." Quint shrugged. "Then it looked like nothing but a traffic accident."

"We must hope for the best. Hope no one saw it."

"The police've had no calls from the press. By now they would've had them, I imagine, if there were going to be any."

Harding nodded. "I suppose so. I hope you're right, Miles. Word of this must not get out. It *must* not."

26

By early evening of the following day, Sunday, Shaalan had told Quint all that Abdullah had ordered him to do and all he and Lawrence had said when they met, and he confirmed that Abdullah had agreed to Lawrence's demand. Quint had been ready to use force if necessary; none had been, but it had taken more than twelve hours of continuous questioning, keeping Shaalan awake when he wanted to sleep.

Later in the evening Gilmour went to 10 Downing Street with Harding's report of the interrogation.

Watching MacDonald read it, he said: "There's absolutely no doubt now that Lawrence is prepared to go."

Still reading, MacDonald nodded. He was very tired. Gilmour saw it was pointless trying to talk to him until he was finished. These days, MacDonald could certainly not read a report and discuss it at the same time.

MacDonald laid it down and leaned back in his chair. "It's quite tiresome."

"Yes." Quite tiresome, Gilmour thought. My God! The man talked about it as though it were a mild cold. "I spoke to Cunliffe-Lister last night. He told me Lawrence wouldn't be dissuaded by him."

"No. I asked him if he thought it might be more effective if I had Lawrence come here and we all three spoke to him."

Gilmour nodded. "He told me. I agree with him that it wouldn't be. In fact, I rather think I was wrong to suggest he go down to see Lawrence. It probably succeeded in doing nothing but satisfy Lawrence's feeling of self-importance."

"I don't know." MacDonald took off his horn-rimmed glasses and rubbed his eyes. "Something had to be done."

"Yes. Unfortunately, it still does. As soon as Abdullah's man's out of hospital, they'll meet and make their final arrangements, and Lawrence will go. It's all very clear." Gilmour nodded at the report.

"Yes." MacDonald picked it up and laid it down again. "But what should we do?"

"Lawrence has got to be stopped."

"But how d'you propose we do it? Cunliffe-Lister's talked to him without success. You tell me we'd all three be no more successful. What else can we do? If we tried to coerce him, he'd tell it to the press within the hour. I believe you've mentioned that risk at some time."

"I have. Most definitely we can't do that."

"I don't know." MacDonald shook his head. "I don't know, Gilmour. There's no manner of legal action we can take. We've discussed that too, haven't we? He's perfectly free to go out there if he wishes."

"Yes, yes."

"Then I see no solution." For a moment MacDonald closed his eyes. He wanted nothing more than to sleep. He couldn't think about this any longer. It was a terrible dilemma, yes, and they'd talked about it so often, but there was nothing he could do. Nothing.

"We can stop him," Gilmour said.

"How?"

"Not legally—but he can be stopped, and he'll never talk."

"How, Gilmour?"

"Harding's men could do it. As they stopped those Irgun people yesterday."

218

MacDonald gazed at him. Gilmour insisted on talking about this, and he wanted to sleep. "Could it be done?" he murmured. Oh, but he was tired.

"Yes." It had to be. Gilmour saw no alternative for them. It was imperative that they stop Lawrence from going to Palestine, and there was no other way.

"Will you arrange it, please, Gilmour?" MacDonald felt he couldn't keep his eyes open for another second.

"Yes. I'll speak to Harding at once."

"Yes, please. Have anything done that you consider necessary to resolve this problem of Lawrence. No necessity to tell me any more."

That night Harding drove to Whitehall from his home in Kensington and went to Gilmour's office. When he had telephoned him, after he walked back from 10 Downing Street, Gilmour had not said why he wanted him so urgently, but Harding was sure it was because of Lawrence. It was very rare that they had a meeting on Sunday night. Very rare.

Gilmour told him of the conversation with the Prime Minister and said: "Now it's for you to arrange, Harding."

"Yes, Minister." Harding was amazed that his own voice sounded quite so unemotional. Very little shocked him, but this action Gilmour had ordered against Lawrence was desperate. Not that it was altogether surprising—and that was probably why he'd taken it so calmly; he'd half expected it would come to this, because if Lawrence went to Palestine, the consequences would be disastrous. They had certainly tried to appeal to Lawrence's reason, so Gilmour said. And he didn't doubt what Gilmour had told him; he'd had the report from his own men, who'd seen Cunliffe-Lister go to Lawrence's cottage yesterday. He'd been curious about the reason for that visit. Now he knew. "We'll find a way."

"One thing must be understood by whomever you assign to it: There must be no suggestion of foul play."

"No. Quite. It'll have to have the appearance of an accident."

"That's vital, Harding. The press must on no account ask questions and begin to look into Lawrence's activities over these past few weeks." Even the thought of that troubled Gilmour. He knew he wouldn't be at ease until this terrible thing was finished and enough time had passed for them to be sure nothing was suspected.

"Needless to say, we'll take every precaution," Harding said, but he knew that if anything went wrong they'd all go down: MacDonald, Gilmour, Cunliffe-Lister, himself— anyone who had any connection with it—and it was his duty to warn Gilmour. "Sometimes there are mishaps, however. Someone might find reason for suspicion, and if . . ."

"See to it that no one does, Harding." Gilmour was very firm.

"We'll do all we can, of course. But my point, Minister, is that Lawrence is an extraordinary man, a legend. Everything that happens to him becomes magnified in the press. No matter how he dies, no matter how it happens—in circumstances that, with anyone else, would never be questioned—it'll inevitably cause speculation in the press. I think that has to be expected."

"I'm aware of it, Harding. I'm only too aware of it. We must be prepared, but the speculation mustn't go too far."

"There's the risk that that sort of attention, with journalists prowling about looking for the kind of fantasy they always seem to create about Lawrence, might cause something to be uncovered, Minister. What I'm attempting to explain is that the death of Lawrence will be subjected to unusual scrutiny."

"I repeat that we must be prepared for it." Gilmour leaned suddenly across his desk, glaring at Harding. "You're uneasy about this, aren't you?"

"I'm conscious of the risk, Minister."

"Dammit, man, d'you suppose I'm not?" Gilmour sat heavily back. "This isn't a decision I've reached on a whim, Harding! D'you think I'd order it if there were an alternative? We've tried the only possible one—we've tried to persuade Lawrence not to go, and we've failed."

"Yes, yes, of course, Minister." Harding hadn't meant to rouse Gilmour like this. He'd simply wanted to point out the risk being run by everyone from the Prime Minister down to whichever officer he assigned to this damned unpleasant business—and he knew who that would be. There could be only one.

There was silence in the big high-ceilinged office. They both were tense, unsettled by what had to be done.

"It must be taken care of quickly," Gilmour said. The thought of what they were going to do was terrible, but now that it had been decided, he wanted it finished. He didn't think he'd be able to endure any delay. "As soon as possible."

"Yes." There was something else, and Harding had to mention it. He'd thought of it a few hours ago, when Quint reported on Shaalan's interrogation. He didn't particularly want to raise this matter. He knew what it would mean, had to mean. "There's another point that I think should be given attention."

"Yes?" Gilmour held himself ready for anything.

"Abdullah's man. He's aware now that we know everything. I think he could be an embarrassment."

"Good God!" It hadn't occurred to Gilmour. "D'you think he'd tell Abdullah? That'd be awkward. It's important that we maintain the appearance of good relations with Abdullah. When he sees nothing's come of his attempt to recruit Lawrence, I suspect he'll have no further part in any Arab uprising. We'll have to go on treating each other as friends—and that'd be a very difficult game to play if Shaalan went back and told him we'd interrogated him and knew everything. Abdullah's pride'd be involved and he might be forced to come out openly against us. That's to be avoided, if at all possible. What d'you think, Harding: Might Shaalan tell him?"

"I think he might, Minister. If he did, of course, he'd have to admit that he'd given us the information, betrayed Abdullah's trust."

"Yes. Would he do that, d'you think?"

"I rather think he would." Harding hated to admit it;

he knew what it meant. "He's betrayed Abdullah to us. I think his honor would demand that he confess that to him."

"I'm afraid you're right—and it's a risk we can't take." Gilmour sat staring off across the office. He took a deep breath. "You must see to it that Shaalan doesn't get word to Abdullah."

"Yes, Minister." There it was, Harding thought.

"That'll have to be done carefully too—so Abdullah doesn't suspect we had anything to do with it."

"Of course."

"Are there any others who might give us trouble?"

"I think not, Minister. Lawrence and Shaalan—those are the only two. This has been a closely kept secret."

"Thank God for it, Harding."

"Yes."

"All right. I'll leave them both to you. Keep me constantly informed." Gilmour wished he could forget it all, here and now, but that was impossible. Until this terrible affair was finished he knew he'd be able to think of nothing else.

27

The next morning Lawrence sat writing a telegram for Selim. Their meeting would have to be here at Clouds Hill. He didn't want to go to London again. He wrote:

PLEASED MY CONDITION ACCEPTABLE. COME HERE
TOMORROW 4 P.M. TO SETTLE FINAL DETAILS.

It would do, he thought. He laid it aside. He had another telegram to write, to Henry Williamson, the writer he'd talked to in London a few weeks ago about the Blackshirts and Anglo-German friendship. A letter had come from him on Saturday, an incredible letter, really, full of the kind of thing he'd talked about in London—the need for a new age in Europe, Anglo-German friendship as the basis for the pacification of Europe—but now there was more: Williamson saw him as the man who should lead the movement in Britain, and wanted him to meet Hitler to discuss the idea of a friendship between their countries. It was an interesting notion. Williamson wanted to come and talk about it and said he'd arrive tomorrow unless it rained.

He couldn't decide what to tell Williamson. He wanted to hear more about this, but he didn't want him here when Selim arrived. It'd have to be earlier, early enough for them to talk and for Williamson to be gone before four. He wrote:

LUNCH TUESDAY WET FINE. COTTAGE ONE MILE
NORTH BOVINGTON CAMP.

That should do it. Williamson could come whether it rained or not. Then they'd get their talk over and done with tomorrow. It certainly looked as though Williamson would be wasting his time, anyway. In a few days he expected to be a long way from England—and Palestine would be taking his attention, not Europe. But the thought that the man wanted him to meet Hitler was fascinating enough to be worth a few hours, certainly.

Tucking the two telegram forms into his pocket, he got up. He'd take them down now to the post office in Bovington and send them off. He picked up his goggles and walked out to the Brough. It was a fine day, with the sun out and already warming. The morning was half gone, almost half past ten, and he'd done little but write these two telegrams. In these few weeks since he'd left the air force he'd learned very well how to waste time. But he would do better soon, in Palestine. His life would have purpose there. No more aimlessness. He could hardly wait to be there.

Tugging his goggles over his head, he swung onto the Brough and kicked down on the starter. Carefully he rode through the gateway. There was no traffic. He swung the Brough toward Bovington.

About one hundred yards down the road he felt the lurch as he rode down through the slight hollow, the first of the three on the way to Bovington. He always enjoyed the sinking and lifting he felt when he rode at speed down and up the other two, the deeper ones. God, he loved the feeling that came from riding this bike. It was something he'd miss in Palestine.

But in Palestine there'd be so much more. It was an incredible opportunity he'd been given. A second chance to do for the Arabs what he'd failed to do for them during the war: give them their freedom. It wouldn't be all he'd

224

hoped for during the war, when he'd met Sherif Ali and, because of all he felt for him, had dedicated himself to work for Arab freedom—as a gift for him. It couldn't be as complete a gift now, because the French had control in Syria, but it would be at least some recompense for not having worked wholeheartedly for the Arabs during the war. No, that wasn't true enough: for actually betraying them by being an accomplice in that scandalous Anglo-French plot that tricked them out of their land, and for never—great Arab champion that he was—never working as hard as he should have done against it. Though he'd wanted freedom for them, out of weakness he'd betrayed them. Instead of warning Feisal of that plot, as he would have done if he'd been strong enough, he'd deceived him, and it had all ended disastrously. Oh, if only Feisal were alive now, to see him make this act of remorse. It might blot out the disgrace of what had happened in Damascus near the end of the war.

Late in nineteen-seventeen, when he learned of the Sykes-Picot Agreement from the Turks, Feisal's confidence in the British was badly weakened. In spite of his father's faith in them, he suspected that the British did intend, as the Turks said, to share Arab lands with the French when the war was over, allowing the French to control Syria, which he wanted for himself. Lawrence worked hard to persuade him to keep his troops in the war and to fight even harder.

"To what purpose?" Feisal said. "We are fighting to expel the Turks from our lands. What will it profit us if we do this and the Turks are only replaced by the French?"

"Nothing, if it were so, Your Highness—but it will not be so. And even if you have doubts, the wise course for you is not to weaken your efforts now but to fight even harder, until the war is won. You must one day ride into Damascus at the head of an Arab army and establish your government there in the capital of Syria before the British take control. Once you are in possession, my government would never dare move against you and risk another Arab uprising—against themselves, this time, rather than the Turks. They would be facing a *fait accompli,* Your Highness, and it would be politically expedient for them to accept it. Remember that my government's interest is, above all, Palestine. They would not want an uprising that would sweep through all the Arab lands and make Palestine untenable for them."

Feisal sat studying him. "You believe all this?"

"Wholeheartedly, Your Highness."

"Then we shall continue to fight—even harder than ever, as you advise. When we reach Damascus, we shall see."

"It is a wise decision, Your Highness," Lawrence said, and told himself it was best that Feisal not know that the Sykes-Picot Agreement was indeed part of British policy and they did intend to share Arab lands with the French. He himself privately opposed the agreement and any suggestion that the French should have Syria. He truly believed that if Feisal were installed in Damascus before the British took formal control, Syria would be recognized as an independent Arab state and Feisal as ruler—and Feisal's counselor would be himself, shaping the destiny of an Arab dominion in the British Empire. That was his ambition, to be the controller of a new Arab nation—a free nation within the Empire—and it could never happen if Feisal did not keep his men in the war against the Turks.

It took another year of fighting before the British and Arabs pushed their way north to Damascus. The time came on the evening of the last day of September, nineteen-eighteen, when Australian cavalry under General Harry Chauvel rode into the northwestern outskirts.

Lawrence was south of the city that night, hearing the distant explosions of stores and ammunition dumps that the Turkish and German troops had fired as they withdrew. The glaring white blazes of the explosions lightened the dark, and over Damascus he could see yellow points of shells bursting in the sky, tossed up by the explosions of magazines. He was sure there would be nothing left of Damascus by morning.

At dawn he climbed into a Rolls-Royce tender, and when his driver reached the top of the ridge above the oasis of Damascus, he told him to stop, expecting to see smoking ruins. But the city was there, looking untouched, a haze of morning mist from the Barada River low around it, the early sun sparkling on its domes and minarets. Just one column of black smoke was still rising, and from the direction he knew it was nothing but the storage yard at the railway terminus.

They drove down the straight road to the city, past fields where the peasants were beginning their day's work, and on the outskirts a picket of Indian troops stopped them for a few minutes, the sergeant looking doubtful about Lawrence's Arab dress while he checked their papers. Lawrence sat in the car, wondering what was happening in the city. Perhaps the British had already set up their administration and it was too late for his plans for Arab control.

When the guard passed them, they drove up the long street to the government center, through crowds that packed the walks on both sides and swelled into the road. More people crowded all the windows and balconies and looked down from the flat roofs. All of them were laughing, shouting that they had an Arab government at last, after four hundred years of Turkish rule.

As the car moved slowly through the crowds Lawrence listened to the shouting and wondered what had happened. Feisal was still eighty miles south, in Deraa, and it was more than two days before he would make his triumphal entry, the symbol that Arab rule had arrived.

But at the town hall he found that an Arab administration had taken over before the British troops entered. At noon the day before, as the last of his troops left, the Turkish governor had handed over control to an Arab prince, Mohammed Said, who at once formed a provisional government and declared Syria independent. Lawrence knew Said, and knew he wanted an Arab state that would be completely self-governing, with no kind of involvement with any foreign power. Said was not the man for his plan, and he could not be allowed to stay in office.

Lawrence decided on the man he wanted to govern until Feisal arrived: Shukri el Ayubi, a supporter of Feisal. With men loyal to Feisal, he forced Said out of the council chamber and appointed Ayubi. Then he went to General Chauvel, lied to him that Ayubi was the choice of a majority of citizens, and asked Chauvel to confirm him. Chauvel did. Lawrence also suggested that the general set up his headquarters in the British consulate rather than in the residence of the former Turkish governor, which was being reserved for Feisal. Chauvel agreed to that too, not seeing that he was making a token admission that the British were simply allies of the Arabs and not the controllers of Damascus. Lawrence saw that his plan for Arab control was moving ahead.

And through the first day it seemed that it would work. The Arabs began to reorganize the administration of the city. A police commandant and assistants were appointed. The water supply, out of action because the main conduit was plugged with Turkish and Arab bodies, was made to flow again. The power station was brought back into operation, and by the first nightfall the streetlights were working. Damaged food from the partially burned Turkish stores was distributed to the hungry people who filled the streets. Railwaymen began to go back to work, so the supplies to keep the city alive could be brought in again.

Then on the second day it all ended. The British supreme commander, General Allenby, arrived at one o'clock in the afternoon of the third of October. He had heard of the moves the Arabs were making and he told General Chauvel he wanted to see Feisal at once. Chauvel said Feisal, now waiting outside the city, was not due to make his triumphal entry until three.

"I can't wait till three," Allenby said. "Send a car for him and ask him to come in and see me at once. He can go out again for his triumphal entry."

Chauvel sent an aide in a Rolls-Royce to bring Feisal in quietly, not to be seen by the people of the city, but Lawrence had heard about it and already sent a rider to warn him, and Feisal came galloping into the city with about fifty Bedouin. There was no crowd on the streets to see him—he was an hour too early.

Feisal and Allenby, with their senior staff officers, met in a big salon in the Victoria Hotel. Lawrence was there as interpreter, though Feisal by now was comfortable with English.

Allenby, big and red-faced, hunched over the table, his gold rank badges spread along his wide shoulders, said to Feisal: "Your Highness, there are several points that I must make clear at this stage of our campaign, with Damascus in our hands and total victory not far away. It is necessary that you and we fully understand each other's positions."

Gently Feisal, slim and fine-boned in his robe, said: "I agree, General. Perfect understanding is essential."

"Quite. First let me make it clear that it is my government's intention that France shall be the power that will have the mandate for Syria, in accordance with the terms of the agreement between our two countries. You, Your Highness, representing your father, will be responsible for the administration of Syria—not including, of course, Palestine and the province of Lebanon—under French guidance and with French financial support."

Lawrence felt sick when he heard it. This was why Allenby had come rushing here, to make it all clear so brutally to Feisal, to smash all the ambitions he'd had for proclaiming his sovereignty here—and the ambitions that he himself had had for being Feisal's guide, though Allenby knew nothing of that.

He translated for Feisal, but saw from the way his pale, sad face had turned even paler that he had already understood.

Feisal said nothing, waiting for the rest.

"It is also our intention," Allenby said, "that the sphere which will be under your administration, Your Highness, will be the hinterland of Syria only, and your authority will not extend to the Lebanon, which we define as stretching from the northern border of Palestine to the head of the Gulf of Alexandretta. To prepare for your future coopera-

tion with France, it has been decided to provide you immediately with a French liaison officer, who will work for the
present with Colonel Lawrence."

Lawrence saw Feisal seem to quiver, his long, slim fingers twined tensely together, waiting for the end of the
translation.

When Lawrence was finished, Feisal said: "Is that all
you have to tell me, General?"

"Yes."

Bitterly Feisal said in English: "I do not accept any
of this. I reject it most firmly."

Allenby sat very still. His red face was a deeper red.

"I know nothing of the future of France in the future
of Syria," Feisal said. "I am prepared to have British assistance. For many months I have been willing to accept that.
But not French. I also know nothing of the Lebanon being
subtracted from Syria. I have understood from the adviser
you sent me"—he glanced at Lawrence—"that the Arabs
were to have the whole of Syria, including the Lebanon
but excluding Palestine. Palestine, it has long been known,
is to be a British area of interest. But not the Lebanon.
That is a part of Syria. Without the Lebanon, Syria will
have no port. A country with no port is something I will
not accept."

Allenby sat with his heavy fists clenched on the table.
He glared at Lawrence. "Did you not tell him that the
French were to have the protectorate over Syria?"

"No, sir. I know nothing about it." To Lawrence it
seemed that the words were coming from someone else.
He felt Feisal watching him and was sure he could see that
he was lying. He felt that he might be sick.

"But you knew definitely that he was to have nothing
to do with the Lebanon," Allenby said.

"No, sir. I did not."

For a moment Allenby sat looking at him, then turned
to Feisal. "Whatever you might have been told or not told
in the past, Your Highness, what I have just now told you
is the policy of my government, and it represents the essen-
tials of an understanding entered into between my country

and France. It will be honored by my country and must be similarly honored by you."

"I was no party to it, General," Feisal said, speaking in English and ignoring Lawrence.

"Nevertheless, you must accept it now. The position now is that I am commander-in-chief and you, Your Highness, are at present a lieutenant general under my command and will have to obey orders. My order is that you accept the terms of the agreement I have described to you."

"So long as I am under your command, General. But the war cannot last much longer."

"Perhaps not. In any event, Your Highness, you must accept this situation until the matter is resolved after the end of the fighting, at the peace conference."

Coldly Feisal lowered his head and murmured: "Until then, it seems that I have little choice."

He rose and walked out of the room with his officers. But Lawrence stayed. Later he would try to convince Feisal that he hadn't known of the plan to give Syria to the French. Damn Allenby! How could the man have put him in that impossible position in front of Feisal? All these months he'd been keeping Feisal in the war by telling him he'd have Syria, knowing all the time that France had been promised it but hoping desperately that all that would be changed by the reality of having Feisal established in Damascus, at the head of an Arab government that was demonstrating its ability to govern efficiently. And there were many men influential in London who shared his hopes—not many at the Foreign Office, where the Sykes-Picot Agreement had been drafted, but others with influence. And the dream had come very close to reality, here in Damascus. He'd almost won it for the Arabs—for the Arabs and himself. But the French were winning with the politicians in London—and might carry their success through the peace conference.

"Sir," he said to Allenby.

"Yes? What is it?" Allenby snapped.

"I shall not find it possible to work with a French liaison officer."

"You shall, Colonel Lawrence. That is what you are ordered to do."

"In that case, sir, I'm due for some leave. I think perhaps I should take it now and go to England."

Allenby glared at him. "Yes! I think you should."

"Very well, sir." Lawrence saluted and left the room.

It had really ended there, in that salon in the Victoria Hotel, he thought now, feeling the speed of the Brough trembling through his body. Yes, he'd been able to convince Feisal afterwards that he hadn't known of the plan to give Syria to France. He'd even attempted, in the talks between Feisal and Weizmann in London, only two months after that disastrous meeting with Allenby, to make the arrangement for Zionist financing of an Arab government in Syria, still trying to find an alternative to French control. But that had failed too, and he and Feisal had gone on to Paris, where the Arabs had lost everything. It might've been different in Paris if he'd been able to persuade the British delegation to support his view, but French pressure for Syria had been too strong. He'd been too weak. In the end he'd failed the Arabs—and himself.

It had been very uncomfortable for him to face Feisal after that—but they'd met again, the year after the peace talks, in London at the end of nineteen-twenty, five months after the French had expelled Feisal from Syria. That day in London he and Lord Winterton, acting for the Middle East department of the Foreign Office, had persuaded Feisal to accept the throne of Iraq. He still remembered, and he'd never forget, how bitter Feisal had been then about the way he'd been treated by the British and the French. He'd been especially bitter about the British character in general, and he himself, listening to it all, had had the distinct feeling that Feisal was saying it to him, as the Englishman he knew best. It had been deeply distressing.

Yes, surely Feisal would be pleased if he could be here now, to know that he was going back to try to make restitution. But even now he wasn't being completely honest, was he? Was it only remorse that was taking him back? No.

232

Not just that. There was still the strand of motivation that had tugged at him more strongly than any of the others during the war: intellectual curiosity. Even more strongly than the wish to give the gift of freedom to the Arab people, for Ali, that desire had driven him—the desire to know the feeling of being the inspiration of a national movement, to know he was guiding so many lives with his will. Oh, God, the satisfaction that would come from that! He would do it this time. He must do it—for Feisal, for Ali, and, yes, most of all for himself.

28

Quint turned the black Wolseley off the road from Bere Regis, down the secondary road that led to Lawrence's cottage. It felt strange to be driving the car down here, alone. All the times he'd been down this road in these past weeks, he'd sat on the other side, watching the scenery, while Richmond drove. The poor devil—no more driving for Richmond.

After this morning he wouldn't be driving down here himself, if it all went well. This would be the end of it. Some time ago it had been clear to him that there'd be no other way of stopping this little man. But the politicians had had to go through their bloody act, first pretending the problem wasn't there, then that it'd conveniently disappear without forcing a decision from them, then that it might all be settled in a gentlemanly way, with no discomfort for anyone. But none of that had happened, and now they just wanted it finished, not caring how it was done. That was all right—but if the bastards had decided it a few weeks ago, even a few days ago, Richmond wouldn't be dead, nor that poor damn misguided woman they'd found in the Baker Street flat. Their deaths had been completely unnecessary. Unlike Lawrence's. That little exhibitionist had been playing with it for long enough, causing no end of trouble while he satisfied his need for attention. He deserved it. No bloody regrets for what would be done today.

He'd known, instantly, last night, what it was all about. Coming up from a delightfully deep sleep, which, by God, he'd earned after twelve hours of questioning Shaalan, he'd known as soon as he picked up the telephone and heard Harding's voice. When Harding asked him to his house, which was bloody unusual at any time and unprecedented on a Sunday night, he'd known not only what had to be done but that it had to be done urgently.

In Harding's study he'd heard all about it immediately. That was a damn good thing about Harding: When things were most serious, he became completely cool and businesslike.

"Lawrence must be killed, Miles," Harding had said.

"I see. And I'm to do it?"

"Yes. If you've any objection—for any reason at all— I'll look for someone else."

"I've no objection."

"Good." Harding nodded. "It'll have to be done without delay. Tomorrow, if at all possible."

"I see." Yes, Quint thought, he'd been right. They did want it urgently.

"It'll have to appear accidental, Miles. It's going to be extremely delicate, I'm sure I don't have to tell you. When this happens to Lawrence, the press will be on it in a flash. There must be no cause for suspicion, nothing they can sensationalize and begin speculating about. It must appear accidental."

"Of course." Quint glanced at his watch. "If there's nothing else, I'd like to get back to bed. I'm bloody tired— and I'd like to drive down to Lawrence's place as soon as I can in the morning."

"There is one more thing."

Quint stopped half forward in his chair, ready to rise.

"Your friend Shaalan will have to go too."

Quint said nothing.

235

"We can't risk his going back and telling Abdullah we know all about this, d'you see, Miles? We can't have anything upsetting the applecart out in the Middle East."

"Of course not. But Shaalan'll be in hospital for a week or two."

"We'll watch for him to come out. But it'll have to be done then. That, too, must appear to be accidental."

"Yes, of course," Quint had said.

Shaalan was one he hadn't expected, he told himself now, making the left turn along the secondary road to drive the last mile and a half along to Lawrence's cottage. That poor bastard had simply come over here because he'd been told to. It was damn bad luck for him.

Ahead of him was the T-junction where the road to Lawrence's cottage and Bovington branched off. A black car was parked off the road at the head of the junction, so the two MI-5 men in it could look down the road and watch the cottage. Quint passed the car, beckoning to one of the men, Townsend, and stopped just ahead, waiting for him to come forward.

Townsend looked in at the open window, one hand resting on the sill. "Hello, Quint."

"Where's our man?"

"Out on his motorbike. He went down to Bovington about half an hour ago."

Quint looked at his watch. In a few minutes, a half hour at the most, Lawrence would come riding back. After the first few days of the surveillance they had stopped following him into Bovington. He would have become suspicious, in time—and, anyway, they'd found that he rarely went farther down the road than Bovington, to the post office or the shops, and stayed only half an hour or an hour. But, to be safe, they kept a car on the road south of there, and if Lawrence ever went through Bovington that car would follow.

"What're you doing here today?" Townsend said. "I didn't know you were coming."

"It's finished here." Quint was staring down the road, past Lawrence's cottage, toward Bovington.

"I beg your pardon?"

"We're taking the surveillance off Lawrence."

"Really? May I ask why?"

Quint looked at him. "No."

Townsend stood there, unsure whether to stay or go.

"Drive back to London at once," Quint said. He didn't want to waste another second here. He knew how he could settle this thing very quickly. But he didn't want witnesses— not even two of his own people.

"Very well." Townsend took his hand off the window sill but still stood in the road, uncertain. "Are you coming?"

"No."

"Very well." Townsend stepped back. "We'll go at once. Cheers."

Quint raised a hand to him, between a wave and a salute. He sat waiting. Townsend's car door opened and closed. Then he heard the car start up. It came slowly up behind him, and the driver nodded to him as it passed, moving faster. When it went out of sight around a bend he started the Wolseley and turned down the narrow road toward Bovington.

Before Lawrence's cottage he passed another on the right. From time to time, when he and Richmond had been here, trying to behave like journalists, they'd seen a man or woman, sometimes both, working in the garden. Now he drove quickly past and saw no one. Sunlight through the tree leaves made light and dark speckles on the road.

He passed Lawrence's cottage on the left and drove through the slight hollow in the road. For most of the way to Bovington the road was fairly straight, and he watched for Lawrence on his motorcycle.

Riding toward him he saw two boys on heavy-looking bicycles. They were side by side on a high point of the road, just about to ride into one of the deep, long hollows.

Quint drove the Wolseley down into the hollow toward them. They looked about twelve or fourteen.

As the boys rode down the slope of the road, one of them glanced back as though he had heard something. Quint could not see beyond the far rim of the hollow, but he thought the boy must have seen something coming because he dropped back and swung in behind the other. Driving up the rise, Quint passed them.

Then Lawrence rode over the lip of the hollow.

Quint saw him crouched over the handlebars, his goggles looking dark against his face, his hair whipping in the wind. It had to be now. Quint glanced behind, and the two boys were riding on, not looking back. They wouldn't see anything. Damn them for being here—if there were questions later, they might remember his car—but this was the time to do it. It had to be now.

He eased the Wolseley out to the center of the road. Still Lawrence was coming on. Not very fast, Quint thought: thirty-five or forty. But with his own speed it would be enough. He edged over into Lawrence's lane.

In the moment before they touched, he saw Lawrence's mouth open, and with the goggles he looked wide-eyed. It was as though he were screaming.

Quint felt a slight bump and there was a quick metal-scraping as the Wolseley brushed the motorcycle. Then he was past, driving up to the top of the hollow.

In the driving mirror he saw Lawrence was wobbling but still upright, riding on down the road after the two boys. Damn! He's getting away with it! He's going to stay on the damn bike!

Then the Brough was tumbling, out of control. Quint saw it hit one of the boys. Then he drove out of the hollow, and Lawrence and the two boys were out of sight.

Quint drove on down the road to Bovington.

29

Lawrence lay bleeding from the head. Near him one of the boys was down too. The other one, white and shocked, was getting up from the road, picking up his bicycle. His friend's bike, a wheel buckled, was a few yards along the road. It had knocked him down after the motorcycle had slammed it out from under his friend. The Brough was on its side near Lawrence, badly smashed. A dog was barking somewhere close.

A man called: "What's happened, son?"

The boy looked up and saw a man in army uniform, a corporal, running in from the fields beside the road, a dog bounding and barking along beside him. The corporal jumped through the brush at the edge of the road, glanced at the boy lying there, and at the man and the blood around him.

"That man's motorbike hit my friend," the boy said.

The second boy sat up in the road. He looked dazed. The corporal could see nothing but a cut on his head, but he might be in shock. He turned to the man, and saw how much blood was spreading. Oh, Christ, he thought. It looked as though the road had been painted red-brown around the man, especially around his head and shoulders. It was

239

gleaming in the sun. Blood was all over his face, and he was either dead or unconscious. The corporal couldn't tell.

The dog darted in, sniffing at the blood.

"Get out!" The corporal whipped at it with his leash. "Get back!" Nervous, angry at the dog, he hit at it again and it ran off around the boys.

The corporal stood there. He pulled out his handkerchief and tried to wipe the blood from the man's face. There was too much of it. He didn't know what to do. He heard something coming.

An army lorry swung down the road. The corporal ran to it, waving his arms. "Hey! Stop!"

The driver braked hard and pushed his head and shoulders out of the side window. "Gawd! What's this, Corp?"

"This bloke came off his motorbike. He's caught a packet, I think. Hit one of these boys too."

The driver climbed down from his cab. "What're you going to do?" He looked down at Lawrence.

"Better take him into Bovington, into the camp hospital."

"Blimey! What a bloody mess." The driver stood with the toes of his polished boots carefully back from the edge of the spreading blood. "Is he dead?"

"I don't know whether he's bloody dead! Come on! Let's get him into the lorry. This boy too." The corporal nodded at the sitting boy. "We'll take you to our hospital and let the doctor have a look at you, son. Did you get hit too?" he said to the other one.

"No." The boy looked at his friend. "His bike came down and knocked me off mine, that's all."

"You might as well come with us, anyway. You can stay with your friend."

Carefully the corporal and the driver lifted Lawrence into the back of the lorry, and the boys' bicycles and the wreck of the Brough. The corporal climbed into the back too, with his dog. The two boys sat in the cab with the driver.

On the ride down to the army camp the corporal sat

240

looking at the bleeding man, thinking about what he'd seen and heard from out in the fields while he was walking his dog. He'd seen the black car driving down the road, and the two boys go down into the dip, then the man on the motorbike go down behind them. For a second or two they'd all been down there together, where he couldn't see them. Then the car had come out. Then he'd heard the crash and seen one of the bikes spinning out along the road, with no one on it. Why hadn't that car stopped and helped? Didn't the driver know he'd hit this poor sod?

Quint followed the road past Bovington to the town of Wool. From there he telephoned London and spoke to Harding.

"I got him," he said.

"When?"

"Fifteen minutes ago."

"How, Miles?"

"He was on his motorbike, on the road from Bovington to his cottage, and I jogged him with the car. He went down."

"Is he dead?"

"I wasn't able to confirm it." It troubled Quint to admit that. He liked neatness. "Even if he wasn't killed outright, I doubt he could live. He was probably doing forty, and I was doing the same. Eighty miles an hour when we hit— and he wasn't wearing a crash helmet."

"I see. I trust there were no witnesses?"

"There were two boys on the road, riding bikes. They were ahead of him, and I passed them before I hit him. But . . ."

"Good God, Miles!"

"There was no choice. The moment was there. You wanted it done without delay, and the bloody man doesn't come out of that cottage every day. God knows when another chance might've come."

Harding was quiet on the line. "Could those boys identify you, d'you think?"

241

"No. And they didn't actually see me hit him. They were riding on. But he hit one of them. I don't know how seriously."

"I see. This might be awkward, Miles. I'll have to make sure that it doesn't become a problem. Did anyone actually see what happened?"

"No. There was no one else on the road, and it happened in a dip in the road, quite a deep one, where we were all out of sight from either side—Lawrence and I, and the two boys. We were all hidden at the moment I hit him."

"I see. The nearest hospital would be—where?"

"Here at Wool, I suppose. Or the military one, in Bovington Camp—that's certainly the closest."

"All right." Though it wasn't all right, Harding thought. Not yet. There was a disturbing uncertainty. It was unlike Quint to leave a thing half done like this. "I'll follow this up—to make certain."

Again Quint felt dissatisfied at the way it had gone, but there was nothing more he could do now. "I don't think I should hang about here."

"No. Come back now, Miles."

30

Lawrence, admitted unconscious to the Bovington Camp hospital, was identified at once. The commanding officer was told, and he telephoned the War Office in London.

Little more than twenty minutes later a telephone rang on a small table behind Harding's desk. It had a confidential number and was connected directly to his office, not through the departmental switchboard. As he swiveled around in his chair, reaching for it, he had a premonition about the call. Only half an hour ago, as soon as he'd finished talking to Quint, he telephoned a friend in military intelligence, a brigadier, and said he'd like to know if Lawrence had been admitted to Bovington hospital and what his condition was.

He picked up the telephone, hoping it would be good news, and that this problem was finished.

"Clive here, John," the brigadier said.

"Hello, old boy. What news?"

"He's been admitted. Caused no end of a rumpus at Bovington. The camp CO's telephoned the War Office to ask for instructions."

"Really? What's his condition, Clive, d'you know?"

"Poor, I'm afraid. He's unconscious, and they don't

think he'll pull through. Head's quite badly bashed about, they say."

"I see."

"Anything else I can do, John?"

"No, thanks, old boy. Terribly grateful." Harding put down the phone. The brigadier had asked no questions when he'd first spoken to him, and none now. A real professional. The fewer questions he'd ever have to answer about this matter, the easier he'd feel.

He picked up the telephone again and called Gilmour's office, using a private number like his own, a direct line to Gilmour's desk. He had already called him on the same line a few minutes ago, after speaking to Quint, to tell Gilmour what had happened.

"Yes," Gilmour said.

"Harding again, Minister. I've just learned that Lawrence has been admitted to the hospital at Bovington Camp. He's still alive."

"God!"

"Yes. But he's unconscious and they don't think he'll live."

"But in the meantime he *is* alive, Harding. Dammit, why didn't that man of yours. . . ?" Gilmour stopped. "Well, there's no point in that, I suppose."

Harding said nothing.

"We'll have to make damn certain that no hint of what's happened is made public." Gilmour saw there could be terrible problems in keeping it all secret. He'd have to telephone MacDonald. Whether or not MacDonald wanted to hear any more of this affair, he'd have to know what had happened, because he'd have to see to it that the army cooperated in keeping all this quiet. Damn! The thing was spreading. "The press will have to be kept from it, as far as possible. It's fortunate that Lawrence is in an army hospital. That'll make it easier to control them."

"It will indeed, Minister." It relieved Harding that Gilmour saw some reason to be thankful. "Perhaps I should send some officers down to Bovington too. It might be wise to have a watch placed on Lawrence."

"Yes, perhaps. Yes, I think that should be done."

"And also to Lawrence's cottage."

"Is that necessary, Harding? What I want most of all to avoid is making the press curious. All this activity is hardly going to help."

"I suggest we have no choice, Minister. We know Lawrence has had at least two letters or telegrams from Shaalan. Unless he destroyed them, which I doubt, presumably they're somewhere in his cottage. We can't risk having a journalist break in there and find them. I'm afraid it will happen unless we get there first."

"Yes, you're right. I don't like it, but you're right. Send some of your people there at once, Harding."

"And Lawrence was, of course, in communication with Shaalan," Harding said cautiously. He wondered how Gilmour would respond to what he had to ask next. Whatever Gilmour might say, he had to ask it. It was the politicians, after all, who wanted this kept quiet.

"Yes. What're you saying?"

"It's more than likely that Lawrence sent him telegrams. Copies of them will be in the post office at Bovington. We should have them, Minister."

"Good Lord, Harding!"

"It's imperative. Whatever we do to keep this from the press, they'll be looking for sensational reasons for what's happened. In fact, our efforts to maintain the secrecy are going to encourage them to look harder. We can't risk having one of them extract copies of Lawrence's telegrams from the Bovington post office. We don't know what he might've written to Shaalan. It could be very dangerous."

"Yes," Gilmour murmured. How far could this go? "I'll speak to the Prime Minister. You'll get authority for your men to go and look for the telegrams, Harding."

"Thank you."

"Is there anything else we should do?"

"Those two boys on bicycles," Harding said.

"Yes?"

"They may have seen my officer in the car. They must be persuaded not to speak of it."

245

"Oh, good Lord," Gilmour whispered.

"It's essential, Minister." By now Harding was feeling much more confident about the whole thing. With unlimited authority from the politicians—and he was assured of that, because for the politicians it was self-preservation—he could keep the secret of what had happened to Lawrence today. "Those boys mustn't speak of that car."

"I'll see that it's taken care of. Where are they, d'you know?"

"If they were hurt, probably at the hospital in Bovington."

"All right." Gilmour was quiet. "This is an awful bloody mess, Harding."

"Yes, it is, Minister. There is, however, one thing in our favor."

"What is it? I should like to know."

"Because of all the mystery Lawrence has always created around himself, anything we do now is apt to be taken by the press as simply a continuation. They'd expect a degree of mystery about anything that happened to him—even a simple road accident. With luck, things we do that might otherwise be suspicious will be discounted as simply part of the Lawrence legend. He's put out so many stories about himself that by now no one knows what to believe. We might have to endure some sensationalism in the press, Minister, but I fancy no one will treat it very seriously. I think they'll be so taken with the myth that they won't go probing very deeply for the reality. Lawrence's romanticizing might work for us."

"Unless he lives and tells it all, Harding."

"We must hope that doesn't happen."

Less than an hour after he was admitted to the hospital, all officers and men at Bovington Camp were ordered to say nothing of Lawrence to anyone and were reminded that as serving soldiers they were restricted by the Official Secrets Act.

Before the local police began their investigation an officer at the camp issued a statement saying there had been no witnesses to the accident.

But the London newspapers had heard of it. The call from the first reporter to telephone the camp was passed to an officer who had been assigned to answer inquiries from the press.

"What's his condition?" the reporter said.

"I'm afraid I can't tell you anything," the officer said.

"But he's in the hospital there, isn't he?"

"Yes—but all inquiries must be made at the War Office."

"The War Office? But he's a civilian!"

"Yes—but he's been admitted to an army hospital."

"Then why can't you tell me anything? Why must I ask the War Office?"

"Because those are the orders we have. There's nothing more I can tell you."

One by one all the other reporters who telephoned during the afternoon were told the same thing: All information on the accident would be given only by the War Office.

The army doctors who first examined Lawrence found a large fracture across the left side of his skull and thought he had no chance to survive. But in London someone decided that the public should believe that everything was being done to save his life, so four of the best surgeons in the country were sent to Bovington, including two of the King's doctors.

247

31

At Bovington Camp the two boys identified themselves as Frank Fletcher and Albert Hargreaves, both sons of soldiers there, and both had just left school at fourteen. Hargreaves was found to be suffering from shock and was put to bed. Fletcher was taken to a room in the camp headquarters building to be interviewed by an officer, a major.

"How d'you feel, son?" The major looked very friendly.

"All right, sir, thank you." It was the first time the boy had ever talked to a major. They were very important officers.

"That's good. Sit down, son." The major motioned to a wooden chair in front of his desk.

The boy sat, keeping his back very straight in the chair, like a soldier.

"Now. Tell me everything you remember about this accident, from the beginning. Tell me exactly what happened—not just when the motorbike hit you and Albert, but before. Tell me all you saw."

"Me and Bertie were riding up the road. We were side by side, and then we heard the motorbike coming, and Bertie came in behind me, so we were in single file. A car passed us, going the other way, coming down toward here, and the motorbike was coming closer behind us. Then I heard a big bang, then something crashed into me and knocked me off my bike."

"What was it that hit you, son?"

"Bertie's bike, sir. The motorbike hit him and knocked him over, and his bike came flying over and hit me."

"I understand. Where was the car after that? Did you see?"

"No. I didn't see it, sir. When I got up, it was gone."

"What d'you remember about the car, son?" The major was very casual about it, as though it was not really important.

"Not much, sir. I think it was black. I don't know what kind it was."

"How many people were in it? Did you notice?"

The boy shook his head. "No, I'm not sure. Sorry, sir."

"I see. You don't think it hit the motorbike, do you?"

"I suppose it did. I suppose that's what knocked the motorbike over into Bertie."

"Oh, but surely the motorbike ran into Bertie. Isn't that what caused the accident?"

"I don't know, sir. I don't think so. There was a lot of room for the motorbike to go by without hitting us. I think the car must've hit it."

"But you didn't actually see that, did you, son?" The major was very gentle.

"No, sir."

"In fact, you don't seem very sure about this car at all, do you?"

"No, sir." The boy glanced at the floor. "Don't suppose I do."

"Are you quite sure there was one?"

"I don't know now, sir. I'm getting mixed up, talking about it like this."

"Now, now, son. There's no reason for you to be confused. No one wants that. But you don't seem at all sure about this car. Certainly you couldn't say definitely that you saw one, could you? You couldn't swear under oath that you had?"

"No, sir." The thought of swearing under oath made the boy nervous.

"No, I didn't imagine you could." The major sat giving it some thought. "I tell you what, son: I think it'd be best if you forgot everything about that car. The police will be talking to you about this soon, and they'll be asking a lot of questions. Take my word, old chap, in matters like this, where there might be legal complications, it's always best to keep things as simple as possible." He smiled. "We know how civilians can be, don't we? They enjoy complicating simple matters."

The boy grinned. "Yes, sir." He liked it that, because his father was a soldier, the major was talking to him as though he was a soldier too.

"So it's better to just say nothing about the car, don't you agree, son?"

"Yes, sir."

Smiling, the major nodded. "Yes. Simpler for everyone. Have you and Bertie had time to talk about this?"

"Not yet, sir."

"All right. I'll have a talk with him as soon as the doctor allows it." The major rose, and at once the boy got up from the chair. "I expect you and I will have another talk later too, Frank, just to be sure you remember everything exactly as it happened. Other people might ask you in the next few days, so it'll be best to have it all straight, what?"

"Yes, sir."

The major held the door open and the boy walked out.

Next the major spoke to the corporal who had run to help after the accident. His name was Catchpole.

He came to attention and saluted the major.

"Stand at ease, Corporal. I understand you saw this accident with the motorbike and the two boys. Is that correct?"

"I didn't actually see it, sir. I heard it." Catchpole wondered who this major was. He'd never seen him at the camp before.

"Heard it? Where were you, exactly?"

"Walking across the heath, sir. I'd just left the camp

to take the dog for a walk. I was walking north, toward the two cottages out at the other end of the road."

"Were you close to the road?"

"Not very far from it, sir. Perhaps a hundred yards. Close enough to see everything on it. I could see quite a long stretch of it."

"I understand. Tell me what happened."

"Yes, sir. I walked out of the camp at about ten past eleven and started walking across the heath. I'd been walking about ten minutes when I heard a motorbike on the road, coming from this direction, going north. I heard it changing gear as it went into the first dip in the road, and . . ."

"Dip?"

"Yes, sir." Now Catchpole was sure the major was a stranger, or he'd know about the road. "There are three dips along that part of the road: The first one, going from here, is quite deep, the second one not so deep, and the third one is quite shallow."

"I understand. Go on, Corporal."

"Yes, sir. I looked and saw the chap on the motorbike, just going down into the first dip. At the same time I saw a car up the road, coming the other way, just coming out of the third dip."

"How far away would that be?"

"The car from the motorbike, sir?"

"Yes."

"I'd say about five hundred yards."

"I understand. Go on."

"Yes, sir. I saw the two boys on their bikes too, just about to go into the middle dip. Then they went into it, and the motorbike followed them."

"Could you see what was happening then, Corporal?"

"In the dip? No, sir. It's too deep to see anything in there from off the road. But I saw the car come out, coming down this way. Then I heard the crash."

"You clearly heard it, did you ?"

"Yes, sir. Just about the time the car was coming out of the dip."

"I understand. What then?"

251

"I saw a bike twisting and turning over and over along the road. There was no one on it. Just the bike, spinning out of the dip. Then I ran over to see what'd happened. To see how bad it was. I found the chap off the motorbike, with blood all over the place. I didn't know whether he was alive or dead. And one of the boys was down on the road. One of our lorries came up then, and I stopped it, and we brought them all in here."

"I understand. Now what about this car, Corporal? Can you describe it at all?"

"No, sir. It was black. That's all I can say."

"But you're quite sure you saw it?"

"Oh, yes, sir. I reckon it hit the motorbike and just kept on going."

"But you said you couldn't see anything that happened," the major said sharply.

Catchpole was surprised at the sharpness. "No, sir, I didn't see what happened." He wondered why the major didn't like what he'd said about the car.

"And you said you heard the sound of the crash *after* the car came out of the dip."

"At about the same time, sir."

"About the same time. And the car was then in your line of sight?"

"Yes, sir."

"That surely establishes, doesn't it, that the car wasn't the cause of the crash? If you saw it, alone, coming out of this dip, and heard the crash just after—or even at approximately the same time—there couldn't be a connection between the car and the crash, could there?"

"It could've hit the motorbike and sent it into the two boys, sir. That's what I reckon happened."

"Then you'd have heard two crashes, wouldn't you? The car hitting the motorbike and the motorbike hitting the boys."

"Not if the car just brushed the motorbike, sir. Enough to send it off balance."

The major sat staring. "Corporal, my very clear impression is that you're determined to involve this car in this accident. Why is that?"

"Excuse me, sir, but I'm not trying . . ."

"Then why do you insist on saying that it hit the motor-bike? Surely the logical assumption is that the motorbike simply ran into the boys."

"I don't know, sir. I don't see why it should've done that. There was plenty of room for it to pass them."

"Then certainly there was plenty of room for the car and motorbike to pass—going in opposite directions?"

"Yes, sir." What this major said made sense, Catchpole had to admit—but why didn't the major want to listen to him when he said the car had hit the motorbike? "I just have the feeling that the car hit the motorbike."

Slowly the major sat back. He was making a great effort to be patient. "Tell me clearly once again: Did you actually see the collision?"

"No, sir."

"Then say no more about this car, Corporal. I particularly order you to say nothing of it to the press. Since you didn't see the accident, anything you said about that car could only cause confusion. You could also prejudice possible legal proceedings—and that would cause you serious trouble."

"Yes, sir." Catchpole had the feeling that there was already serious trouble here. He wished he hadn't gone walking the dog at that particular time this morning.

"You're dismissed," the major said.

Catchpole saluted and marched out.

At once the major telephoned London and spoke to a senior officer at the War Office. He reported that one, at least, of the two boys should cause no concern, but Corporal Catchpole was quite confident of what he had seen, and would not be moved from it—and though he had been ordered not to speak to the press of the car, his testimony at a trial or inquest, where he would be sworn to tell all he knew, could be embarrassing.

32

On the second day Lawrence had still not regained consciousness, and now two men in civilian clothes guarded his room at the hospital, one sitting beside his bed, one outside the door. No one, not even the commanding officer, knew who they were, but he knew they had come from London with credentials from the highest authority.

That day the King telephoned Bovington and asked to be told at once when there was news of Lawrence's condition.

From all over England and many other countries, reporters were gathering around Bovington Camp. Although the only statements were being issued from the War Office, in London, they stayed there, watching to see who came. More and more they asked why there was such rigid security around Lawrence.

One of the reporters went up the road to Lawrence's cottage and found men in civilian clothes there who would not let him through the gateway. The reporter told some of the others about the guards, and soon the story spread that the Air Ministry had sent men to the cottage to remove secret papers that Lawrence had been working on since his retirement from the Royal Air Force.

Civil and military police went to Frank Fletcher's father and told him that the boy must not be interviewed by anyone about the accident unless there was permission from the War Office.

At once neighbors and some of the reporters heard about it, and the story began to spread that the police were trying to conceal something about the accident.

On the third day Lawrence was still unconscious, and although the army was now issuing statements on his condition twice a day, the tight security had stimulated the reporters' imaginations. Newspapers were printing stories that said Lawrence was working for the secret service and foreign agents had tried to kill him, and that there was confusion in Whitehall because he was lying in a hospital with the plans for the defense of Britain in his head and no one else knew what they were.

To try to stop the rumors that had been spreading since the day before, the army now allowed a reporter from a local newspaper, the *Dorset Daily Echo,* to interview Frank Fletcher. The boy told how the motorcycle had knocked his friend down, and his friend's bicycle had knocked him down. The details he gave of the accident were essentially the same as he had given the major on the first day except that he told the reporter there had been no car or other vehicle on the road at the time of the accident.

"I'm frankly becoming very nervous, Harding," Gilmour said. "It's been four days now, he's still not dead, and the very thing I didn't want to happen is happening: The press are becoming very inquisitive."

"But they've found nothing, Minister." Harding thought Gilmour had probably had very little sleep since Monday. He looked terrible. And the fact that Gilmour had asked him here to his office, simply to talk about it like this, was an indication of how upset he was. He'd never have thought Gilmour would allow anyone to see him as agitated as this. "I did say that the harder we tried to keep this from them, the harder they'd look for our reasons for doing so. They're doing that, but they've found nothing."

"They've come too damn close for my taste, with this nonsense about Lawrence working for the secret service and foreign agents attempting to kill him. I don't like the way this is developing."

"There's been some sensationalizing—and I said we should expect it—but the very volume of it is, I think, working to our advantage. It's all beginning to sound too outlandish to be taken seriously. I don't believe the press will go very much further with it. In any event, so long as it's foreign agents they're writing about, we have no cause for concern."

Gilmour looked unconvinced. "Why did the military police go to that boy's father and tell him there must be no unauthorized interviews? That was damned unnecessary. The boy had taken very well to the briefing he'd been given at Bovington. It was very heavy-handed of them to do what they did."

"Someone at the War Office had become carried away with enthusiasm, Minister. It was unfortunate. It certainly won't happen again. The War Office is doing nothing now before talking to me. They're cooperating very well."

"But what the devil will happen if Lawrence lives, Harding?" Gilmour sat leaning forward, gripping the edge of his desk.

"I very much doubt that he will."

"He's lived for four days! Your man was supposed to kill him, but he's lived for four days!" Gilmour's voice was beginning to rise.

"Yes, Minister, but the doctors say he can't go on much longer." A confidential report that had come to Harding that morning said Lawrence was expected to survive for another week at the most, and it was unlikely he would regain consciousness. He had told Gilmour that on the telephone, but evidently it hadn't reassured him.

"I'm not going to be easy about this till he's dead, Harding. And probably not for a long time afterwards. I feel this is something that isn't going to be easily forgotten. If I'd known what would come from this, I almost think I would've recommended letting the damn man go to Palestine. I almost think I would."

"In a couple of weeks it'll all be forgotten, Minister." Harding wasn't certain that he believed that, but he hoped it would help Gilmour.

33

To Lawrence it was as though he was struggling to the surface from a very, very long way down in something that held him tight, like quicksand pressed in all around his body, all around his head. Especially his head. He could feel nothing. There was only the knowledge that he could not move. Everything was pressing on him. He tried to open his eyes but something was pressing on them too. He could see nothing and feel nothing. He was simply aware that he was somewhere. He was somewhere and completely powerless. Was this death? What had happened?

There was the Brough. He'd been riding the Brough along the road to Clouds Hill.

Then there had been that black car. It had moved over on the road, coming directly for him. Yes, the car. It had brushed him and sent him into a wobble. It had been no accident. That had been clear in the face of the driver. The man had intended to do it. Why? He'd never seen him before. Why had he done it?

Because he'd been sent to do it. Yes, it had to be that. They'd sent the man to stop him. To keep him from going to Palestine. Oh, yes. There was no other reason. They must have wanted very badly to stop him. They'd sent Cunliffe-

Lister to persuade him not to go, and he hadn't been persuaded. What had Cunliffe-Lister said, just before he left? If you go to Palestine, it'll be in defiance of the wish of the Prime Minister. That should have warned him, but all it had done was flatter him. He'd been flattered at the attention, as he'd always been flattered to be noticed by prominent people. So he'd defied the Prime Minister. But he hadn't imagined they'd do this.

What, precisely, had they done? Was he going to die? Possibly. For weeks he'd been thinking what a relief death would be. Now was it going to happen? Was this how it was going to come to him? Yes, it had to be. It wasn't possible to be like this and not be dying.

God, it was ironic. They'd done it to keep him from going to Palestine, but if he'd gone he would probably have made no difference there. How much had he really done before, during the war? Very little that was valuable. Certainly much less than he'd claimed. He knew it too well. So much of his life had been sham. Most of it. A sham that he'd created to keep hidden all those parts of himself that he'd never wanted to become known.

To keep so much secret he'd had to work very hard, all those years, creating the stories that would reveal him and yet keep him hidden. The urge to have people know about him had been so strong. He'd always tried to provoke interest in himself and yet always loathed the thought that someone might see him clearly, too clearly, and he'd have nowhere left to hide. So he'd written so much fantasy, distorting the truth, hoping people would believe him, yet hoping at the same time that they might see through the inventions and recognize him as he really was.

What he'd written in *The Seven Pillars* about Deraa, for instance. It had never happened. The Turks had never beaten him and raped him. No. Something like it had happened, but not at Deraa and not with the Turks. Writing about that, the experience that had changed his life, he'd reshaped the reality, wanting as always to show a little and conceal more.

259

That night in November, nineteen-seventeen, after the disaster at the Yarmuk bridge, they all rode south, hearing the Turks still firing occasional shots into the dark, where they thought they saw figures moving. Lawrence was hardly conscious of where he was riding. He could think of nothing but the failure. How could he explain it to Allenby? He'd wanted so much to blow up that bridge, and he'd failed. And, worst of all, Allenby would know he'd failed. It would be impossible to hide. And there was no excuse. It had been completely his fault—his fault that the Indian soldier had fallen. He should have foreseen that something like that might happen, with the boots the Indians were wearing, and taken some sort of precaution. He'd failed because he hadn't given it enough thought. He deserved to be punished, and he undoubtedly would be.

Ali rode up beside him, moving his camel at a trot. "What should we do now, Lawrence? I still wish to accomplish something on this trip." He sounded cheerful, and in the moonlight Lawrence could see he was smiling.

"There is nothing we can do, Ali. Nothing but ride back to Akaba."

"To Akaba!" Ali moved his camel in closer. "You say this in seriousness?"

"Yes." God, didn't Ali understand? Didn't he understand how important it had been to destroy that bridge? How could he dismiss a failure like that so simply?

"We still have explosives. We did not blow up the bridge, it is true, but we have the means to blow up something else. Let us go and blow up a train."

Lawrence saw how much he wanted to do it. All that was in Ali's mind now was that he wanted to blow something up. Their failure at the bridge meant nothing to him. God, he envied Ali his freedom from guilt. But he was still a boy. A leader of men, but still only nineteen. And if he wanted to blow up a train, perhaps they should do it. It might be good for the men's morale. Certainly better than riding all the way back to Akaba with nothing to show for their long ride. Nothing but the explosives that hadn't been thrown into the Yarmuk gorge!

"All right, Ali. We shall blow up a train."

Ali laughed. "Good, Lawrence!"

They stopped, and Lawrence told the others what they were going to do. The Indian troops and Selim with his Howeitat he told to ride down to Akaba. Only he and Ali with his Harith men would stay to wait for a train.

While the others rode off south, Lawrence and Ali and thirty men turned east for the railway. They stopped at a section of the line between Mafrak and Deraa, and buried their explosives beneath the track in the best site they could find for an ambush, with two machine guns on a ridge over-looking it. When the mine was laid and all their tracks hidden, they sat behind the ridge to wait.

By the end of the day they had seen only two small, unimportant-looking trains. Nothing worth exploding the mine it had taken them so long to bury.

"I think I should send men along the line to obtain information," Ali said. "If there might be a valuable train passing soon, I should like to know. If not, by God, I should like to blow up the next train that passes, big or small."

Lawrence nodded. "Yes. Send one man north and one south, Ali."

They waited all the next day, and again there was no worthwhile train. In the evening Ali's man rode back from Deraa. They saw him from a distance, galloping fast, and when he rode onto the ridge he swung down from the saddle and came running to Lawrence and Ali.

"A beautiful train is coming tomorrow, Sherif!" he called to Ali. "Lawrence, Mehmet Jemal Pasha is coming!"

"He will be on the train?" Lawrence said.

"Yes, Lawrence, yes!"

"It will be worth the waiting." Lawrence smiled at Ali. Mehmet Jemal Pasha was commander of the Turks' Eighth Army Corps. "Worth the waiting, Ali." It wouldn't compare with blowing up the Yarmuk bridge, but they would, at least, put a senior Turkish general out of the war, if they had luck.

Next morning they saw the white woodsmoke coming from the north. Lawrence watched through his glasses, and soon he saw the moving train beneath the smoke. When it was closer he saw the corps commander's flags fluttering stiff in the wind on the front of the locomotive. The train was nothing but passenger carriages, not one freight wagon, and he could see no car with general's flags. Mehmet Jemal Pasha knew better than to draw that much attention to himself. It was as well for him, or he would have had a mine exploded under him. But it was enough that he had his flags on the locomotive.

"This is the one, Ali." He brought down his glasses.

"I see the flags, Lawrence." Beside him on the ridge, Ali was staring up the line. He turned on his side and signaled to the machine gunners and riflemen spread along the ridge.

Lawrence knelt beside the exploder box, watching carefully across the top of the ridge for the moment to blow the track. Even without the glasses now he could see the sandbagged machine-gun positions on top of the first and last carriages.

When the locomotive was close to the mine, he tensed himself. "Be ready, Ali," he muttered.

Ali raised his hand, ready to drop it and signal to the men.

The locomotive clattered over the spot where the mine was buried, and when the first carriage was halfway across Lawrence heaved down on the handle of the exploder box.

In a red-black roar the locomotive and the first carriage burst into the air in a storm of sand, broken steel, and shattered wood. Machine guns and rifles along the ridge were firing into the train as the next three carriages toppled and rolled off the track, and there were men screaming in them, thin screams above the sound of firing.

Blown-up sand sprayed back along the track and over the men on the ridge, and in the sand were whistling chunks of steel and wood. As Lawrence reached for his rifle, moving to a firing position beside Ali, something hammered his left shoulder, and as he went down it bounced up against the side of his head and dropped in the sand. His eyes were not focusing sharply, but he saw it was a ragged-edged length of steel rail. He felt himself drifting and everything ended.

Something was hitting his face. Someone's hand. He opened his eyes and Ali was kneeling over him, slapping his face. Near him a machine gun was firing.

"Get up, Lawrence! Get up!" Ali hit him again, pulling at him with the other hand to get him up.

Lawrence spun over and was up on his knees, keeping his head down. A burst of machine-gun fire crackled and splintered along the top of the ridge, and a man was flung back beside him, his head shattered.

"They are too many for us!" Ali shouted through the firing. "Mehmet Jemal Pasha escaped! He is down there leading them personally!"

Lawrence turned to look along the top of the ridge. He couldn't think clearly.

"Come, Lawrence!" Ali pulled at his robe. "We must leave this!"

Already some of the men were at the foot of the ridge, on their camels, holding the reins of the others, waiting. Lawrence scrambled down beside Ali, and they went down with the rest of the men, the Turkish fire whipping the rock and sand along the ridge.

Lawrence pulled himself up on his camel, and beside him Ali jumped up on his. The men were waiting for them, and they all turned and galloped south. Lawrence saw there were some camels without men.

"How many did we lose, Ali?"

"Seven!" Ali's mouth was tight. "Damn the Turks! There were hundreds of them in that train. Not counting whatever was in the first carriages, there were four hundred of them. By God, Lawrence, if there had been more of us, it would have been good to stay there against them." Then he smiled. "But at least we inconvenienced a Turkish general. No small thing."

Lawrence said nothing. He was feeling sick from the pain in his head and shoulder. He'd come to blow up a train, as consolation for the failure at the bridge, and now he'd failed here too. They were running from the Turks.

263

Mehmet Jemal Pasha was still alive, and they'd left seven of Ali's men behind.

Next day they rode into the oasis at Azrak, where they had stopped on the way up to the Yarmuk River, and Ali smiled when he saw the grass again. They rode their camels at a trot through the grass and the palm groves that grew all around the chain of wells, up to the old basalt fort on the ridge.

"We will rest here for a few days," Ali said. "Until your shoulder is strong enough for the ride back to Akaba."

"Well. The camels need resting." Lawrence smiled tiredly. "Yes, and I need it too."

Ali moved into the corner tower on the southeast wall of the fort. Lawrence moved into a room in the tower on the north wall, and when he had spread his sleeping robe on the stone floor he stood staring out through the square window opening. They were going to rest here but, God, he hadn't earned the right to rest. What had he done? He'd failed at the Yarmuk and again at the train. He didn't deserve to rest. For those failures he should be punished.

He walked down to the courtyard and across to the southeast tower, up the Ali's room. Ali was lying on his robe, flat on his back, head propped on his arms.

"It is good here, Lawrence." He smiled.

"Yes. Very good. Too good for me, Ali."

Ali frowned. "What?"

Lawrence stood looking down at him, at the way his strong arms were flexed as he lay there with his head on them. "I don't deserve to be resting in this place."

"And I? Do I deserve it?" Ali stared up at him.

"Yes, of course. You have done well." Looking at him, Lawrence could think of nothing but the first time he'd seen him, a year ago, at the oasis a day's ride from Rabegh, when Ali had beaten his cousin, Sherif Mohsin. He could still remember Ali's muscular arm rising and falling, beating his cousin with his camel stick. "It is I who have failed, Ali. My general ordered me to destroy that bridge on the Yarmuk, and it still stands. It was important that it be destroyed. Much depended on it."

"It will be destroyed another time, Lawrence. Yesterday we robbed a Turkish general of his train." Ali smiled. "Think of that, and be cheerful."

Ali didn't understand. Nothing touched this young animal. Yesterday, for a few minutes, he'd been dejected because they'd lost seven men and left a Turkish general and four hundred troops alive. Today it meant nothing at all to him, and he could smile. How could he make Ali understand?

"I must be punished for my failure, Ali."

"Punished? What will your general do to you, Lawrence?"

"No, not the general. There will be no punishment from him. Certainly not a fit one. I must be made to feel pain, Ali. You must do it."

"I?" Ali brought his head up but his strong arms stayed folded on his robe. "Are you mad?"

"No. It must be done. You must beat me—with this." Lawrence reached down and snatched up Ali's camel stick, and held it out to him.

Ali stared at it.

"You must do it, Ali. You must make me pay." He saw the change in Ali's face, in the movement of his heavy lips, and knew he was going to do it.

"By God, I will!" Snatching the camel stick, Ali swung up to his feet, grabbing the hem of Lawrence's robe with one hand and tugging up at it. "Bare yourself!"

Lawrence dragged the robe up and over his head, tossing it aside on the stone floor.

"Bend!" Ali cut him across the buttocks with the stick.

He saw now that Ali was going to get pleasure from it, and for a moment he was afraid. It was going to hurt terribly, as it always had when he was a boy and his mother had whipped him with his trousers down. But he had to be punished. He bent over, with his hands braced on his knees. He waited for it.

The slash of the stick felt as if someone had cut across his buttocks with a sword. It came again and again. He counted ten, fifteen. He could hear Ali beginning to take

265

deep breaths as he swung with the stick. Now it lashed around his ribs too, and he felt the wetness of his own blood on the stick when it landed.

"Ali! Oh, God!" He was calling out and crying, the tears running into the corners of his open mouth and dripping to the floor. "Oh, Ali!"

The stick lashed at him again and again, around his buttocks and up his back, and he could hear Ali's breath sounding forced, and now he was grunting as he raised his arm to lash him.

Then there was no sound, and he could feel nothing but the pain all down his back to his thighs. Where was Ali? He couldn't straighten to look.

He heard the stick flung down on the stone floor.

"Lawrence!" Ali's strong hands grabbed his shoulders, holding him, pulling him back, and he felt Ali against him. "Ah, Lawrence!" Ali grunted, and pushed into him.

He stayed there with his hands on his knees, Ali's hands pulling him back by the shoulders. Now Ali wrapped his strong arms around his waist, holding him still, and Ali's bare body bent along his back, very tight against him, Ali's smooth, beautiful flesh against his own ripped, bloody, filthy body, forcing into him. It was beautiful.

Yes, it had been Ali who had done that terrible, beautiful thing to him, not any Turks. And he had wanted so much to have Ali do it. That day in the fort at Azrak he had at last accepted the truth about himself. After that there had been no way to deceive himself.

And the massacre of the Turks at Tafas, ten months later. That had not been revenge for Deraa, but a simple thirst for blood. He'd been unable to control his desire to know how it felt. He'd had to experience an orgy of killing and blood. For that he had ordered them to take no prisoners. No other reason. Oh, God, he was worthless. He didn't deserve to live.

And he wasn't going to live. He believed he was going to die. It had to be close now. In a way, he regretted it. He would have liked to try once more. If he could have gone to Palestine, back to the desert, he might have achieved something true and valuable at last. Now he'd never go. It was too late. He could feel it. It was ironic. Because of the myth he'd created, they believed he was much more than he'd ever truly been, and they'd been afraid to let him go to Palestine—so they'd killed him. Oh, God, but he was satisfied that it was over at last, and he'd be finished with all of it.

34

Six days after the crash he died, on Sunday, the nineteenth of May, nineteen thirty-five, a little after eight in the morning.

Two days later, in the morning, an inquest was held by the East Dorset district coroner, in a small dining room at Bovington Camp. Entry to the room was tightly controlled by the army, and very few members of the public were allowed inside.

There were few witnesses. The main one was Corporal Catchpole. He said that, from the sound, Lawrence had been riding at somewhere between fifty and sixty miles an hour at the time of the collision. He also said he had seen a black car on the road, but Lawrence had passed it safely before he heard the crash.

One after the other the two boys were questioned, and both said they had heard Lawrence's motorcycle behind them, and had then moved from riding abreast into single file. They had ridden one behind the other for about one hundred yards when Lawrence crashed into the boy riding behind.

They both said they had not seen or heard any kind of car on the road.

Corporal Catchpole was recalled to the witness stand and was asked again about the black car. He insisted he had seen it.

The conflicting testimony about the black car was disturbing to the coroner, and he told the jury that that conflict was rather unsatisfactory, though it did not mean that the car had been involved in what had happened.

In two hours the inquest was over. The jury's verdict was that Lawrence had died an accidental death.

On the death certificate Lawrence was called Thomas Edward Shaw, the name he had used for the last twelve years of his life, in the army and air force. Cause of death was congestion of the lungs and heart failure, following a fracture of the skull and laceration of the brain sustained on being thrown from his motorcycle when colliding with a pedal cyclist.

No one ordered a search made for the black car.

In the afternoon after the inquest a funeral service was held in the village church at Moreton, Dorset, one and a half miles from Lawrence's cottage. A special train had brought distinguished guests from London, and more than one hundred of them knelt for the service in the church. Winston Churchill was there, Lady Astor, Lord Winterton, General Wavell, and many others who had known Lawrence or worked with him. The body was buried in the churchyard.

Ten days after the burial Selim Shaalan was discharged from a hospital in west London. Walking with a cane, he was crossing the road to wait for a taxi when he was knocked down and instantly killed by a sports car traveling at high speed. It did not stop but turned into Cromwell Road and moved off to the west. Some witnesses told police it was an MG, some said a Frazer-Nash. It was never found.

This accidental death of a visitor who had been staying obscurely in London was treated briskly and routinely by the police and was never reported in the press.

Epilogue

The Prime Minister, Ramsay MacDonald, resigned on 7 June 1935, nineteen days after Lawrence died. MacDonald died on 9 November 1937, aged 71.

In April 1936, the Arab Higher Committee for Palestine was formed to direct the Arab movement, and in August the Arab rebellion opened. The British security forces did not declare it ended until August 1939, the month before the outbreak of World War II. The casualties of the rebellion have never been accurately known, but the official estimate is 5,614 killed and wounded—Moslem and Christian Arabs, Jews, and British troops and police.

On 20 July 1951, King Abdullah of Jordan, formerly Transjordan, was shot dead at the Al Aksa mosque in Jerusalem by a Palestinian supporter of Haj Amin el Husseini, the former Grand Mufti. King Abdullah was 69. His grandson, Hussein, is now King of Jordan.

Haj Amin el Husseini left Palestine in the second year of the rebellion, and at the outbreak of World War II he was in Iraq, where he worked with German and Italian secret agents. He moved to Europe and advised the Nazis on subversion in the Middle East; they called him the most distinguished antagonist of England and Jewry. After the war he was arrested by the French in Paris, but escaped and eventually settled in Lebanon, from where he directed a propaganda campaign against Israel. He died in Beirut on 4 July 1974, aged 77.

Dr. Chaim Weizmann, president of the World Zionist Organization and the Jewish Agency for Palestine in 1935, was elected President of the provisional government of Israel on 16 May 1948, and President of the state on 17 February 1949, after the first general election, He died on 9 November 1952, at his home at Rehovot, south of Tel Aviv, aged 77.

Sherif Ali fought beside Feisal in the summer of 1920, in a last attempt to keep the French out of Damascus. Later he went to Saudi Arabia, and he was living there with his Saudi wife at the time of Lawrence's death. The details of his later life are obscure.

Sir Philip Cunliffe-Lister, later Lord Swinton, died on 27 July 1972, aged 88.

Sir John Gilmour died on 30 March 1940, aged 63.

Lawrence remains an enigma, and the circumstances of his life and death are still mysterious. The telegram he sent to Selim Shaalan on the day of his death has never been recovered, only the one he sent to Henry Williamson, who died in August 1977, aged 81. The black car that Corporal Catchpole saw has also never been found.